ATTACKING POVERTY

IN THE

DEVELOPING WORLD

ATTACKING POVERTY

IN THE

DEVELOPING WORLD

Christian Practitioners and Academics
in Collaboration

Edited by
Judith M. Dean, U.S. International Trade Commission
Julie Schaffner, The Fletcher School, Tufts University
Stephen L.S. Smith, Gordon College

Authentic

Published in partnership with World Vision Resources

Authentic
We welcome your comments and questions.
129 Mobilization Drive, Waynesboro, GA 30830 USA authentic@stl.org
and 9 Holdom Avenue, Bletchley, Milton Keynes, Bucks, MK1 1QR, UK
www.authenticbooks.com

If you would like a copy of our current catalog, contact us at:
1-8MORE-BOOKS
ordersusa@stl.org

Attacking Poverty in the Developing World
ISBN: 1-932805-43-5

Published in 2005 by Authentic Media

Published in partnership with World Vision
34834 Weyerhaeuser Way South
P.O. Box 9716
Federal Way, WA 98063 USA
www.worldvision.org

Cover design: Paul Lewis
Cover images: World Vision/Jon Warren and World Vision/Margaret Jephson
Interior design: Angela Duerksen
Editorial team: Carol Pitts

Printed in the United States of America

Contents

115978

Section III
The Evaluation of Christian Development Efforts

Section IV
Christian Engagement in Poverty
Reduction Policy-Making

Preface

Moved by the tremendous needs of the poor in developing countries for more productive and satisfying ways to earn their livings, and for better nutrition, education and health care, Christian development organizations administer a wide range of poverty reduction programs. Many Christian academic economists, moved by the same tremendous needs, hope to inform and promote these development efforts through research and teaching. Christian development practitioners and academics—with expertise related to such diverse poverty reduction efforts as microcredit programs and tuberculosis control—have much to learn from each other, and much to share with the concerned Christian public, about how to reduce poverty in the developing world.

In celebration of the twentieth anniversary of its founding, the Association of Christian Economists created a forum in which Christian practitioners in development organizations and Christian academic economists could come together, to learn from each other and to find new ways to collaborate in the attack on world poverty. The conference, entitled "Economists, Practitioners, and the Attack on Poverty: Toward Christian Collaboration," was held in Washington, D.C., on January 5–6, 2003. Despite differences in professional incentives and training, the academics and professionals who attended the conference found themselves on firm ground for collaboration, because of their shared faith in Jesus Christ and shared desire to serve the poor of the world. This volume draws on the spirit and content of that conference. It seeks to share the encouragement and wisdom of the development experts who participated with a larger community, while also forging ahead in responding to the challenges issued there.

For readers who are just becoming interested in the Church's relief and development efforts, the short papers collected here provide an expert and accessible introduction to the choices and challenges that Christian development organizations face in today's world. For those who are already familiar with the landscape of development efforts, these papers challenge them to question received wisdom and to consider ways of improving upon the status quo. For academic researchers, these papers highlight areas in which their research and participation might be especially useful to Christian development efforts.

Section I

Christian Collaboration in Poverty Reduction Efforts

1

Christian Collaboration in the Attack on Poverty

Judith M. Dean (U.S. International Trade Commission)[1]
Julie Schaffner (The Fletcher School, Tufts University)
Stephen L.S. Smith (Gordon College)

Over the last thirty years tremendous progress has been made in raising the standard of living in Asia, Africa, and Latin America. Yet the extent and severity of poverty is still enormous. The World Bank's *World Development Report 2000/2001, Attacking Povery,* reports more than one billion people still living below an international poverty line of $1.00 per day (as of 1998). More than 85 percent of these people were living in Sub-Saharan Africa or South Asia.

Even in countries that have made concerted, well-considered efforts towards development, poverty remains acute. After the end of the long civil war in Mozambique in 1994, for example, the country greatly improved growth and reduced poverty through major policy changes. The change was so dramatic that it drew the President of the World Bank, First Lady Hilary Clinton, and other officials to visit the country in 1997. International investment began flowing into Mozambique again, and international aid increased. Yet even in 2003, Mozambique's gross national income per capita was about $210, as compared to the U.S. figure of about $38,000. Recent World Bank estimates show 25 percent of Mozambican children under the age of 3 to be malnourished. For every 1,000 live births, 147 Mozambican children die before the age of 5. More than half the population over 15 years old is illiterate.[2]

India is about twice as wealthy as Mozambique. In the early 1990s, India made remarkable changes to its domestic and foreign economic policies, which contributed to significant growth and development. But here, too, the poverty problem is still overwhelming. World Bank estimates show that Indian gross national income per capita was only about $540 as of 2003. About 29 percent of the Indian population lived below the national poverty line. For every 1000 live births, 87 Indian children still die before the age of five. Thirty-nine percent of the population over 15 years old is illiterate.[3]

Christians cannot ignore the plight of the poor. God's call to help the poor rings out throughout the entire Scripture. In a very poignant verse, the author of Proverbs stresses that our response to the poor is a reflection of our attitude towards our Lord: "He who oppresses the poor shows contempt for their Maker, but whoever is kind to the needy honors God" (Proverbs 14:31). Remarkably, a believer's generosity—both of heart and of hand—to the poor, is seen by our Lord as an offering to Him: "He who is kind to the poor lends to the Lord, and He will reward him for what he has done" (Proverbs 19:17). But how should Christians respond?

At times God moves individuals to take specific actions on sudden inspiration. More often He moves them to address problems after careful thought and planning. Rather than providing specific blueprints, He allows his people to exercise their God-given powers of reasoning. In the case of poverty reduction, sound reasoning would lead believers to search out the root causes of poverty in order to attack the problem at its source. This would mean eliminating the root causes, where possible, and providing for the on-going needs of the poor where the cause is irreversible (as in the case of severe disability, for example). Special expertise is called for, both to discern the root causes of poverty and to design responses that will succeed in improving people's well-being. In His mercy, God has raised up many individuals who have acquired tremendous expertise of the sort required to do this. Two such groups are economic researchers, working in academics and in government organizations, and practitioners working for relief and development organizations.

Economic researchers and relief and development practitioners have spent many years attempting to find the causes of poverty and address them. A few fundamental factors have been isolated, which are at the root of the problem. The poor lack income and assets. They own few physical assets, such as land, and few human assets, such as skills, education, or good health. The return on what they do have is low and often volatile. Access to financial assets, such as savings and credit are often non-existent. The poor also lack protection from corruption. The consequences of the absence of rule of law, or corruption in law enforcement fall most heavily on the poor. They are often victims of usury, bribery, and indentured servitude despite laws which prohibit these practices. Finally, the poor are vulnerable to shocks. Having few assets and low returns, they have little to sustain them through adversity. Floods, crop failures, job loss, and sickness, can easily push them into dire poverty.

For the most part, researchers and practitioners have pursued their work in surprising independence. Researchers studying economic development have analyzed how to best respond to the lack of income and assets among the poor, and to their vulnerability. They have collected data and studied the results of many programs designed to address these problems, and have examined the relationships between local solutions and national and international policies which may impact those solutions. Yet the results of their study very rarely reach the practitioners who carry out this work "on the ground." Practitioners have designed programs which, very literally "lend to the poor" to meet their lack of financial assets. They have designed schools to meet their needs for education, and clinics to meet their health needs. They have brought technical expertise to help poor people improve the yields from their farms, and learn how to shield themselves from the risks of bad harvests or floods. Recently, they have even brought advocacy skills to help local officials turn back corruption and implement laws that help protect the poor. Yet the lessons they have learned from years of field experience very rarely reach the researchers engaged in the same endeavors.

Researchers and practitioners tend to interact little, even though they have much to learn from each other. The professional rewards of collaboration are meager at best, and the practical costs are high. However, Christians should be better able than others to bear these costs, as their calling is to something larger than a profession. This book is evidence of Christian collaboration, and aims to initiate what the authors hope will be a long and productive conversation among Christian development professionals.

Part I casts the vision. It brings together researchers and practitioners to discuss the need for and scope of potential collaboration. Part II examines efforts to help the poor in the areas of microfinance, agriculture, health and education, sharing what is already known about good program design, and brainstorming about how to collaborate in answering remaining questions. Part III presents a broader discussion of the steps that must be taken to develop feasible and desirable impact assessment tools, for use in continued and expanded study of poverty reduction efforts. Finally, part IV looks at poverty reduction through a global lens. Researchers and practitioners examine the impact of national and international policies which affect the poor, and opportunities for Christian collaboration in shaping those policies.

Christian Collaboration in Poverty Reduction Efforts

Christian researchers and practitioners have much to gain from greater interchange of ideas. They share the desire to find productive means for reducing poverty, but differ in experience, in the sorts of questions that their instincts and training lead them to ask, and in their approaches to the analysis and evaluation of development policies and projects. Practitioners can help academics to identify research questions that are more useful, conceptual models that are more reasonable, and research methods that are more feasible and reliable. Academics can help practitioners to apply analytical and statistical tools, as well as insights available in the academic research literature, in brainstorming about project selection, design and evaluation. But interchange is made difficult by differences in experience, assumptions and vocabulary, as well as by professional pressures rendering it personally costly to devote time to these activities.

There may be even more to gain from the development of truly collaborative research projects, a more challenging task than the interchange of ideas. For example, researchers and practitioners together can design and implement the collection of comprehensive base line and follow up data for use in evaluating the costs and benefits of a variety of development projects. Such data would allow them to answer many practical and important project design questions that cannot be answered with any other sort of data. When collected from comparable treatment and control groups, such data also yield more reliable answers to questions that have been studied using other sorts of data, in which it is difficult to distinguish true project impact from the effects of the traits that cause individuals or communities to become beneficiaries. But data collection requires money that could instead be spent directly on poverty reduction, and the creation of comparable treatment and control groups may conflict with practitioners' criteria for choosing which communities should receive help first. Large field research endeavors furthermore require large inputs of time, which could instead be devoted to activities with greater professional rewards.

Part I presents a challenging call to costly but valuable Christian collaboration. Speaking as a practitioner, David Beckmann (Chapter 2) discusses God's special concern for the poor, and emphasizes the great value and unfortunate scarcity of collaboration between practitioners and academics in the attack on poverty. He then gives examples of potential collaborative efforts from the work of Bread for the World. Ken Leonard of the University of Maryland (Chapter 3) provides an academic counterpoint, exploring the scope for and challenges to mutually beneficial collaboration between academics and practitioners in non-governmental organizations. He then puts forward a provocative model for future collaboration. James Foster of Vanderbilt University (Chapter 4) describes two exciting cases of productive collaboration, in the areas of microfinance and poverty reduction transfer programs. These chapters suggest the importance of collaboration in three areas of Christian development work: the design of projects and programs, the evaluation of these projects and programs, and engagement with the government, donors and other development organizations in policy-making.

The Design of Christian Poverty Reduction Efforts

Many government efforts at promoting education in the 1960s were shaped by the compelling notion of providing "free schooling to all." Many schools were built, and their doors opened to all comers free of charge, but they did not draw all children into school. Recent decades have brought the recognition that while "free schools for all" sounds good (and *is* good compared to many alternatives), it grew out of a very narrow view of the ways in which governments might intervene to improve educational attainment. It was shaped by the implicit assumptions that (1) the education subsidies offered to all children must be the same, (2) the right level of subsidy to offer families is the one that just eliminates their need to pay tuition, and (3) adequate education will be provided in new locations by schools employing standard curriculum, materials and organization. Efforts to think broadly and flexibly about policy options raised many questions about these assumptions. Might there be reason to consider subsidizing the poor more than the non-poor? Might some of the poor need even more subsidy than that associated with free schooling; might they need stipends to cover hidden costs of schooling? Might the benefits of charging tuition fees of some non-poor students, in order to spread a limited budget further, outweigh the costs? Might students learn more, and parents find schooling more attractive, if teachers were better motivated, curriculum more relevant, or if school administration was altered in other ways? Such flexible thinking has led to much experimentation, excitement and forward momentum in the education policy field in recent years.

Governments and NGOs alike need to think flexibly and ask questions like this. God, in his grace, moves people and governments to contribute money, skills and other resources for poverty reduction. But the resources forthcoming from a fallen world are limited, and the call to exercise good stewardship over them is pressing. Christian development organizations, Christians working in other development institutions, and development professionals more generally, have been entrusted by God with "talents" to use in poverty reduction efforts, not only in the form of money and goods, but also analytical capacities. God calls these servants to thoughtful stewardship. He places poverty reduction objectives on his servants' hearts, and calls them to apply their intellect and energy in a good faith effort to get the most of what matters to them from the limited resources available.

Thoughtful stewardship begins with recognizing, first, that people entrusted with resources for poverty reduction face a range of choices about how to use them; and, second, that it is useful to consider thoroughly the advantages and disadvantages of each possible choice before selecting one option. In the language of economists, development organizations must see themselves as making program design choices, trying to maximize the attainment of their objectives subject to the constraints or limitations presented by fixed budgets, access to specific expertise, legal restrictions, and other factors. Thoughtful stewardship thus requires careful thought about constraints, objectives, and the range of design choices available.

While many constraints on program design are easy to identify, others are more subtle. At least in the near term, development activities must be shaped by obvious constraints of fixed budgets, staffs of given size with given sets of training and experience, and restrictions imposed by governments, donors or parent organizations on the range of an organization's activities. Less obvious constraints arise out of the need to draw beneficiaries or clients into programs. In many cases the poor will be served only if they find participation in a program sufficiently feasible and attractive. Thus their hopes, fears, and desires, as well as their economic and social circumstances, constitute constraints not only on their own behavior and well-being, but also on the program designer's problem. New schools may do little good if families are too poor to send their children to them, or if travel by road is so difficult and dangerous that parents fear to send their children. The development of crop or livestock varieties that produce much higher yields on average may do little good if the new varieties are also more susceptible to disease, rendering them too risky for a poor population to accept, or if the new seeds must be purchased with credit, which the poor lack. Thus analytical thinking about the economic and social circumstances in which the poor live is crucial to effective program design.

The objectives of program design, too, contain both obvious and more subtle elements. At a very general level all Christian development organizations share the objectives of serving the poor and advancing God's kingdom. At a more specific level, however, the objectives that shape relief and development work may vary greatly. Some organizations and individuals are called to serve the destitute in large Third World cities. Some are called to work with small-scale entrepreneurs. Some are called to provide health care in rural villages, some concerned primarily with infectious diseases while others focus on reducing the risks associated with childbirth and trauma. Some are called to provide practical material help to church members as just one small component of a larger effort to pastor a growing spiritual community. Some are called to lobby for legislation in the U.S. and Europe that benefits less developed countries. Within each of these callings, organizations must sometimes wrestle with more subtle choices. Is their objective to improve the health and nutrition of all children in a region, or are limited resources to be targeted more narrowly on the poor and malnourished among the region's children? Is the objective to help "the poor" or to target limited resources more narrowly on the "very poor"? Even fine distinctions between objectives can have important implications for the desirability of specific programmatic efforts.

Identifying the range of program design choices available, too, can be a tricky task for program designers. In day-to-day involvement with a particular project, it is easy to begin assuming that things are done the way they are for a purpose, and perhaps even to begin feeling that the way things are being done is right or fixed in stone. They come to represent givens rather than choices.

Seeing the full range of ways in which things might be done requires "thinking outside the box."

Conversation and collaboration with colleagues in other development organizations and with academics in relevant disciplines has great potential to speed or improve the identification of constraints, objectives and options for program design. Colleagues outside an organization bring different skills and experiences and different ways of looking at the world, which add energy to brainstorming efforts. Academic economists, in particular, may be especially helpful in analyzing the constraints on program design posed by the economic and social context in which the poor live, and in identifying the range of design options available. Their research and teaching exposes them to a wide range of studies regarding the motivation of and constraints on the poor in developing countries, and on the efforts of diverse organizations to reduce poverty. Trained to break programs and problems down into their component parts, they can transform large and complex questions into series of smaller questions more amenable to fruitful study and discussion. Trained to recognize similarities across superficially different problems, they can also derive insights for the design of specific programs from the experience of a wide range of related programs.

Once program designers pull together their understanding of objectives, constraints and options in program design, they will recognize that they face choices that involve tradeoffs. For example, program design choices that increase a program's ability to improve school attendance of poor children (given limited resources) may also reduce its ability to improve the current consumption levels of the children's households (if school attendance requires children to work less and contribute less to current household income). Similarly, program choices that target cash benefits to the working poor with little leakage to the non-poor (as, for example, through an employment program) may do a very poor job of reaching the most destitute households (if they lack able-bodied workers).

The existence of tradeoffs implies that before choosing one design over another, designers much judge that the benefits of doing so outweigh the costs. They must appeal to facts to determine the likely sizes of the benefits and costs in practical terms. With facts in hand, they must then appeal to values to determine the weights employed when comparing the benefits and costs, which take different forms and accrue to different people. For example, when deciding whether or not to increase interest rates in a microlending program, program designers face a tradeoff. The increased interest rate may allow the organization to achieve "sustainability" and the associated ability to expand operations without searching for donor support. This would allow them to reach a larger number of borrowers. The interest rate increase will also, however, reduce the extent to which borrowers enjoy increased income and may drive some of the poorest borrowers (who face less productive investment opportunities) to withdraw from the program. An appeal to facts (or best guesses about them) is required to determine how much the reach of the program would expand at higher interest rates, and how many of the poorest would drop out. Even once the facts are in, an appeal to values will be required, as designers must determine whether the expected expansion of services (among the less poor) associated with the interest rate increase is "worth" the cost of the reduced participation among the poorest.

In weighing tradeoffs, as in the identification of objectives, constraints and options, collaboration with diverse colleagues can be of great value. Most obviously, through colleagues designers may learn what is already known about the facts, and with their help they may make better guesses about the facts that are not yet fully known. Less obviously, the desire to communicate effectively with colleagues whose training and experience are different pushes them to work hard at distinguishing the roles of facts and values in decision making. Failure to make such distinctions is the frequent cause of impasses in which debaters argue at cross-purposes. It is important to note that the role of academic economists in such program design discussions is not to force their values onto development practitioners, but to bring out more clearly the nature of the relevant tradeoffs.

Chapters 5 through 13 seek to promote flexible thinking about poverty reduction program design, and to synthesize current understanding of the facts, in five areas of interest to Christian development organizations: microfinance, agricultural and rural development, education, health, and the development of north-south partnerships. Authors from differing backgrounds and training, but who share a commitment to thoughtful stewardship, offer their perspectives on the range of program design choices available in each area, on the facts Christian development practitioners and academics already do and do not know about related tradeoffs, and on the additional evidence that would be required for making future advances in the attack on poverty.

Microfinance programs seek to help poor people help themselves by offering them access to flexible mechanisms for borrowing or saving, and are tremendously popular with both Christian and secular development organizations around the world. Microcredit programs are based on the idea that many poor people can improve their material and social circumstances if they have access to reasonably-priced financial services with which to begin or expand small businesses. Kenneth Graber and Robert Gailey (Chapter 5) set out many of the design choices embodied in these programs, and describe how recent growing interest in "financial sustainability" alone may reduce these programs' potential to help very poor people. They raise the possibility that Christian development organizations should resist this trend, and describe some ways in which research could enlighten these design choices.

Programs promoting the development of informal savings and credit institutions, such as Rotating Saving and Credit Associations (ROSCAs), are based on the idea that many of the poor are willing to save and invest but lack access to financial institutions through which they can do this. These programs provide such means. Brian Fikkert (Chapter 6) examines recent experience with such programs, explains why Christian development organizations might find them preferable to microcredit programs, and challenges these organizations and academics to collaborate in further experimentation with this approach to poverty reduction.

Agricultural and rural development is an area in which NGOs have a long tradition of helping the poor, offering diverse support to small farm agriculture and to the rural economy more generally. Doug Brown and Chris Barrett (Chapter 7) describe features of the local economies that must be understood by practitioners if projects are to be successful, thereby emphasizing the contribution that economic researchers can make to good decision-making by Christian development organizations. Tom Reardon (Chapter 8) shows, through discussion of a provocative example, how academic research on a critical issue can yield important implications for development practitioners. He reviews recent academic research on the rapid replacement of informal agricultural produce markets with a few large supermarket chains in many regions of the world, and shows how the results of this research challenge two common assumptions made in development work. The first assumption is that the poor always know what they most need. The economic landscape may be changing too rapidly for the poor to predict its implications. The second assumption challenged by this research is that small-scale assistance to small farmers, encouraging them in their agricultural production, is always effective. Christian development organizations may do better to offer substantial assistance to farmers with the potential to become successful players in the new markets, while helping others transition into the production of another crop or even non-farm employment.

Christian organizations have also played a large role in the provision of literacy training, and primary and secondary education to poor populations around the world. Diana Weber (Chapter 9) describes the great variety of modes in which literacy education may be offered, and the great importance of local participation in designing programs that meet local needs. Paul Glewwe (Chapter 10) then digs into a more detailed design question—regarding what materials and oversight to provide to primary schools in efforts to produce the greatest student achievement possible on a limited budget—and describes how collaborative research can be shaped to shed practical light on it.

Yet another area in which Christian organizations have a long tradition is in the promotion of improved health in poor countries, whether by providing health care services for the ill and injured or by promoting public health efforts aimed at preventing illness and injury. Paul McNamara (Chapter 11) sketches out the dimensions of diversity in Christian health efforts, and describes several analytical tools developed by health economists that can be useful to practitioners as they set priorities and design health programs. Ndunge Kiiti, Claire Boswell and James Oehrig (Chapter 12) then dig further into the importance of a development paradigm that encourages and builds on local participation and collaboration at different levels in the design and implementation of these programs.

A set of practical choices that cuts across microfinance, agricultural and rural development, education and health has to do with the extent to which Christian development organizations headquartered in the developed countries can improve their work in developing countries by partnering with local organizations. Roland Hoksbergen (Chapter 13) identifies the potential benefits to partnership that underlie the current enthusiasm about partnership, draws out the characteristics partnerships must have if they are to produce these benefits, and derives practical lessons about partnership-building from the experience of Christian Reformed World Relief Committee.

The Evaluation of Christian Development Efforts

The authors of Chapters 1 through 13 are unanimous in their belief that improved evidence-gathering activities—many of which fall under the labels of "impact assessment" or "monitoring and evaluation"—would provide important fuel for improving and expanding Christian poverty reduction efforts. Careful empirical study of what works well under what circumstances, and of the tradeoffs associated with specific design choices, would clarify the scope and nature of the choices program designers face, thus allowing them to make better use of the resources already available for poverty reduction. Improved documentation of achievements might also increase the quantity of resources available for poverty reduction, by persuading potential donors to expand their contributions.

While development professionals understand the potential benefits of improved impact assessment, the prospect of involvement in such activities produces debate and anxiety, because the costs of impact assessment also appear rather daunting. Methods put forward as "state of the art" involve the collection of massive amounts of information, often using data collection methods with which organizations have little experience. They may also involve sophisticated statistical procedures, and, because they focus on an excessively narrow range of concerns, appear not to be worth the effort. Or worse, they may seem to be shaped by alien values and skewed in an unwelcome direction.

In the face of such difficulties, what can be done to increase the attractiveness and frequency of impact assessment? Two general steps suggest themselves. First, it is useful to recognize that impact assessment approaches must be designed and tailored, not adopted ready made. Just as development workers must make careful choices regarding the design of poverty reduction programs, so must they make careful choices regarding the design of impact assessment. If approaches to which they have been exposed appear too narrow, then the approaches must be adapted or replaced with more appropriate ideas. Brainstorming with diverse professionals is a natural way to develop this more flexible view of assessment options. A more flexible view of impact assessment options should increase the potential benefits of the undertaking, spurring investment.

Second, it is useful to search for ways to lower the costs of good impact assessment through collaboration, both with practitioners in other organizations, and with academics. Collaboration may open the door to cost reduction through at least three channels. First, brainstorming with both practitioners from other organizations and academics may raise awareness of a wider range of methodological options, some of which fit the organization better. Second, academics may be able to perform some of the specific tasks involved in an impact assessment at low cost, and may well be willing to volunteer their services, in exchange for the opportunity to do some good and gain access to information. Third, academics and others could be convinced to undertake independent research aimed at identifying lower-cost but effective impact assessment methods. Chapters 14 and 15 offer encouragement and tools for this collaborative approach to the design of impact assessments in two ways. Julie Schaffner (Chapter 14) offers an economist's observations on how impact assessments could be tailored to meet the needs and constraints of Christian development organizations and on how collaboration between individual development organizations and researchers could improve the effectiveness and reduce the cost of such efforts. She also urges broader collaboration among NGO development practitioners and academics, who together could approach the World Bank and other large development actors with a proposal for the creation of an NGO impact assessment facility. Such a facility could offer matching funds for impact assessment, and could serve as a repository of information on the aims, methods, costs and results of impact assessments carried out by a wide range of organizations. Jaisankar Sarma and Bernard Vicary (Chapter 15) dig deeper into the need to identify outcomes and measures that reflect the organization's values and objectives, and the practical importance of involving many stakeholders in the design and implementation of evidence gathering efforts, drawing on World Vision's ground-breaking experience.

Christian Engagement in Poverty Reduction Policy-making

The efforts of Christian development organizations do not take place in a vacuum. Christian and other non-governmental development organizations are increasingly aware of the impact of developed and developing country policies on the poor, and are showing keen interest in advocating good policy. Development professionals have seen sound efforts by Christian organizations undone by poor policy or frustrated by poor government administration. They increasingly appreciate the role good policy can play in improving nutrition, education, health and income. Christian economists, for their part, are also aware of the importance of good policy and have been active in researching development-related policy questions. Practitioner and economist collaboration in advocacy thus in principle offers a rich field for action.

Advocacy takes place at three levels: local, national, and global. Christian development organizations have always been willing to advocate at the local level—making sure, for instance, that local hospitals get medicine through available government programs. One thing that makes Christian organizations especially valuable in development is that they are trusted and involved at the local level. Of necessity, they often work very closely with local government authorities in delivering their aid and development services. They are thus very well placed for local advocacy.

Policy advocacy at the national level is a natural outgrowth of local advocacy. Christian development agencies see first hand the problems inherent in poorly-designed national social welfare and macroeconomic policies, and often have particular insight about how those policies affect the poor. In recent years the World Bank's Poverty Reduction Strategy Paper (PRSP) consultations have opened up a potentially fruitful way for Christian development organizations to participate in national policy discussions in those countries engaged in such a process. The promise of the PRSPs has not always been realized and, in every event, it takes hard work for a development agency to offer cogent policy advice at the national level. To do this well requires not only a detailed knowledge of grassroots conditions but an understanding of possible important tradeoffs in policy choices and in short-term versus long-term goals, and the ability to communicate in a language that is understood by policymakers.

Both local and national advocacy can be complicated by the uncertain and at times dangerous political ramifications of speaking clearly to government authorities. While northern-based NGOs enjoy some advantages in becoming policy advocates in such cases, they also face some disadvantages. They are sometimes able to speak as "outsiders"—perceived as fair players across ethnic groups and parties. They may also be in a key position to equip local indigenous groups to advocate for their community interests. At other times they may be less able to speak out because they are vulnerable to expulsion, or because they are not viewed as representing the local community. Collaboration with academics may at times be useful for finding an indirect voice in policy discussions.

Christian development organizations are increasingly active in global advocacy. They played a prominent role in the Jubilee movement and, along with secular NGOs, have taken part in a wide range of international advocacy movements relating to areas as diverse as HIV/AIDS pharmaceutical policy and World Trade Organization (WTO) negotiations. Christian development organizations have entered global policy debate most prominently in the new World Faiths Development Dialogue (WFDD) sponsored by the World Bank. This initiative, in which the Bank is attempting a structured, formal dialogue with development organizations from all faiths, is a sharp break from past practice in which there was no institutional way for Christian development organizations to convey their views on matters touching the Bank's work. The WFDD offers a forum in which to express their views—often detailed and critical views, well-informed by their grassroots networks—and expect to be heard by the Bank and other development actors. Again, however, taking full advantage of this opportunity is not a trivial undertaking.

The potential benefits for Christian development groups of collaboration with economists in advocacy is enormous, especially at the national and global levels. Policy questions at these levels are often framed in terms more familiar to academic economists than to practitioners. Economists also bring a wealth of academic research to substantiate their points, and may be able to facilitate translation of NGO concerns into the language of policy consultation.

The nature and extent of that collaboration is likely to differ across local, national and global levels, and across policy issues. Collaboration may be the easiest in policy areas of traditional interest to Christian organizations. The large scope for economist-practitioner collaboration in research in the areas in education, health and microfinance, discussed earlier in this chapter, naturally should allow for economist-practitioner collaboration in advocacy in these fields, as well. Here the applied research of development economists pairs easily with Christian organizations' grassroots networks to yield fruitful local and national advocacy.

By contrast, collaboration may be more difficult when it comes to advocacy about trade and domestic macroeconomic policies—policies that are central to World Bank and International Monetary Fund (IMF) work in developing countries. Here mutual stereotypes and misperceptions abound, along with some real differences in view among diverse economists and practitioners. Practitioners may be tempted to characterize trade and macroeconomists' strong policy preference for global economic liberalization as a kind of "deification" of the market economy, callously imposed irrespective of the human costs. Economists may be tempted to discount practitioners' views as short-sighted, excessively focused on the immediate costs of policies which should deliver broad-based long-run benefits. Effective collaboration is possible only after all parties become open to expanding their views of the potential tradeoffs involved in deciding what to advocate, and to engaging in careful study of the facts and values to be weighed in drawing conclusions.

One reason these stereotypes persist is that they touch upon several key differences between practitioners and academic researchers. Economists are trained to evaluate policies in the aggregate. They have elaborate models for assessing the overall, long-term costs and benefits of particular courses of action. This sets the stage for tension with practitioners who, of necessity, are often more focused on the local status quo, highly aware of the deep costs of economic dislocation imposed by new trade and macropolicies, and perhaps more ambivalent about the merits of economic growth given their awareness of the tremendous social changes that that entails.

Yet collaboration between economists and practitioners on national and global policy issues is essential if both groups are to have a good understanding of the relationship between national trade and macroeconomic policies and poverty. Academic researchers have much to offer at this point—they have long worked on these issues, and despite some disagreements with practitioners on some points, there is convergence on views on a large number of issues. Researchers can help development agencies see where this agreement exists and how it would impact their work. Researchers can also help practitioners see where convergence does not exist, and where agencies' experiences might contribute useful information to policy debate and formulation. To engage each other more effectively practitioners and economists need new equipping, and need to speak in a language that better communicates with each other.

Chapters 16 through 18 offer encouragement and guidance to Christian organizations interested in becoming more involved in national and global policy advocacy. Katherine Marshall (Chapter 16) describes the genesis and nature of two new modes of involvement for faith-based organizations in poverty reduction policy debates: The WFDD and country level PRSP consultations. While the extent to which true participation has occurred varies greatly across countries, these new institutions do offer some real opportunities for Christian organizations that are equipped for participation in policy debates. Academic economists can offer practitioners both conceptual guidance, as well as a voice that communicates in a language understood by the major development actors.

The recent convergence of views between two radically different groups—the WTO and Oxfam—on the benefits of freer trade for the poor highlight the importance of a better understanding of the role of trade policy. In chapter 17, Judith Dean analyzes the relationship between international trade policy and poverty. Dean points out that the relationship between trade reform and poverty is complex and sometimes ambiguous. Yet some clear conclusions do emerge: changes in both industrial and developing country trade policies will be necessary to help the poor. Over the last few decades, many macroeconomic policies have been criticized as detrimental to the poor. Andrew Levin and Stephen Smith examine the design of some key macroeconomic policies more closely in Chapter 18. They argue that macroeconomic stability is necessary to improve the well-being of poor people. Reducing a high rate of inflation, for instance, often helps the poor more than the wealthy. This implies that macroeconomic stabilization programs, while criticized by many Christian development organizations and NGOs, have in some cases a claim to moral legitimacy. These macroeconomic stability issues, frequently absent in populist debate, are vital in understanding how some reforms can help the poor.

These chapters neither provide all the answers to policy debates, nor pretend that Christian development practitioners and economists will always agree on those answers. Rather, they point out what can be agreed on by a large group of economists about macroeconomic policies and the poor and offer this consensus to practitioners to assist them in thinking about their advocacy, to help equip them to participate in the policy discussions with economists and international agencies, and to encourage mutually sympathetic thinking between practitioners and economists. Differences of opinion about policy advocacy are unavoidable; but mutual understanding is valuable and worth pursuing.

Moving Forward

These chapters offer insight into a new collaborative approach to poverty reduction. Drawing on the strengths of both Christian academic researchers and Christian practitioners, they propose new ways of approaching project and program design, program assessment, and participation in national policy-making. Though collaboration is difficult and sometimes costly, these chapters highlight the wide scope for and benefits of joint work. Uniting skills, knowledge, and experience in thoughtful, effective ways, Christian researchers and practitioners should make greater progress in addressing the needs of the poor.

Individual Christian development professionals may wish to take advantage of a new resource created by the Association of Christian Economists, for facilitating connections between Christian academic economists and Christian development practitioners. The new "Development Connections" web site (http://www.gordon.edu/ACE/devconnect/devconnectWelcome.html) helps Christian academics and practitioners interested in conversation and collaboration to locate one another. It also points them to a variety of helpful resources, through postings of conference announcements, book reviews, and links to useful websites.

By God's grace, God's people are given the opportunity to work together in Christian development efforts, thereby showing kindness to the poor and honoring our Maker. The contributors to this book hope that the discussion here will be a catalyst for conversation and collaboration that will benefit impoverished people around the world.

Notes

[1] The views expressed here are solely those of the author. They do not represent in any way the views of the U.S. International Trade Commission, or any of its individual Commissioners.

[2] World Bank, *World Development Indicators, 2005.*

[3] World Bank, *World Development Indicators, 2005.*

2

What Christian Development Practitioners Need from Christian Researchers

David Beckmann (Bread for the World)

When I was ordained as a Lutheran pastor, I was called to be a "missionary economist." My calling was to help bring Christian faith and moral teaching to bear on issues of economics, especially poverty issues. The phrase "missionary economist" has always seemed like an oxymoron to most people. So it is my delight to address in this volume an audience of people who desire to combine compassion and analysis in helping the poor. As we explore ways in which academics and practitioners can work more closely together in the attack on poverty, we are all serving as missionary economists.

The Importance of Addressing Poverty Concerns Together

It is fitting that this book brings together Christian economists and practitioners to discuss the attack on poverty, because what is most distinctive about the economics of the God of the Bible is God's special concern for the poor and oppressed. The seminal experience of the Old Testament is the exodus—the liberation of poor and oppressed people. God did not send Moses to Pharaoh's courts to take up a collection of canned goods, but rather to insist on political and economic change—the liberation of the slaves. Then, in the wilderness, God gave his people a law, the Mosaic Law, which is shot through with provisions to protect poor people, especially widows, orphans and immigrants.

Centuries later, God's prophets focused on two offenses—idolatry and neglect of social justice. The clearest mark of worshipping the true God, rather than an idol, was not that you used the right words but that you did right by people in need. The prophets insisted on both personal charity and social justice. They held the kings—the government of the day—especially accountable for protecting poor people. At a time when our own nation is preoccupied with national security, it is important to remember that the prophets taught that the way to achieve national security was to worship the Lord and do right by poor people.

A few more centuries later in the biblical history, we come to our Lord Jesus—healing the sick, casting out demons, feeding the hungry and preaching good news to the poor. Jesus disobeyed laws when they hurt people or marginalized people, and he was crucified for the threat he posed to religious and political authorities. Jesus' resurrection is our guarantee of forgiveness and life beyond the grave, but it is also our guarantee that poor people will be rescued. The day will come when there will be hunger no more. Christians wait and work for that day.

Sharing was certainly a mark of the New Testament Church, and the crying need for such sharing is even greater today. Despite strong Christian influence, however, our country is no impressive model of sharing. We are Christian economists at a time in history when the whole world is bound together economically, when about 800 million people are still routinely undernourished, and when our nation is the world's major power. Many Americans—around 25 percent—are in church every Sunday. Even so, our country doesn't do nearly what it could do to reduce hunger and poverty in the world. I have watched our presidents and Congress closely over the last decade, and I am sure that reducing world hunger and poverty has never been even among the top 100 concerns of our elected officials at the national level.

The integrity and gospel witness of U.S. Christianity in our time depends on more faithful response to hunger and poverty in our country and around the world. A more serious commitment from U.S. Christians would, without any doubt, dramatically accelerate progress against poverty worldwide. So the topic of this book—the attack on poverty—is exactly what Christian economists should be talking about.

This book stresses especially improving collaboration between those of us who are working every day in practical ways to reduce poverty and those of us who do research in academic settings. The unfortunate, and somewhat surprising, truth is that these two groups haven't tended to work very closely together. But the potential is great. This volume—and the conference which preceded it—should give rise to a number of specific new initiatives and collaborations. I certainly hope that Bread for the World Institute will develop new partnerships during the course of this conference. Finding specific ways to work together will lead to much more practical progress than talking about "big ideas."

Bread for the World

In initiating a dialogue with academics, it is useful for practitioners to provide academics with a "wish list." In the spirit of getting practical, I'll set out what I think practitioners want, drawing on my own experience at Bread for the World. Before providing my list, it is useful to provide some background on BFW.

Bread for the World is a national Christian citizens' movement against hunger. Our 50,000 members, including 2,500 churches, lobby Congress on issues that are important to hungry people in our country and worldwide. We rely on long-standing relationships with a wide range of denominations and with Christian agencies such as World Vision and World Relief.

Bread for the World Institute is a partner organization that does research and education on hunger issues. Bread for the World can't lobby effectively if we don't think clearly, and Bread for the World Institute is the think tank and teacher for Bread for the World. For example, the Institute is about to issue a major report on how the agricultural policies of the industrialized countries depress agriculture in developing countries. That is not an easy issue, but U.S. church people who care about world hunger need to understand it.

Bread for the World and the Institute do draw on academic research, especially for the Institute's annual report on hunger. But I think we rely much more on other sources of knowledge—U.S.

and U.N. agencies, private agencies such as World Vision and
Church World Services, and policy think tanks. We have much
to gain from opening new doors of communication with Christian
academics.

What Practitioners Would Like from Academics

Let me suggest three areas in which practitioners in organizations like BFW could use help from academics. I hope that discussion of these and other needs will give rise to new partnerships
between academics and practitioners.

First, we need help in developing better *measures* of the poverty and other problems we are trying to fight, and of the success
of various efforts to reduce them. In general, we need measures
that are fast, feasible, easily comprehended and easily disseminated back to policy makers and donors in middlebrow fashion.

For example, at BFW we need better and more timely measures of hunger around the world. The best data come from the
United Nations Food and Agriculture Organization, but they are
rough estimates and always a couple of years out-of-date.

At BFW we also need studies of the impact of international
development assistance. For nearly 30 years we have worked with
some success to win funding for selected development assistance
programs. Most Americans are deeply skeptical about how effective international development assistance has been. Now, most
foreign aid has been driven by foreign policy interests, so we
shouldn't be surprised that it hasn't been very effective in helping poor people. But I wish we had more and better information
about some of the best development assistance programs—the
Child Survival Revolution, for example, or Africa's Famine Early
Warning System. I wish we had more stories about how these
large governmental initiatives have affected particular communities and families. That would help us convince U.S. Christians to
speak up for new initiatives of this sort.

Similarly, we would love to have more evidence on the beneficial impacts of debt relief for poor countries. In 1999 and 2000,
Bread for the World and many other church groups worked to-

gether as part of the global Jubilee campaign to win debt relief for some of the world's poorest countries. We insisted on processes that would translate debt relief for poor countries into help for poor people. The Jubilee campaign included churches and other groups in poor countries, and the process we won—the Poverty Reduction Strategy process—promotes public discussion. Our sense—based on what we learn from grassroots groups and church groups—is that debt relief is working remarkably well—that many more children are in school, that more medicines are in rural clinics, and that, in some countries, the process of debt relief has helped to reduce corruption and strengthen democracy. But more systematic evidence on these effects would be much more persuasive in convincing Christians who helped achieve debt relief to push on other issues that are important to poor people around the world.

A second need of development practitioners is help in *designing programs and policies* that do the best possible job of meeting our organizations' objectives. For example, grassroots groups might need help in designing microcredit programs to reach specific populations.

As an advocacy group, our design needs are somewhat different. At BFW, we need help designing a reform proposal for U.S. nutrition assistance programs. Federal nutrition programs, such as the Women, Infants, and Children Supplemental Food Program (WIC) or the Food Stamp Program, work well. Expanding these programs would be the most direct, fastest way to reduce hunger in our richly blessed nation. But these programs could also be improved. They could be more efficient and less bureaucratic. They could be better connected to all that communities are doing through food banks and anti-hunger coalitions to help hungry people. Reform ideas that would deliver more real help for hungry people for each taxpayer dollar would help us win voter support for expanding nutrition assistance. We at BFW would also benefit from research that can teach us how to design programs that build up U.S. political commitment to reducing poverty worldwide. Researchers might start to answer this question by undertaking a critical history of Bread for the World itself. What campaigns had the biggest impact for hungry people? Which of Bread for the World's outreach efforts are most effective in engaging U.S. Christians as agents of global justice? What should Bread for the World do differently over the coming decade?

We also have much to learn from research on other social movements and lobbying campaigns. What approaches are effective for engaging low-income Americans and people of color in changing our country's poverty policies? What can research teach us about how to mobilize Christian congregations and individuals as agents of global justice? How do evangelical Protestants tend to think about these issues? Nondenominational community churches are growing by leaps and bounds; what are they doing about global poverty, and how can they be engaged in advocacy for public policy change that would help hungry and poor people?

The third thing practitioners need from academics is not actually research, but *activism*. As respected members of civic and religious communities, academics command attention, and could use it to promote thoughtful giving and active involvement in the politics of poverty reduction. All Christian development organizations will benefit as academic economists develop courses on poverty, give lectures and teach Sunday school classes.

At Bread for the World, our need for academic economists' involvement in advocacy is even more acute. Such activism can help change U.S. government priorities. I hope academic economists will all become members of Bread for the World. They clearly have the necessary commitment and knowledge. They could do a lot to help us convince our elected officials to make poverty reduction a higher priority.

Bread for the World is campaigning to increase the effectiveness of development and health assistance to poor countries. The terrorist attacks convinced President Bush that reducing poverty in the world is important to U.S. national security. So he has proposed a major expansion of U.S. funding for poverty-focused development assistance—an additional $7 billion a year. President Bush wants to make sure that this new money is used effectively and that it supports what poor countries themselves need to do to overcome poverty. So he has proposed that most of this additional money be channeled through a new Millennium Challenge Account and go to poor countries with relatively good governments. By good governments, he means governments that are democratic, allow markets to work, and invest in the health and education of their people. President Bush has also proposed an expanded U.S. initiative to help poor countries cope with the HIV/AIDS pandemic.

Democrats and Republicans in Congress have reached agreement, in principal, that the United States should do more to reduce hunger, poverty and disease globally. But the promised increase in funding will not actually be approved unless tens of thousands of Christian people and other people of good will actively, passionately push the elected leaders to keep these promises to poor people around the world. I hope that both practitioners and academic economists will become part of this campaign and will engage their institutions in it. If academic economists help Bread for the World come alive on their campus, they will definitely have an impact on their members of Congress. Thirty years of Bread for the World experience makes me sure of that. They will also teach their entire student body that they can and should speak to the elected officials on issues that are important to poor people worldwide.

This is a very tough time for poor people. The slowdown of the global economy means that coffee farmers in Guatemala are only getting a third as much income as they did five years ago. Parts of Africa that are already plagued by HIV/AIDS are now facing famine, too. President Bush's highest priorities are homeland security, war against Iraq and terrorism, and big tax cuts, mainly for rich people.

At this somber time the vocation of Christian economists— missionary economists—is serious business. We need to think clearly, work resolutely, and collaborate. We are called to speak out with God's own passion on behalf of people in need.

3

Collaborations of Mutual Benefit to Academics and Practitioners

Kenneth Leonard (University of Maryland)

What can development scholars and researchers gain from conversation and collaboration with development practitioners? How could scholars approach such interactions to make them more fruitful? Would collaborations that are fruitful for researchers be worthwhile for practitioners? In this chapter I argue that researchers and practitioners have much to gain from four modes of interaction: engagement in knowledge forums, development of practitioner-oriented academic programs, informal conversations, and collaboration in joint research projects. I offer my views on how to shape each form of interaction for greatest mutual benefit. Of the four modes, the last merits the most lengthy discussion. Collaboration in joint research projects has tremendous potential value, but is daunting for reasons that must be acknowledged and accounted for. I propose a model of intensive collaboration that combines elements of research design more familiar to academics, with elements of action research or participatory research more familiar to practitioners, to produce a hybrid which capitalizes on the strengths of each group. I argue that such collaborative research has greater potential to achieve the goals of both academics and practitioners than current modes of research pursued by either group independently.

The Benefits of Collaboration

We are considering here the potential for collaboration between academics in both research and teaching positions at universities, and practitioners who work for local or international non-profit organizations (called non-governmental organizations or NGOs) working in some form of poverty alleviation in developing countries. The definition of an NGO is elusive, but I specifically intend it to include religious service organizations. This is different from collaboration with practitioners in international development organizations, or national development agencies, which have long histories of collaboration with development scholars. Individual academics and practitioners in smaller NGOs do not typically work in an environment with direct incentives for such collaboration.

Collaboration between these groups can have many important benefits. Development scholars and practitioners have significant overlap in goals. We are all fighting poverty and believe that there are and should be deliberate actions to facilitate the achievement of this goal. The benefits of collaboration come from the obvious fact that scholars and practitioners have different and complementary skill sets and access to resources. The practitioner is the one in the field doing the work and has at his disposal a functioning institution with experience and local knowledge. Importantly, practitioners often have access to two very important groups: policy makers and the poor. Access to policy makers offers the possibility of rapid dissemination of new ideas or results. Access to the poor means that, in a research framework, the questions asked and the results discovered have a greater chance of being helpful. Scholars bring practical research tools, a broader view of international development experience and the analytical tools to view local experience in this light. Collaboration offers opportunities for the exchange of knowledge, skill and access for the creation and dissemination of knowledge and for the alleviation of poverty.

It is important to emphasize at this point how difficult it is for almost any scholar to get true access to the poor. I can travel to a poor country, but the people I meet will be the elite of that country. I can travel to poor areas of poor countries, but I will most likely interact with the elite of those poor communities. I can find the poorest people of the poorest communities, but I will have no way of understanding the social structure they inhabit. I cannot tell the difference between a social safety net and a glass ceiling. Even if I were to be able to clearly see all the paths and obstacles to poverty alleviation, I would still have no mechanism for effecting change. Cooperation with the community I am trying to help would be necessary to achieve progress, and trust is a prerequisite for cooperation. When there exists an institution that has gained the trust of the poor, I should deal with it. The fact that a majority of such institutions in the developing world are religious based organizations suggests that scholars who are willing and able to work with such organizations can achieve otherwise unobtainable results.

Knowledge Forums

The conference organized by the Association of Christian Economists is one obvious example of a forum designed for the exchange of knowledge between development practitioners and scholars. Importantly the conference was not designed for academics to talk and practitioners to listen. The communication must be in both directions. Such meetings are also a good way for practitioners and scholars to make contact that might allow for future, more intense forms of collaboration. When such forums are general, covering all topics of development in all parts of the world, there is a danger that little information is actually exchanged. It is possible to divide up such groups along service lines or along geographical lines. However, such divisions might rule out important opportunities for collaboration. In my opinion, general combinations of services and areas are acceptable as long as every participant is careful to communicate the context of his work. Practitioners working in Chile should be able to learn from those working in Nigeria, and people working in health care should be able to learn from those working in education.

Outside of formal gatherings, individuals can further these goals of communication directly. I try to maintain parallel version of some of my papers, with one version for my colleagues and another for practitioners. However, it is very difficult to disseminate the second version such that it can be found and accessed by practitioners. I have used the web but have found that more formal mechanisms (such as a World Bank newsletter) are more likely to catch the practitioner's eye.[1] Scholars and practitioners should try to make themselves aware of such resources where they exist.

Development of Practitioner-Oriented Academic Programs

As with most scholars, I am both a teacher and researcher. I had the privilege of teaching for many years in a Masters program designed for mid-career professionals from the public service sector of developing countries. These were students who were similar in many ways to the people who work in international development organizations. Many practitioners can benefit enormously from continuing education programs that are designed to meet their needs. Too many Masters programs are designed either for students to continue on to PhD programs or for American students to enter the international job market. Columbia University, with both a school of international and public policy and an economics PhD program with a strong field in development economics, saw the need to develop a program specifically for these international students.

That program had the following necessary characteristics. First there were generous scholarships available for students coming from developing countries. Second we substituted a formal set of pre-requisites for a flexible and individual-specific application review process. Third we had an intensive course work program designed not to teach students the answers, but to teach them how to find the answers that were specific to their own working environments. Fourth we had faculty who were dedicated to teaching in the program, not a rotating series of star professors. And lastly there was a clearly defined set of future employers for our students and we actively sought feedback from these employers every year.

A successful program creates a professional ethic among the students and generates a sense of membership in a professional cadre. In an ideal world these shared professional values can help people to transcend the pressures of daily life. I have had the experience of meeting veterinarians from many countries in Africa who got their advanced degrees in Edinburgh, Scotland, from a program they all described as difficult and transforming. One such man, living in a country destroyed by civil war, still went about his day measuring his work against what he imagined his fellow students from twenty years ago would have done, relatively immune to the immediate pressures around him. In addition, a successful program should be aware that awarding credentials often allows the best students to leave the very sector in which they would have had the most significant impact on poverty alleviation. I do not know if it is possible to escape this trap. One common method is to focus on short courses that offer certificates but not degrees. However, these short programs do not offer students the chance to escape the pressures and immediate concerns of their jobs and to see the larger picture, to compare their own experience to that of the rest of the world.

That an essential element of the successful program is a well-defined set of employers, points to the important role that practitioners must play in any such program. Not only must they aid in the design of the program by discussing what they expect students to learn, they should remain in contact with the teachers and administrators of the program to provide feedback. Students who discover that their education is not useful in their jobs rarely write back to their professors, but when this happens scholars need to hear from the practitioners who employ these students.

Informal Conversations

I worked for a short while with an Italian doctor on a successful research project in Tanzania. In retrospect I learned more from the conversation we had over dinner the night I left town than I did from the project itself. He had spent a lot of time in the field and had thought carefully about the issues he was facing. His ideas for how to improve the system were not the kind of things you can learn simply by studying the current system. He had thought about issues I had never questioned. This came not just from his experience but from his fundamentally different training and perspective.

Just as scholars and practitioners possess complementary skills and resources, they also posses complementary perspectives. These will necessarily come to bear in the context of designing a collaborative research project, though conversations of this type should not be restricted to such a format. Informal conversations do not need to generate either knowledge or impact and should therefore be freer. These are conversations about possibilities, not probabilities; ideas and experience, not necessarily knowledge or impact.

What should be discussed will of course depend on the context and the actors. My advice to both practitioners and economists is to realize that economists will often have useful contributions to offer even before they know many specifics of the situation. In my experience, economists (and probably all social scientists) have more training in thinking about the unintended or far reaching consequences of actions. The narrow or highly stylized view of human behavior that characterizes economists also allows them to think through the broader implications. Local actions can have far reaching consequences, both positive and negative. You can serve the poor but end up benefiting the elite (if they simply have to pay a lower wage to the poor because someone else guarantees their survival). You can serve one person and end up benefiting both that person and someone else (by reducing the prevalence of a communicable illness, for example). You can pay someone to perform a particular action and find that you have in fact encouraged him or her to do the exact opposite.

Practitioners, of course, are not ignorant of these impacts. Even when they do not anticipate all of the possible impacts of a program, they do witness the realized impacts. And the real world is complex enough that often programs have impacts that economists would fail to anticipate. The juxtaposition of theory and reality is precisely what makes these conversations so fruitful. The economist is trained to expect such impacts and to know where to look for them and the practitioner knows what is actually happening in the community.

Collaboration in Joint Research

Collaboration in joint research projects will happen only if it can be designed to deliver benefits to both researcher and practitioner, but it can be hard to design collaborative projects that deliver what matters most to both parties. Although poverty alleviation is a common goal of both practitioners and researchers, it is not the only goal of either party. Scholars are judged by their ability to create and disseminate knowledge. Practitioners are judged by their ability to help their target population. Unfortunately, for most academic institutions, the dissemination of knowledge usually implies dissemination to other scholars (publication in journals or academic presses). For the practitioner, the need to satisfy organizational stakeholders means that his immediate goal is to help his target population. The larger and more forward thinking the organization, the more likely that it will explicitly devote resources to the creation of knowledge, but creation of knowledge is rarely the primary concern of the practitioner in the field. The scholar lives in a world in which it is not productive to say "this project had a positive impact on the welfare of the targeted population, but we don't know whether it can be replicated." The practitioner lives in a world in which it is not productive to say "the project failed, but we have now conclusively identified the reason why it failed." Thus while both scholars and researchers might take an interest in studying the impacts of poverty reduction projects, their goals and preferred methods will tend to differ.

It is useful to highlight some characteristics of research design about which researchers and practitioners might be inclined to make different choices, in particular the care taken to ensure that the results can be generalized and the approaches taken to what economists call "identification" of true impacts or causal effects. These are closely related and the subject of more lengthy consideration in Julie Schaffner's discussion of impact assessment in Chapter 14. In research aiming to measure the effect of some action on some outcome, identification is achieved when the research design insures that the measured relationship between action and outcome is a reflection of true causal impact. For identification, the research design must allow researchers to prove that the outcomes observed were not caused by something other than the action. Identification is important both to practitioners wanting to learn about the impact of their specific programs, and to scholars who want to learn more general lessons, but scholars may tend to prefer research designs that take a more rigorous approach to identification. The difference in preferences lies in the fact that while scholars' primary interest is in advancing knowledge (thereby improving poverty reduction efforts in the future and in other places), practitioners place more weight on helping current target groups.

To illustrate the potential conflict between rigorous identification and maximized current impact, let me pick an example: research about the impact of supplying desks to rural schools in developing countries. Such research poses a simple question: "Do desks make students learn better?" The action is replacing nonexistent or old desks with acceptable desks. As an outcome the scholar will pick something measurable, like attendance or test scores (or some combination of the two). Researchers seeking to identify the true causal impact of desks on schooling outcomes must design the research so that they can isolate the impact of desks on test scores. They will want to compare outcomes in schools with desks to outcomes in schools without desks, while insuring that there are no other differences between the two types of schools that might explain differences in test scores. The gold standard for such experiments is randomization, where schools are randomly chosen to belong to the control group (no desks) or the experiment group (desks). In general, the less systematic (or the more random) the process by which people are exposed to any particular action or policy, the more useful it is to compare the outcomes between the two groups. Knowledge is furthered by being able to isolate the impact of a particular program from other influences on the outcome.

Unfortunately, the closer the research design is to the gold standard of randomization, the less scope practitioners have to add value through careful selection of recipients. Practitioners seeking to get the most benefit out of a limited number of desks would not choose schools randomly. Understanding the differential ability of communities to absorb and benefit from programs is one of the benefits of being a local organization. The practitioner will not put desks in schools that already have nice desks, nor will he add desks to schools that don't have any teachers or buildings. He will not add desks if he thinks they will be stolen, or if he knows that the poor in that community are being excluded from access to that school. He knows that if he adds desks randomly he will have significantly lower impact than if he adds desks selectively. When practitioners make interventions available selectively in this manner, rigorous standards of identification cannot be attained, because it impossible to distinguish the extent to which differences in test scores between schools that did and did not receive desks are the result of receiving the desks rather than the result of pre-existing differences that led to selection. The true "impact" of receiving the desks may be overstated by the differences, if selected schools had characteristics that tended to increase test scores even without desks, and may be understated if the selected schools tended to be particularly needy along multiple dimensions.

Even when academics and researchers agree on an approach to identification, they may differ in the lengths to which they are willing to go to guarantee that their results produce lessons of general value (i.e., value to many development actors, not just the organization involved in the research). Identifying the impact of a particular program may be the primary objective of the practitioner, who may not place great weight on deriving more general lessons about poverty reduction approaches from the research. Academics are, at least in principle, more concerned with generalization. Returning to the school desk example: suppose the following compromise approach to identification has been achieved. Practitioners select schools to receive desks in the way they see fit, and academics attempt to measure impact by comparing outcomes in these schools before and after the introduction of the desks. (Even better, they may have collected additional information on outcomes for schools that did not receive desks and verified that in the absence of the desk distribution, schooling outcomes were not changing for other reasons.) Despite identification of the true impact of this desk distribution program, the results cannot be used to make predictions about the impacts that other organizations would achieve if they give desks to schools. If the practitioner has done a good job of selecting schools where impact will be especially large, then the impact observed in this comparison is larger than the impact to be expected from giving desks to a random set of schools, and quite possibly larger than the impact to be derived by other organizations giving desks to schools through different selection mechanisms. The researcher could draw some conclusions about the impact of *this organization's* desk distribution program, but not the more general impact of desks alone.

Designing Collaborative Research for Mutual Benefit. The first step toward mutually beneficial collaboration is recognition of the obstacles to collaboration. Research that best accomplishes the objectives of both academic and practitioner is designed to acknowledge both the organization's need to practice selection and the potential obstacles this poses to the achievement of generalizable research results. In many cases, mutual collaboration would have two characteristics, the combination of which would render it an exciting new alternative to the research carried out by either academics or practitioners.

First, mutually beneficial research designs will often allow practitioners to practice selection, while taking a rigorous approach to identification of true impact. It rules out the possibility that observed differences between groups that have and have not been given program benefits (like the "desks" discussed above) are driven by pre-existing differences between groups, by randomly selecting groups for treatment *among groups already selected by the organizations.* For example, Michael Kremer of Harvard convinced Internationaal Christelijk Steunfonds Africa (ICS) to randomize over the dates on which they were to begin a program in different schools (Miguel and Kremer, 2004). The practitioner produced a list of schools to receive the program and a random device (like picking names out of a hat) produced a group to receive the program in the first round and a group to receive it in the second round. The scholar can then compare the outcomes between the two different groups in the first round. Randomization allows the scholar to say that the schools receiving the program first are not different from the schools not receiving the program in the first round. But all of the schools were carefully selected by the NGO and since the NGO would have had to stagger start dates anyway, this randomization comes at little cost to them, but great benefit to the research and ultimately, knowledge. It is important to recognize that this knowledge is of tremendous value to the practitioner organization. If the effects of pre-existing differences are not ruled out, then the organization learns little about true impact. This process can easily be replicated for many types of programs. It requires coordination and a willingness on the part of the practitioner to allow some degree of transparency (he must select all the schools that will receive the program up front, and not change his mind when his favorite school is not chosen for the first round).

The second characteristic of mutually beneficial research wrestles with the difficulty of generalizing from the research design just described. Randomization among entities selected by the practitioner organization identifies the specific impact of a particular organization's poverty reduction efforts. Rather than trying to avoid this, the mutually beneficial research design highlights the importance of this to drawing truly useful conclusions, and digs more deeply into understanding exactly how the program was carried out. Institutions are as central to the development process as interventions. While it is important to know which interventions work, it is just as important to know how effective institutions make sure that they work. This type of research must communicate information about the institutions that implement policies, if it is to be of any use. When it can clearly communicate this information, it not only tells us the impact of a policy, but maps out how the policy might be replicated. We should not be asking the question, "do desks make students better off," but rather, "how does an effective organization identify needs, implement a program based on these needs, and ensure success?" To answer this question, academics must move outside the bounds of the research methods with which they are most familiar.

The Distinctiveness and Importance of this Mutually Beneficial Research. Collaboration of this sort between practitioners and academics can be characterized as a novel, and for some purposes superior, alternative to what are sometimes labeled "conventional" and "participatory" research.[2] Under conventional research (of the sort familiar to academics), the researcher identifies the research question, collects data (with the help of enumerators), analyzes the data in the light of disciplinary concepts and pre-existing academic literature, and presents the results to other academics and large development agencies. Under participatory research (at least ideally), local people identify the research questions, collect data, analyze the data in light of their experience and with an eye to their own empowerment and learning, and take immediate local action in response to the results. Each approach has its advantages and disadvantages. Conventional research draws on the expertise of academics in designing research for identification and generalization, and on the ability of thoughtful outsiders to "think outside the box," but may fail to connect with what matters to the poor themselves and may fail to produce practical results. Participatory research fosters strong links between research and action, but, by failing to resolve identification problems or by employing small and non-representative samples, can produce misleading conclusions.

Working in collaboration, academics and practitioners could develop a new hybrid approach to research that would do a better job than either of these extremes at achieving the goals of both academics and practitioners. Academics could make more valuable contributions to knowledge if their research designs were more sensitive to the concerns of the poor and more informed about the institutional details of the organizations trying to help the poor. It is very difficult for academics to work directly with the poor, but they can gain indirect access to the poor by collaborating with NGO development organizations that do work closely with the poor. Practitioners could obtain more reliable and complete answers to the questions of importance to them with research designs more sensitive to problems of identification, but may find the required methods daunting. They can acquire expertise in these areas through collaboration with academics.

Such "action collaboration" would lean on the skills and resources of both the practitioner and the scholar with the immediate goal of helping the poor. Problem identification and topic choice would be driven by the practitioner. The methodology would be chosen so as to further both impact and knowledge. The research must provide interpretation and analysis that allows the practitioner to learn, in a timely manner, about the success of his program and how to improve it. The research must also provide knowledge about how this positive impact is achieved and it should be able to identify the elements of both the program and the NGO that contributed to the success.

Action collaboration puts the scholar in four different relationships with a development practitioner. He *listens* to the priorities of the practitioner, learning about goals and projects. He *uses* the practitioner's organization and that organization's projects to implement an appropriate research project. He *studies* the practitioner and his organization within the context of the project. And he *enables* the practitioner to improve by providing timely and appropriate feedback and analysis. Effective practitioners are characterized not by the fact that they are always successful, but rather by the fact that they learn from their mistakes and adapt successfully. Action collaboration puts the practitioner in his normal relationship with the target population, but also into a new relationship with both his organization and the scholar. The practitioner is both partner and subject to the scholar. The research is performed both with and on the practitioner and his organization.

None of this makes either the scholar's or the practitioner's jobs easier. Adding the elements of the institution to the research question only makes identification more difficult. But, I have agued that to properly identify the answer to a less important question is no real gain. The real challenge to action research comes in choosing the right problem to study and in picking the right questions to ask. The scholar and practitioner will not generally be examining the impact of a clearly defined policy like adding desks, but rather a less well-defined poverty alleviation approach. This is a process that should be driven by the development practitioner who has the interests of the poor in mind. He must have control over the types of programs to be studied and the time frame in which analysis is produced. But the training of the scholar is an essential element of success. As discussed in the section on informal conversations between practitioners and scholars, each party has a very different perspective on the world. The scholar must be aggressive in asking questions about who is to be served, how outcomes are to be measured, the opportunity cost (alternative uses) of the funds and what constitutes success.

Conclusions

I think we do not collaborate enough. The shared goals and the diverse skills and resources of practitioners and scholars are a vast resource waiting to be tapped. I have offered a number of cursory examples of how we might collaborate. Importantly we must not be blind to the fact that each of us seeks slightly different objectives in collaboration especially in a research framework. Cooperation should be pursued only when both participants have their eyes wide open. Trust does not mean we have the same interests, but that we believe cooperation can be mutually beneficial.

Forums for the exchange of ideas and informal conversations are both ways in which collaboration can begin immediately. These should be actively pursued by both practitioners and scholars. These will automatically lead people to begin talking about more intensive forms of collaboration. The deeper the collaboration, the more openly scholars think about success and impact and practitioners think about general knowledge, the greater the potential benefits. Teaching programs for development practitioners is a more formal commitment, and even if it is not possible to design programs that serve this population exclusively, it is possible that currently existing programs can be altered so that they were more inclusive of the needs of these types of students.

The collaborative research described in this chapter is both an outline for successful collaboration between two parties with differing goals and a call for better research—research more likely to answer the questions that really matter to poverty alleviation. The scholars' concern with identification is something that practitioners should share and the practitioners' use of selectivity to achieve impact is something the scholar should seek to understand. With proper collaboration the joint product is vastly superior to anything either party could produce on their own. It is not just a matter of sharing resources and skills but of pushing towards a deeper understanding of what is necessary to achieve true poverty alleviation.

References

Cornwall, Andrea and Rachael Jewkes. 1995. "What Is Participatory Research?" *Social Science & Medicine*. 41:12, pp. 1667–1676.

Leonard, Kenneth L. 2003. "African Traditional Healers and Outcome-Contingent Contracts in Health Care," *Journal of Development Economics*. 72:1, pp. 1–22.

Leonard, Kenneth L. 2001. "African Traditional Healers: The Economics of Healing," *Indigenous Knowledge Notes*. No. 32 (May).

Miguel, Edward and Michael Kremer. 2004. "Worms: Identifying Impacts on Education and Health in the Presence of Treatment Externalities," *Econometrica*. 72:1, pp. 159–217.

Notes

[1] A paper of mine on traditional medicine is tailored to different audiences and in three different formats: a refereed publication (Leonard, 2003), an article in a World Bank magazine (Leonard, 2001), and as a paper on my research website ("African Traditional Healers: are they as good at economics as they are at medicine?" www.arec.umd.edu/kleonard/research.html).

[2] For a detailed contrast of these two research approach extremes, see Cornwall and Jewkes (1995).

4

Productive Collaborations between Development Practitioners and Academics

James E. Foster (Vanderbilt University)[1]

> There are different kinds of gifts, but the same Spirit. There are different kinds of service, but the same Lord. There are different kinds of working, but the same God works all of them in all men. 1 Corinthians 12:4–6

Poverty is fundamentally multidimensional, with significant complementarities across its constituent dimensions.[2] This observation has important implications for practitioners who provide services to the poor, and for academic researchers seeking to understand and explain poverty: collaboration is crucial. Practitioners addressing one component of development can enhance their effectiveness by coordinating their efforts with NGOs, churches and government organizations providing other services for the poor. Similarly, researchers from one academic discipline can gain a better understanding of poverty by seeking out other disciplinary perspectives. The most fruitful studies of poverty are likely to involve collections of scholars willing to transcend disciplinary boundaries.

At the same time, such "within group" collaborations can be challenging to implement. Different development practitioners often have diverging missions, time horizons, and target populations, and this can hamper their ability to work together to help the poor. Coordinating the efforts of several organizations—even those with congruent long run objectives—can entail significant transactions costs. Within the academy, there are substantial barriers to the cross-disciplinary collaboration needed to study poverty in all its dimensions. This arises in part from the longstanding academic tradition that rewards are decided within the faculty member's home department with contributions across disciplinary lines being undervalued, thereby discouraging interested faculty from venturing outside disciplinary bounds. Early-career researchers, in particular, have a strong disincentive to engage in the multidisciplinary research needed to understand poverty. Even so, when there is a shared vision and a common purpose among participants, such "within group" collaboration can thrive despite the presence of structural impediments.

"Across-group" collaborations between development practitioners and academics face even more daunting challenges. To begin with, practitioners and academics have rather different incentive structures. Academic institutions reward faculty on the basis of their research and teaching (with greater emphasis on research at most research universities); outreach efforts are typically not part of the equation. Consequently, faculty have little institutional incentive to participate in collaborations with practitioners. In contrast, academic research and teaching are not high on the development practitioner's list of concerns; effective outreach is typically the main objective. Academics have the luxury of time and can spend long hours crafting a paper for publication or presentation. Practitioners have more immediate and tangible concerns. Even the very language used by academics and practitioners can be vastly different. In light of this, a natural question to ask is: what basis is there for collaboration across the groups?

Benefits to Academic Researchers of Collaboration with Practitioners

My contention in this paper is that despite fundamental differences in incentives, orientation and even language, there are significant potential benefits from partnerships between practitioners and academics, at both the individual and institutional levels. The laboratory of the academic social scientist is the real world—an environment where development practitioners work on a daily basis and have amassed substantial practical and institutional experience. Their familiarity with the community makes them valuable to the academic researcher; they have information on local conditions and can even provide access to key populations that the researcher is interested in studying.

A dialog with practitioners can lead to the identification of important research problems. Informed observations by practitioners can help shape the models developed by theorists as well as the hypotheses that applied researchers will later test. Case studies of practitioners' programs can provide insights helpful for formulating general development solutions for policy researchers. Some innovations in development practice, such as the Grameen Bank discussed below, have led to entirely new fields as academic researchers try to understand and evaluate them. Practitioners can take a more active role in knowledge creation by working with researchers to design experiments for evaluating the effectiveness of alternative development strategies. And partnerships between the university and groups providing services to the poor can advance the university's outreach mission while at the same time offering new educational experiences for students—such as internships and service learning. In sum, the potential benefits to academic researchers and their institutions from collaborating with practitioners are not unsubstantial.

Benefits to Practitioners of Collaboration with Academic Researchers

In a similar fashion, links with the academic research community can help the development practitioner in several ways. The typical academic has a great deal of knowledge—both general and specific—that may have value to the practitioner. At the most general level, the economist can provide a clear picture of how markets work and when they don't work, the role of the government, and many other contextual features in an economy. An academic with specific experience in the practitioner's field can help by anticipating future needs in the target population. The academic can be a valuable partner in the design of new programs and the improvement of existing programs. Most important of all, academics can provide an independent evaluation of ongoing programs to ensure that they are doing what they are meant to do. The feedback from such an evaluation can lead to improvements in the operations of the practitioner's organization, while an unusually favorable evaluation can push it into the spotlight as an example for other practitioners to follow—an excellent example being Mexico's Progresa-Oportunidades program described below. An ongoing link with a university can add credibility to the practitioner's organization and expand its resource base to include student and faculty effort and expertise. And since academia is a network, affiliation with a key node on that network places the practitioner in a position to access a remarkable reservoir of resources. Thus, significant benefits from collaboration may travel in the other direction as well.

Collaboration in the Grameen Bank

To bring this point home, let us examine the cases of two organizations that have had particularly successful collaborations over the years. The first is the Grameen Bank, a remarkable nonprofit from Bangladesh created to address a central problem of the poor—the absence of a functioning credit market for persons whose only asset is their own labor. Without the ability to borrow funds, it is impossible for potentially productive, but poor, small-scale entrepreneurs to start up or expand. The hopeful picture painted by economic theory—in which scarce resources move rapidly to their most efficient uses—breaks down. What form of institution can redress this "market failure" and allow the poor to become participants in the marketplace? One answer is the Grameen ("Rural" or "Village") Bank of Bangladesh.

The Grameen Bank is a credit union-like non-profit organization that provides small loans to the landless poor in Bangladesh using a fund that has been built up from grants from various sources, including individual gifts, foundation grants, and payments from previous borrowers. Over 90 percent of recipients are women, who typically use loans to buy tools and equipment necessary to engage in small-scale, income-generating enterprises, such as "paddy husking, lime-making, manufacturing such as pottery, weaving, and garment sewing, storage and marketing and transport services."[3] No explicit collateral is required to obtain the loan. Instead, the Grameen approach requires participants to adhere to certain norms of behavior and to join a network of participants that supports the efforts of borrowers. Central to this structure is the five-person local borrowing group, whose members receive individual loans in series, contingent upon the performance of other group members. Consequently the group members are highly motivated to support and monitor each other.

There are several aspects that make the Grameen Bank a notable example for development specialists. First is the relative *sustainability* of the system, as the default rate for Grameen loans is quite low—less than 5 percent—despite the absence of collateral. This ensures that the scarce resource, financial capital, is recycled among many borrowers. Second is the *targeted* approach with which participants are selected. To concentrate its efforts on the poor, a series of criteria have been established for identifying potential participants and encouraging them to participate. Third is the *gender* focus of Grameen, which acknowledges that women are the primary agents of development and directs most of its loans accordingly. Fourth is the *scale* of operations of the Bank. There are approximately 3.2M members of the Grameen Bank across Bangladesh and since its inception the Bank has disbursed a total of \$4.2B with about \$35M in loans being made in any given month. Fifth is the fact that the program has been *replicated* many times across the world. Grameen has been as much responsible for the microcredit revolution as any organization and has from its earliest days been concerned with documenting its approach and advising others on how to set up local versions to provide credit to the poor of other countries. As of today, there are approximately more than 150 microcredit programs worldwide that model themselves after Grameen Bank.

For purposes of the present discussion, it should be noted that Grameen has a stated policy of collaboration with other likeminded organizations, and has joined forces with many such organizations.[4] While the direct impact of academic research on the Bank's methods has been limited, the influence of the Grameen Bank on development policy and theory has proved to be quite significant, resulting in a new literature on microcredit institutions.[5]

Dr. Muhammad Yunus, the founder of the Grameen Bank, received his graduate training in economics from Vanderbilt University, and was an economics professor at Chittagong University in Bangladesh when the devastating conditions in his country led him to take on the mantle of practitioner and create Grameen.[6] He found the problems of his country to be beyond the ken of the economics of the day and instead sought out a novel and practical solution to the problems facing the poor. The Grameen approach was developed over time through trial and error, and while this process was primarily guided by practical considerations, there is no doubt that the innovative structure of Grameen benefited from the academic background of its founder.[7] Indeed, the design of Grameen relies on a fundamental appreciation of the role of incentives—a key theme of modern economics that is perhaps less emphasized in other academic fields and is often overlooked in the fashioning of social programs.[8]

The emergence of a financial institution that lends money to landless poor with high rates of repayment sparked interest among academic economists to understand the underlying incentive structure that could sustain it, and so the Grameen Bank has been the subject of a great deal of academic research. Over the years, Grameen has been visited by faculty, interns and students, who have documented the methodology used by Grameen and explored it from various disciplinary points of view. In addition, there have been a number of formal evaluations of the Grameen Bank done by independent research organizations—a fact that is noted on the Bank's website and provides additional validation for its activities to outside parties and potential supporters. The interaction between practitioner and academic researcher has played a key role in this innovative organization and it has clearly made its mark on subsequent academic research.

Collaboration in Mexico's Progresa-Oportunidades Program

A second example of productive collaboration can be found in an innovative government program designed to encourage poor families in Mexico to invest in the health, nutrition and education of their children. For poor parents, the opportunity cost of allowing children to continue in school is relatively significant and rises with age, which results in a much higher dropout rate among poor children and especially among poor girls. The absolute cost per student is often quite small in comparison to the long run benefits to the family and society, since education is one of the main avenues by which the cycle of poverty can be broken. Is there a strategy that might be used to address this market failure? The home-grown solution implemented by Mexico in 1997 was Progresa, or the Programa de Educación, Salud y Alimentación (the Education, Health, and Nutrition Program), which was later expanded by the Fox government under the name Oportunidades.

Progresa-Oportunidades is a program that uses a system of contingent monetary transfers to encourage a participating family to make human capital investments in its children. Mothers receive a cash transfer when children go to school regularly and are taken to the health clinic; a second grant ensures they receive proper nutrition. The transfers are substantial—on average, they represent approximately 22 percent of family income. The program initially focused on rural families, but was recently expanded to include urban dwellers and to provide incentives for students to complete secondary school.

The program is of interest to the development specialist for several reasons. It has exhibited an unusual degree of political *sustainability*, since it was initiated by one party and then retained and expanded by an opposing party when it took office. This is likely due to the general perception that it is an efficient, locally created program that is actually working. A central component of the program's structure is its *targeting* method, which ensures that more funds are made available to objectively poorer areas.[9] The result is a cost effective program with a lower level of leakage than many comparable programs. The *scale* of the program is likewise notable as it serves more than 2.5M rural families in Mexico (about one ninth of all families) and has an annual budget of approximately $780M.[10] The program is sensitive to *gender* in two important ways. First, its payment scheme provides a higher transfer for girls in order to reverse the existing trend for girls to drop out more readily than boys. Second, payments to the family are made to the mother in expectation that she will make the best use of them on behalf of the family. Finally, the success of the program has led to its being *replicated* in the region and worldwide, with countries such as Honduras and Nicaragua modeling or modifying programs in line with the Mexican approach.

Of particular relevance to the present discussion of collaboration, there has been a pervasive influence of academic researchers on Progresa-Oportunidades since its inception—a strong link that continues to this day. The origins of the program can be traced to a paper entitled "Poverty Intervention in Mexico" by Santiago Levy, who was then a professor at Boston University (and currently the Social Security Administrator in Mexico). A central theme of this paper is the multidimensionality of poverty and the need to address several dimensions at once (education, health and nutrition) to break the intergenerational transmission of poverty. He also noted that such a multifaceted investment program would require a close targeting of the resources directed to the poor, a process that could be aided by the use of decomposable poverty measures which had just been developed by researchers.[11] In August 1997 President Ernesto Zedillo of Mexico (himself an Ph.D in Economics from Yale) inaugurated the new program.

Under the guidance of Dr. Levy, who became Deputy Finance Minister, Progresa was rolled out in such a way to facilitate subsequent research and evaluation of the program. Base-line surveys were taken and, in order to differentiate between the treatment and controls groups in subsequent surveys, the timing of a community into the program was randomly assigned. The resulting quasi-experimental design yielded data that allowed a sophisticated evaluation of many of the intended impacts on the education, health and nutrition of children. The International Food Policy Research

Institute was called in to undertake a formal, independent evaluation of Progresa; reports were delivered to the government in 2000/1 and made available on the IFPRI website.[12] This exhaustive evaluation and the substantial academic literature on Progresa that followed provided significant support for the program, strengthening the political will behind it and allowing it to survive a change in government. Indeed, the Fox administration has embraced the program, providing a new name (Oportunidades) and expanding coverage to urban areas and to the final years of secondary education.[13] In order to design and evaluate the changes, the government has standing panels of leading academic experts who convene from time to time. It is safe to say that the impact of academic researchers on this real-world program has been, and continues to be, fundamental.

Facilitating Productive Collaboration

The above two examples were selected in part because of my familiarity with them. More importantly, though, they are two successful development programs that illustrate the kinds of relationships that are possible between practitioners and academic researchers. I suspect that there are a great many other potential partnerships out there that would provide substantial gains to both parties. If so, a natural question that arises is: how can productive collaborations between academics and practitioners be facilitated? The simple answer is to create supportive spaces where potential collaborators can meet and learn about each other, with a prime example being the conference sponsored by the Association of Christian Economists that gave rise to this book. But the venue can be much less formal, such as regular lunches for academics at a local NGO, or invitations to practitioners to present seminars at the local university. A thematic website can go a long way to bring various parties with common interests together, virtually speaking. In general, creating social capital, either from the ground up or more traditionally from existing social structures, provides a fertile source for future collaborations.

The university can play a central role in providing infrastructure for cooperation. My own institution, Vanderbilt University, has recently embarked on a bold program of new trans-institutional centers to encourage faculty from the various schools and colleges to address research questions that are broader than any single department or school. In addition to supporting the research and educational missions of the university, these centers will be a portal through with the external community can connect with university faculty and students on outreach and research activities. For my own part, Douglas Meeks of the Divinity School joins me in leading a study group in our new Center for Religion and Culture to explore the intersection between religion and economy and the implications for economic development and poverty. Through this group, and through a second center I direct in the Arts College,[14] we hope to create an environment that supports the kinds of collaborations between academics and practitioners discussed above.

Finally, we should not overlook the key role that our shared beliefs can play in directing academics and practitioners toward a common purpose. As Christians, our fundamental goals, our orientation, and even our "language" are aligned. Christ said we are to have compassion for our neighbor (whoever and wherever the neighbor might be) and we are invited to act upon this compassion to fulfill God's purpose. While the skills that practitioners and academics bring to the table are different, the Spirit within us is the same, and we all serve the same God. This is indeed a firm foundation for productive collaboration.

References

Foster, James; Joel Greer and Erik Thorbecke. 1984. "A Class of Decomposable Poverty Measures," *Econometrica*. 52:3, pp. 761–766.

Morduch, Jonathan. 1999. "The Microfinance Promise," *Journal of Economic Literature*. 37:4, pp. 1569–1614.

Sahota, Gian. 2000. "Microcredit and Economic Theory," *Grameen Dialogue*. No. 42 (April).

Skoufias, Emmanuel. 2001. "PROGRESA and its Impacts on the Human Capital and Welfare of Households in Rural Mexico: A Synthesis of the Results of an Evaluation by IFPRI," mimeo. International Food Policy Research Institute.

World Bank. 2001. *World Development Report 2000/2001*. Oxford: Oxford University Press.

Notes

[1] This research was supported by the Center for the Study of Religion and Culture at Vanderbilt University, through its Study Group on Religion and Economy.

[2] See, for example, World Bank (2001).

[3] See http://www.grameen-info.org/bank/bcycle.html.

[4] Examples include the Family Planning Association of Bangladesh, Hewlett-Packard, and Monsanto. The Grameen website http://www.grameen-info.org/ agrameen/ states the following: "We welcome people and organizations from all over the world to contact us and let us know how they would like to work in partnership with our existing organizations and/or propose new ideas that may lead to new business ideas which fulfill the social development objectives and organizations in the Grameen Family."

[5] See the list of research papers at http://www.grameen-info.org/bank/biblio.html or the references in Morduch (1999). Note that a substantial portion of this literature is theoretical in nature—an interesting example where theory followed the lead of practice.

[6] Dr. Yunus started with the Graduate Program in Economic Development, a Master's program that I currently direct, and completed his training in Vanderbilt's Ph.D program.

[7] See the article by my colleague Professor Gian Sahota (2000). Professor Sahota served on the Ph.D committee of Dr. Yunus.

[8] Academic interest in incentives and strategic behavior has greatly increased in recent decades, which partly explains the great interest in Grameen.

[9] This is in contrast to a predecessor program which studies showed distributed resources regressively.

[10] As of 2000; see Skoufias (2001).

[11] He suggested the use of the FGT indices (developed in Foster, et al., 1984), the formula of which became part of the associated Mexican Law. In his speech inaugurating PROGRESA, President Ernesto Zedillo explicitly mentioned its use of poverty measures in target resources appropriately. See http://zedilloworl d.presidencia.gob.mx/PAGES/library/sp_06aug97.html.

[12] See http://www.ifpri.org/themes/progresa/progresa_report.htm.

[13] It is interesting to note that the extension to the final years of secondary school involves the creation of a fund similar to an Individual Development Account for each student—a structure that has been used by churches and other organizations to help the poor build wealth. See http://www.cfed.org/main/indivAssets/ main.htm.

[14] The Center for Research on Economic Development and Information Technology (CREDIT) will explore strategies to harness the new information technologies to help the poor help themselves.

Section II

The Design of Christian Poverty Reduction Efforts

5

Sustainability in Microfinance —What's the Bottom Line?

Kenneth Graber and Robert Gailey (World Relief)

Many development organizations, both Christian and secular, are devoting time, energy and resources to microenterprise development (MED) and microfinance (MF) programs. They hope to help poor people help themselves by providing them with access to small loans and savings services with which to acquire capital to begin or expand a small business. MED encompasses any financial, non-financial or ancillary service commonly associated with developing small (micro) businesses among poor people. MF is the provision of financial services (savings, loans, and insurance) for businesses or general consumption purposes. A microfinance institution (MFI) is the development of a formal institution for the long-term delivery of financial services.[1]

The number of players in the MED and MF industry has expanded rapidly in recent years. The Microcredit Summit's 2002 Practitioner Directory lists 2,091 organizations currently operating worldwide. Within the Christian MED field the number of Christian practitioners continues to grow. As new players enter the field, they are confronted with a variety of decisions to be made in order to design and implement an MED or MF program. These decisions have important implications for the extent to which the resulting programs can attain the economic, social, and spiritual development goals of the implementing organizations.

A little over a decade ago, the MF industry was fairly confident that MED programs could provide the breakthrough needed to overcome poverty. Such confidence, however, is no longer certain. John Hatch, founder of FINCA International, and one of the "gurus" in the industry, recently stated,

The longer I remain in this business, the less certain I am about how it should be conducted. I now see more questions than answers, more issues than solutions. Village banking was created to reach the poorest; yet I see large number of the poorest families being left behind. Within the context of mission drift, the topic of scale and sustainability raises a dust cloud of ambiguity. (Churchill, Hirschland, and Painter, 23)

As Hatch so aptly points out, the MED industry is at a critical juncture in its development. During the past twenty years, a wide spectrum of program interventions has been developed and a lot of lessons have been learned. However, many questions remain unanswered. One major question facing the industry is whether programs can continue to respond to the original intent of serving poor people while addressing the growing pressure to reach full financial self-sufficiency—meaning that the organization covers all its operating and financial costs through program income.

Recently, the MED industry has become increasingly segmented. This segmentation is driven by difficult choices often mandated by donors regarding program design and strategic directions. While a few donors and many practitioners are focusing their efforts on ensuring greater social and/or spiritual impact through their programs, there is also rising interest among some donors and organizations to ensure that design choices are driven solely by financial sustainability objectives. World Relief strongly encourages and supports its partner MFIs to keep pace with the financial reporting standards endorsed by the industry. However, since financial self-sufficiency ratios only capture part of a program's success, World Relief seeks to broaden the parameters by which its MFIs are measured to also include social and spiritual transformation measurements. Some of these options are outlined below. The chapter's conclusion suggests research considerations that can help organizations make more informed and better design choices, which in turn, can hopefully lead to a broader perspective on how to measure and achieve success.

Design Choices in Microfinance Programs

Many practical and often difficult choices must be made when designing and implementing microfinance programs. Because resources are very limited, MFIs must carefully choose which of the many demanded services they should offer and to whom the services should be offered. At a general level, organizations need to determine which country to operate in, which methodology to employ (see Ledgerwood, 1998, for more detailed description of the various methodologies), and where to obtain the majority of its initial funding. Specific decisions must be made regarding loan size and terms, what training or other auxiliary services to offer clients, and whether guarantees are enforced using groups, individuals, or physical collateral. Also, specific considerations need to include what, if any, savings products to offer and to whom services will be provided based on poverty level, types of businesses, or particular demographic groups. Christian agencies have the added decision of whether and how to involve local churches in training, staff hiring, client selection, and other forms of collaboration.

For Christian organizations, the issue of context is also influenced by a country's openness to Christian agencies, the availability of Christians to staff positions, and the overall strength of the Christian community. Consideration of presence and witness will affect decisions of where to start work, where to expand, and how easy it will be to service new areas. While some Christian agencies seek to specifically target and help the body of believers with access to financial services, others consider the use of financial services as an opportunity to reach non-believers and choose to work in areas often closed to typical mission agencies but open to sound financial and/or business training programs.

Another important consideration that can affect the decision of where and to whom (as well as when) MED services should be provided is the precedents set by other microfinance organizations. Good precedents are set when most programs exhibit "sound practices" in the delivery of services. Sound practices at a minimum include charging rates of interest commensurate with the types of investments being financed, keeping efficiencies high and subsidies minimal or intentionally focused, being serious about collecting loan repayments and having a plan for clients to be able to access financial services over a long period of time, often indefinitely.

Unfortunately, many well-intentioned organizations do not follow these basic sound practices. This can create "unhealthy competition," characterized by unsustainable services being offered for just a short period of time (at the most a few years). These organizations often call their products "loans" but never fully expect or care if the loans are paid back. Also, they do not plan to create or offer permanent financial service to the communities they are serving so they are less concerned with what happens to their investments.

To give "loans" with little expectation of return is shortsighted. This creates an unhealthy climate within communities towards credit programs that can affect other operators in a country/region for years after the unhealthy competition runs out of money or has moved on to another of the world's "hot spots." By failing to exercise discipline in lending, these organizations give borrowers some short-term benefits but at a potential cost of not having long-term access to financial services. Prudent lenders may shy away from these areas as it is often more difficult to create healthy and enduring microfinance institutions where unhealthy lending practices have existed. This is particularly common in post-conflict or natural disaster type situations that attract relief-oriented, quick-fix, short-term donors and organizations.

Challenges and Opportunities Facing the MED Industry

HIV/AIDS. The newest and perhaps most serious challenge for MFIs is the high incidence of HIV/AIDS in many countries. HIV/AIDS affects programs in two significant ways—portfolio quality and staff costs. Portfolio quality can decline due to illness and death of clients or of someone within a client's extended family who takes on the increased economic responsibility and time demands caring for orphaned children or sick relatives. A few deaths in a community group caused by HIV/AIDS can devastate group solidarity. Some of the clients will not want to interact with those who have tested positive while others may decide to pull out all together for fear of being left to cover the outstanding loans of members who die or who are too sick to work. The disease affects MFI staff as well. Time is lost due to illness or caring for sick family members. The untimely death of a staff member and the costs of replacing and training new staff all add to a program's operational costs.

Interestingly, HIV/AIDS has also created a challenging opportunity for MF programs. The services offered by MF programs are considered key coping mechanisms in the struggle against the disease and its impact on families. Not only can business loans be used to effectively increase people's incomes and help them cope with increased expenses associated with HIV/AIDS, but savings services can also play a key role in stabilizing the economic situation of affected households.

Post-conflict situations. For years, industry leaders were adamant that MFIs were not appropriate tools to employ in post-conflict or extremely challenging environments. World Relief is one of the very few organizations that resisted this conventional wisdom and started MFIs in situations that most organizations sought to avoid. After years of building successful programs in these difficult situations, World Relief has come to enjoy a strong reputation within the industry for being a leader in managing MFIs in post-conflict settings.[2]

World Relief and a few other organizations have demonstrated that successful use of MFIs can help individuals and communities recover more quickly from conflict (Larson, 2002). This has changed many people's perceptions on the matter. The goal now is to shorten the period of relief time and move as quickly as possible towards sustainable economic development practices. The reason for this is that economic growth has proven to be a powerful tool to bring about peace and reconciliation in war-torn areas.

As noted earlier, organizations operating in challenging environments must be aware of and be willing to respond to healthy and unhealthy competition in the field. Many post-conflict settings attract large numbers of relief-type organizations that are not focused on building long-term sustainable financial institutions. Many of these organizations try to adopt some MF methods but their overall approach and lack of technical expertise often means that what gets started does not follow sound principles and practices. When these programs eventually collapse, they can weaken or destroy the credit culture for other better-run MFIs.

Regardless of whether or not unhealthy competition exists, doing sound MF work in challenging environments is often more costly than operating in more stable environments. In immediate post-conflict situations, there is often a lack of basic infrastructure such as commercial banking services, communication systems, transportation, effective police forces, educational programs, or fair judicial systems. This raises the overall costs of doing business in that environment. Likewise, in conflict-affected areas, there are usually limited local technical human resources. The basic law of supply and demand can mean that the cost of hiring a qualified Mozambican accountant immediately following an extended period of conflict may be higher than that of hiring an expatriate accountant to live in Mozambique, despite the country having a per capita GNP of less than $200 at the time.

In locations where there are no commercial banking services operating, cash is used for all transactions. When handling large amounts of cash, safety for staff and clients becomes a major concern. A few years ago in Cambodia, World Relief had the tragic experience of having two of its loan officers killed in an apparent robbery after the staff had collected a loan repayment from one of its community banks. When an institution has to manage many of its own services directly (like electric generators, guards, safes, high vehicle repairs, etc.) its operating costs can significantly increase.

While costs are greater, the MFI's income is often lower than in other countries because the average loan size needed by clients recovering from complex disasters and trying to rebuild shattered economies is normally much lower than the average loan size demanded by clients in more stable economic and political environments. Subsequently, MFIs operating in post-conflict settings find it difficult to achieve and maintain full financial self-sufficiency within a time frame of 4–7 years, a "standard" often set by donors and leading MFIs operating in much more stable environments where costs are lower and market demand for loan products much higher.

Thus, as long as all of the industry's measurements for success of MFIs focus on financial performance indicators alone, MFIs operating in extremely challenging environments will lag behind the standards set by others. However, if the industry is able to adopt and incorporate non-financial measurements for success, including social and (for Christians) spiritual impact measurements, then MFIs making a conscious choice to operate "sound practice MFIs" in devastated economies (where the majority of the world's poorest people live), can compete and be compared to their peers who operate in more stable environments.

Credit with Education. An important advantage of providing financial services through a group methodology, as World Relief does in most of its partner programs, is the ability to more efficiently provide other, non-financial services to clients. An organization called Freedom from Hunger has developed a trademark *Credit with Education* methodology that many other organizations, including World Relief, have replicated. The basic concept behind *Credit with Education* is that with minimal additional costs, a MF program can provide highly valued and useful non-financial services to its clients (Dunford, 2002; Freedom, 1996). Since groups are already formed and meet on a regular basis for their credit and savings transactions, adding a short training on maternal health, child health, HIV/AIDS, or literacy or numeracy can be cost-effective and achieve multiple benefits. The *Credit with Education* methodology utilizes the loan officer to deliver the additional education and training. A variation on this is when a separate trainer—often a volunteer in the community—provides the messages during the regularly scheduled bank meetings.

Within the MF industry there are some who argue that any

non-financial additions to programs are inefficient and unnecessary. They claim that non-financial services are not driven by client demand and therefore encourage subsidies by making the financial services offered to clients more costly and inefficient to them. Advocates for *Credit with Education*-type methodologies counter that to consider clients only as purely *Homo Economicus* (every decision made is based on an attempt to gain maximum material wealth) misses fundamental truths about how people relate to their culture and to each other within their society in terms of decision-making, resource allocation, and ability to gain access to relevant information. They further argue that the additional financial costs needed to incorporate critical non-financial services are far outweighed by the social (and sometimes financial) returns on investment in terms of healthier families, more informed citizens, and more active participants in business, social and political affairs.

Poverty Measurement, Impact Assessment, and Market Research Tools. At the beginning of the current MED movement, an organization's commitment to using MF interventions in their fight against poverty went unquestioned. It was widely accepted that if institutions operating in poor countries focused their efforts on poorer communities with a primary target group being impoverished women, then there would be little need to measure the poverty level of clients or monitor whether their engagement in the program actually made a difference in their lives. A proxy indicator for the level of poverty was often the initial loan size or the loan size as a percent of per capita GNP.

The situation is quite different now. Some donors require MFIs to verify that the clients they serve fall at or below the nation's poverty line. They are encouraging/mandating the development and use of appropriate tools to measure the poverty levels of clients included in programs.[3] Other donors insist on the use of impact assessment or impact monitoring tools to validate a program's effectiveness in alleviating poverty.

A recent phenomenon sweeping the industry is interest in market research tools like those developed by MicroSave-Africa.[4]

Market research is popular because it shifts the emphasis of program and product design from the institution to the clients. In order to respond to client preferences, new methodologies and new systems are required. However, design changes must be approached carefully and prudently since the current methodologies and systems so widely used were developed and fine-tuned with operating efficiencies in mind—efficiencies that may be lost when tailoring products and services to individual clients. When catering a program's products to client demands, staff must remain diligent to ensure mission drift does not occur, especially in regions of the world where people who are not poor have limited access to financial service options. These non-poor people may be very attracted to the customer-friendly products an MFI is offering and seek to manipulate access to the program and subsequently "push out" clients who are in more impoverished situations. For instance, offering a housing improvement loan product to individual clients may create a huge demand from the middle class, requiring a shift in staff time and resources away from serving very poor entrepreneurs and towards responding to an unmet demand in the housing market.

Additionally, a thorough analysis of product/service costing and returns needs to be done before offering more flexible financial services in order to determine if the proposed changes will have a positive or negative impact on the financial standing of the MFI, both in the short-term and the in long-run. Extending repayment periods from four months to six months or to one year will have an impact on cash flow, return on equity, portfolio at risk, repayment rates, drop-out rates, and income statement to name just a few. Some will be impacted positively while others may be impacted negatively. In the end, the quality of the portfolio and the income generated from it is what matters most to the survival and success of an MFI.

Spiritual Impact. For World Relief it is important that MF programs not only achieve significant financial self-sufficiency and have a positive measure of social impact, it is critically important for MED programs to also have a level of spiritual impact on clients and their communities. Obviously, the nature of the impact desired will vary by country context and the strength and breadth of local churches. Additional services require additional resources, limiting the types of interventions possible as programs strive to reach full financial self-sufficiency. One way to minimize such costs is for programs to share their resources with each other. In so doing, implementers are spared the cost of investing in individual research, development, and pilot testing of options while seeking to design new methodologies. To support such efforts, World Relief partnered with and helped to spearhead an informal global coalition of Christian practitioners in publishing a toolkit of biblically based training resources used by MED programs, so that other practitioners could have access to this resource compendium (Gailey, et al., 2001).

Not only are Christian MFIs required to respond to the industry-wide tension of achieving greater financial self-sufficiency while maintaining a strong commitment to social impact, they must also respond to a desire (often mandated by their donor constituency) to ensure programs obtain a level of positive spiritual impact. Successful MFIs realize that achieving excellence in the eyes of churches or mission agencies while satisfying the demands and restrictions placed upon programs by secular donors requires deliberate and careful planning, along with strong accountability. A danger always exists that purists on either side of the equation (pure evangelistic organizations or pure financial programs) can attack the balanced work being done as not strongly focused enough on their particular bottom line.

The Push for Full Financial Sustainability and its Impact on Design Choices

Mission drift by MFIs has become a significant concern for many in the industry. The most over-riding tension for MFIs today is being able to maintain an appropriate balance between profitability (or, at a minimum, cost recovery) and social impact, particularly in regards to reaching quite deep into impoverished communities (Gibbons and Meehan, 2002). Pressure within the industry often pushes MFIs to achieve 100 percent Financial Self-Sufficiency (FSS)[5] within four to seven years of their start-up, meaning that all operating and financial costs are covered by the income earned by the program. Some within the industry advocate for the elimination of all forms of financial and operational subsidies within this time period in order to determine which MFIs can survive and thus offer a reasonable return on investment in global capital markets. They believe that any that can't measure up should be shut down and deemed "unsustainable."

Unfortunately, the same yardstick is often used industry-wide, whether an MFI operates in Costa Rica or Northern Mozambique, provides credit with education or uses a minimalist (credit only) approach, or operates in a capital city as opposed to remote rural regions. MFIs sometimes dramatically change their programs to adapt quickly to the strict FSS standards advocated by some within the industry. These changes can include raising loan sizes, lending to individuals rather than groups, minimalist focus on lending, the dropping of auxiliary services and activities, and shifting the program's focus to serving wealthier clients.

The drive towards FSS has brought pressure on ancillary services included in many programs. Recently, an argument has been put forth for a "blended value" approach (Emerson, 2000). According to this approach, "all investments are understood to operate simultaneously in both economic and social realms. There is no 'trade off' between the two, but rather a concurrent pursuit of value—both social and financial (Emerson, 2000: p.36)." According to Dr. Gary Woller, Business professor at BYU, "Unlike the current conceptualization of microfinance, a blended value approach is not about financial self-sufficiency or social impact per se; it is about *value creation* in the pursuit of both economic and social objectives (Woller, 2001: p.16)."

Other Measures of Success aAnd Sustainability:
A Triple Bottom Line Approach

Christian Microfinance Institutions (MFIs), like other development organizations, should make program design choices that best achieve all of their primary objectives with the resources available to them. This may mean resisting popular trends and balancing decisions when primary objectives conflict. As the benchmark for obtaining financial sustainability within the industry continues to be raised (from meeting all operational costs, to meeting subsidized financial costs, to achieving competitive, non-subsidized market rates of return), some organizations may decide that on-going subsidies (non-financial and sometimes even financial) are justified because they allow achievement of non-financial objectives, including sustainable impact in terms of social and spiritual measurements. In other words, it may be legitimate to achieve a "less than financial market rate of return" on financial resources invested in an MFI in order to obtain sustainable rates of return in social and spiritual development achievements, focusing on a triple bottom line approach. When Christian development organizations measure success using a triple bottom line, they gauge their sustainability using both social and spiritual terms, while not neglecting the significance of obtaining greater financial sustainability.

Important Research Questions to Help MFIs Make Better, More Balanced Decisions

MFIs that take a more balanced approach to tracking success beyond just financial self-sufficiency have greater freedom and greater responsibility to make design choices that are best for meeting their multiple objectives. This freedom and responsibility, however, requires extensive knowledge of the local context to be able to understand the best design choices for any given culture and situation. Thus, research is needed to inform product design (interest rate, loan size, individual or group lending, etc.) in specific settings, while reflecting the objectives specified under a triple bottom line approach. Research that sheds light on the relative merits of various approaches is important. Some of the most critical questions needing to be asked include:

- While the microfinance industry has developed excellent financial health ratios to clearly measure financial success, what social and spiritual impact measurement tools are appropriate, reliable, and affordable?

• Which additional non-financial services should be run either with or parallel to microfinance programs? How can they be made more cost-effective and achieve significant impact?

• How should programs decide which clients receive services on a global scale or in a specific country? What about Christian organizations? How should they go about targeting the population they serve?

While programs seek to expand services and develop their outreach, asking these larger questions and seeking to find answers to them will go a long way towards helping organizations determine their bottom line measurements of success and sustainability.

References

Churchill, Craig; Madeline Hirschland and Judith Painter. October 2002. "New Directions in Poverty Finance: Village Banking Revisited," SEEP Network.

Doyle, Karen. March 1998. "Microfinance in the Wake of Conflict: Challenges and Opportunities," prepared for USAID Microenterprise Best Practices Project. Bethesda, MD: Development Alternatives Inc.

Dunford, Christopher. 2002. "Building Better Lives: Sustainable Integration of Microfinance with Education in Child Survival, Reproductive Health, and HIV/AIDS Prevention for the Poorest Entrepreneurs," in *Pathways Out of Poverty: Innovations in Microfinance for the Poorest Families*. Sam Daley-Harris, ed. Bloomfield, CT: Kumarian Press, Inc., pp. 75–131.

Emerson, Jed. 2000. "The Nature of Returns: A Social Capital Markets Inquiry into Elements of Investment and the Blended Value Proposition." Social Enterprise Series No. 17, Harvard Business School.

Freedom from Hunger. 1996. *The Case for Credit with Education*. Davis, CA: Freedom from Hunger.

Gailey, Robert; Hollie Smith, Alexis Beggs Olsen and Makonen

Getu. 2001. "Spiritual Transformation Through Microenterprise Development: A Compendium of Tools For Christian Practitioners," version 1.0. Baltimore, MD: World Relief.

Gibbons, David and Jennifer Meehan. 2002. "Financing Microfinance for Poverty Reduction," in *Pathways Out of Poverty: Innovations in Microfinance for the Poorest Families*. Sam Daley-Harris, ed. Bloomfield, CT: Kumarian Press, pp. 229–261.

Larson, David. 2002. *Microfinance Following Conflict. Technical Briefs Nos. 1–8*, prepared for USAID Microenterprise Best Practices Project. Bethesda, MD: Development Alternatives Inc.

Ledgerwood, Joanna. 1998. *Microfinance Handbook: An Institutional and Financial Perspective (Sustainable Banking With the Poor)*. Washington, D.C.: World Bank.

Microcredit Summit Campaign. 2002. "The Microcredit Summit Campaign: 2002 Practitioner Directory," Washington, D.C.

Woller, Gary. 2001. "Poverty Lending, Financial Self-Sufficiency, and the Six Aspects of Outreach," Poverty Lending Working Group Paper, SEEP Network.

Notes

[1] See Chapter 6 by Brian Fikkert for more details on these definitions.

[2] World Relief staff has been asked to develop and edit technical briefs on the subject for USAID (see Doyle, 1998, and Larson, 2002) and to significantly contribute to the development of training materials for UNHCR/ILO. WR staff members have also spoken on the subject at several global events and have been selected by mainstream media for interviews on the topic. USAID also chose a WR affiliate to visit during their investigation into how MFIs can function in post-conflict settings.

[3] Recent legislation passed by the U.S. Congress requires USAID to allocate 50 percent of their MED funds to programs that employ approved poverty measurement tools and are reaching very poor people.

[4] For more information on MicroSave tools, please visit their website at, http://www.microsave-africa.com

[5] "Financial Self-Sufficiency" (FSS) is defined as operating revenue (mainly interest on loans)/operating expenses plus loan loss provision expenses plus financial expenses, including inflation and subsidy costs.

6

Fostering Informal Savings and Credit Associations

Brian Fikkert (Chalmers Center
for Economic Development at Covenant College)[1]

Maria walked to the front of God's Compassion Church (GCC) of Manila and testified, "My child would have died had it not been for the help of the members of the Accumulating Savings and Credit Association (ASCA). I was able to get a loan for the medicine, and they also prayed for me, and visited my sick child." Maria sat down, and then Camilla stood and explained how the ASCA members had encouraged her to borrow some money so that she could start a small, cookie-selling business. As a result of this business, she has been better able to meet the daily needs of her children.

The 300 mothers in the audience listened intently as Maria, Camilla, and the other twenty-four members of GCC's ASCA shared how God had used the ASCA to bless their lives. The economic benefits were obvious to all in attendance. Lacking access to formal banking services, these mothers had always struggled to save and were usually unable to borrow at all, except possibly from loan sharks who charged them exorbitant interest rates. In contrast, the ASCA had enabled the mothers to save and to lend these savings to one another much like a credit union does. The results were nothing short of phenomenal. A total of 41 relatively low-interest loans had been made with a 100 percent repayment rate. The interest paid on these loans enabled the ASCA members to earn dividends on their savings averaging 50 percent in annual terms.

But the blessings were more than economic in nature. The ASCA members testified that a strong sense of community had developed as the mothers prayed for each other and their families. God had steadily answered their prayers as their husbands found jobs, their children were healed, and their broken relationships were mended.

The ASCA enabled its members to be salt and light in the community as well. Neighbors of the ASCA members commented about the love and concern that the members showed to one another, so the ASCA members invited these neighbors to attend their weekly meetings and Bible study. These non-members were allowed to borrow money from the ASCA at an interest rate much lower than that available from local loan sharks. And when the ASCA started its second cycle, these non-members were allowed to become members.[2]

While GCC's ASCA is part of the global microfinance movement, it is certainly not representative of the mainstream of that movement. Historically, the microfinance industry has been dominated by microfinance institutions (MFIs) that raise capital from donors in industrialized countries in order to make loans to low-income people in the developing world.[3] MFIs are highly-complex financial intermediaries, often lending millions of dollars in small increments to tens of thousands of clients. As a result of their complexity, MFIs require staff with high degrees of technical expertise, large-scale management information systems, and strong governance and management procedures. In contrast, GCC's ASCA relies on no foreign capital for its loans, offering its members the opportunity to save and lend their own resources to one another. Furthermore, GCC's ASCA has only two dozen members, who both own and manage the group's small savings and loan fund, an amount totaling only about $250.

GCC's ASCA presents some exciting possibilities that merit further exploration, but it is dangerous to generalize from anecdotal evidence. Implementation of ASCAs on a large scale in diverse cultural settings must be combined with systematic data collection and analysis in order to determine whether GCC's ASCA is an aberration or the norm. As will be discussed further below, a number of secular organizations have started large-scale implementation, but the Christian community has not yet promoted ASCAs extensively. And like the entire microfinance field, there is a paucity of sound empirical research establishing the impacts of ASCAs on economic, social, and spiritual variables.[4]

Is there any reason for Christian development practitioners to consider promoting informal savings and credit associations, such as GCC's ASCA, when operating MFIs is an option? If so, how exactly should they go about it and under what circumstances? What are the pros and cons of these very different approaches to addressing the financial service needs of the poor? While there is not yet sufficient experience or evidence to answer these questions fully, this chapter argues that promoting informal savings and credit associations appears to have considerable potential for addressing both the spiritual and economic needs of *very* poor people. Whether this potential is realized will depend, in large part, on the extent to which Christian development agencies, missions organizations, and academics collaborate on implementing, testing, and refining this approach.

Appropriate Financial Services for the Poor

Microfinance attempts to meet the financial service needs of low-income people, but which types of financial services do the poor need? As Rutherford (2000) notes, the poor need financial services that enable them to obtain lump sums of cash for lifecycle expenditures such as weddings or funerals, for emergencies such as illnesses or natural disasters, and for opportunities to purchase consumer durables or business assets. The poor need financial services that enable them to obtain these lump sums in a secure, timely, and convenient fashion.

While the characterization in the preceding paragraph is true, it is important to note that there is considerable heterogeneity amongst the poor in terms of their economic situation and the financial services that they need. At one extreme, the income levels of the very poorest households exhibit considerable fluctuation over time, sometimes hovering above and sometimes below the poverty line. These households are generally one crisis away from disaster, making them extremely vulnerable to the multitude of shocks that characterize their social, economic, political, and climatic environments. As a result, they are often unwilling to pursue potentially high-yield investments if they perceive those investments as increasing the overall risk of their income stream. Furthermore, since taking out business loans to fund such investments would increase their risk exposure even more—making them beholden to the lender—the poorest households often shy away from obtaining such loans either from informal sector moneylenders or from micro-credit programs.

What then are the financial services that are most appropriate for the poorest households as they try to acquire lump sums? There is increasing evidence that the poorest households desire to use savings and small, contingency loans in order to reduce their vulnerability.[5] Unfortunately, it is difficult for the poor to save because: 1) hiding cash under the mattress is not very safe in slums where people live in close proximity to one another; 2) there are many moral claims on one's savings, as friends and relatives are constantly in need of financial assistance; and 3) like all people, the poor have trouble being disciplined enough not to spend money that is hiding under the mattress (Rutherford 2000). Furthermore, obtaining small, contingency loans is nearly impossible since the poor lack acceptable collateral, and the loan sizes they desire are too small to be attractive to lenders.

Households which are a bit better off than those just described are often sufficiently stable economically to bear the risks associated with taking business loans. Hence, in addition to desiring savings services, such households may be eager to obtain loans to capitalize or expand their microenterprises. However, lacking acceptable collateral and wanting small loans, these households are unable to access credit from banks, forcing them to rely on local, informal moneylenders, who lend to them at interest rates that often exceed 300 percent annually.[6]

Clearly, different types of financial services are required to meet the various needs of different segments of the low-income population. The loans offered by MFIs often meet the demand of middle-to upper-poor households for business credit, but such loans are typically too large and too risky for the poorest households, which tend to prefer savings services and very small, contingency loans.[7]

What Does Promoting Informal Finance Look Like?

Records indicate that Rotating Savings and Credit Associations (ROSCAs) existed in China at least 1200 years ago. The concept is simple: A group of people meet together on regular basis and contribute a pre-specified amount to a pot. A different member of the group takes the pot at the end of each meeting until every member has received the pot once. After every member has had a turn, the group can disband or repeat the rotation.

A ROSCA is a simple and efficient means of financial intermediation. In every meeting prior to an individual's receiving the pot, that individual is saving and is, in effect, putting her savings for that meeting on deposit with the person who takes the pot at that meeting. When an individual gets the pot, she is receiving a sum that is partly her accumulated savings and partly a loan. In every meeting after the individual gets the pot, that individual is repaying the loan portion of the pot that she has received. Variations on ROSCAs are found all over the world and are used by people at all income levels to save and lend their own resources to one another.

ASCAs are closely related to ROSCAs, but unlike ROSCAs, the funds contributed to an ASCA in a regular meeting may or may not be completely distributed to the members; hence, an ASCA's funds may accumulate over time. Furthermore, ASCAs are typically more flexible than ROSCAs: An individual might be able to take one or more loans of multiple sizes upon request, and—depending on the rules—the members might be able to draw on their savings contributions throughout the ASCAs' life. While ROSCAs pay no interest,[8] ASCA members earn interest on their savings that arises from the interest paid on loans and from various fines that are sometimes levied on members. Because of their greater complexity, ASCAs involve higher levels of trust, management and record keeping.[9]

While ROSCAs and ASCAs are simple conceptually, one should not presume that they are easy to start or maintain. If savers doubt the safety of their funds, or if borrowers perceive that there are no serious consequences for failing to repay their loans, the groups are likely to collapse, bringing both economic and social harm to the members. In order to foster sufficient confidence amongst the members, groups must design and consistently implement sound policies and procedures regarding membership, governance, management, monitoring, and operations. There is considerable nuance in this process, and small differences can have dramatic effects. For example, the criteria used for selecting group members can have enormous implications for the degree of trust amongst group members. Furthermore, the membership criteria that seem appropriate to the development worker might be entirely inappropriate for a particular target group. Unfortunately, there is no blueprint for creating strong, user-owned and managed groups that fits all cultural settings and demographic profiles, and considerable experimentation and research is needed to understand the nuances of group dynamics more fully.

Despite these challenges, in the past several years a number of organizations have started to experiment with promoting—as opposed to providing—informal financial mechanisms such as ROSCAs and ASCAs, with enough successes to create optimism for further development. In standard microfinance, an MFI provides financial services—usually loans—to the poor indefinitely.[10] Should the MFI close down, the financial services will end. In contrast, as discussed by Ashe and Parrott (2002, p. 138), a promotion strategy is one in which a non-government organization (NGO) acts as a "time limited catalyst of group development," training clients to form and manage their own savings and credit associations without any long-term help from the NGO. If the NGO should close, it may be irrelevant, as the savings and credit associations theoretically can live on indefinitely without it.

One apparent success story pertains to Pact's Women's Empowerment Program (WEP) of Nepal, which has been promoting ASCAs since 1999 when it hired 240 local NGOs to recruit, train, and support groups of women to operate ASCAs and to adopt a literacy curriculum. Within the first year of operation, WEP was reaching 6,500 ASCAs with 130,000 members. In contrast, Ashe and Parrott (2002) note that most credit-based MFIs would be fortunate to reach 3,000 clients in the first year. Savings rates increased from $.20 per member per month in June 1999 to $.45 per member per month in July 2001. In June 2001, the total assets of all the groups amounted to $1,900,000 and were projected to reach $3,000,000 by July 2002 (Ashe and Parrott, 2001).

While no systematic statistical work has been performed, the impacts of WEP appear to be impressive: (1) ASCAs formed by WEP spontaneously started and trained an additional 800 ASCA groups on their own without assistance from WEP staff; (2) 97 percent of WEP ASCA group funds are currently on loan to 45,366 group members, making WEP the second largest village banking program listed in the MicroBanking Bulletin; (3) Only 4 percent of the ASCAs made loans that defaulted, and 82 percent of the groups keep their own records without any outside assistance; (4) An average of 89,000 women reported increased decision-making authority over buying and selling property, children's marriages, family planning and girls' schooling; (5) 63,700 women gained a level of literacy; 6) 86,000 women started a business for the first time; (6) Women earned between 18–24 percent per annum on their savings and were able to borrow at only 24 percent per annum; and (7) The ASCA groups carried out over 100,000 community campaigns and projects to fight against girl trafficking, wife abuse, and alcoholism and to improve their communities (Ashe and Parrott, 2001).

Grant and Allen (2002) describe another dramatic case of promoting informal finance: CARE's Mata Masu Dubara[11] (MMD) program. Building on the ROSCAs that are commonly used by women in Niger, CARE began to train rural women to form time-bound ASCAs in 1993.[12] As the initial groups met with success, news spread throughout the country, and the CARE staff became overwhelmed with requests for training. In order to meet this demand, CARE initiated a "village agent" system in which groups of women who wanted to start ASCAs paid a village agent to receive training from CARE and then to teach them how to start and manage the ASCAs. There are now over 160,000 women in CARE's ASCAs in Niger, and it is estimated that another 40,000 women are in groups that have started spontaneously without CARE's direct involvement. The total savings of CARE's ASCAs have reached $3,000,000, nearly all of which is on loan to the members, making MMD the second largest microfinance initiative in Africa (Ashe 2002). The return that members earn on their savings is quite high, averaging 76 percent on deposits (Grant and Allen, 2002). CARE is now implementing variations of MMD in Mozamabique, Zimbabwe, Malawi, Zanzibar, Mali, Eritrea, Rwanda, and Uganda.

Finally, the Chalmers Center for Economic Development, a research and training program of Covenant College, and Food for the Hungry International (FHI), a Christian relief and development agency, have been collaborating on piloting church-centered ROSCAs and ASCAs in the Dominican Republic, Kenya, and the Philippines. The purpose of these pilots is to create a model in which the local church is better equipped to embody Jesus Christ by caring for the spiritual and physical needs of its own members and others in its community. The Chalmers Center takes the lessons learned from these pilots and then trains missionaries, churches, and Christian NGOs to implement church-centered ROSCAs and ASCAs on their own.[13]

The churches in these pilots do not own the savings and credit groups; rather, their members are mobilized to start, own, and operate ROSCAs and ASCAs as a means of community outreach. Chalmers/FHI staff meet with the groups over time, explaining the technical aspects of informal finance using a biblically-based curriculum.[14] The entire process—including the biblical curriculum—is being tested and refined in order to produce a handbook that others can use and adapt to their own circumstances.

While there is considerable need for further testing and refinement, many of these church-centered savings and credit associations are experiencing positive results, as the story at the start of this chapter illustrates. Financially, these groups permit the poor to save and to earn high rates of interest on those savings. Furthermore, the loans made from the accumulated savings average $10–$11, amounts which are well below the first-time loan sizes of most credit-based MFIs and which meet the need of very poor households for small, contingency loans. Interviews with group members indicate that while they are aware of MFIs in their communities, they do not utilize their services because they are too poor to do so and because they find their ASCAs offer more convenient and flexible services.

Qualitative data indicate that these church-centered groups are doing far more than addressing people's financial needs. Groups' mission statements typically specify broad-based goals such as "to give glory to God's name through building unity, trust, and relationships in the group and through testifying to God's power in the community." And there is evidence that this mission is being met. Meetings often resemble small group Bible studies, with frequent prayers for God's provision for the varied needs of both members and non-members. Staff report that working through money matters and conflicts together is building group trust and unity. Emergency funds are being used to extend mercy to members and non-members in times of crisis, and home visitations to both members and non-members are commonly reported. One group has had such a strong testimony in the community that some non-members are attending the weekly meetings because— as one group member explained—the ASCA members have been "good Samaritans to these people, and these people are drawn to the ASCA because of this." Finally, there are reports of some group members getting involved in the activities of the sponsoring church for the first time.

But the news is not all good. Some groups struggle to hold their members accountable, causing both savings and loan repayments to be in arrears. In addition, a number of groups have experienced very low attendance at their regular meetings, inhibiting financial transparency and reducing opportunities for evangelism, discipleship, and community building. Ongoing experiments seek to uncover the root causes of these problems and to develop appropriate solutions.

Potential Advantages to Promoting Informal Finance?

MFIs that provide micro-credit services are powerful vehicles for rapidly mobilizing large amounts of capital to finance the microenterprises of middle- to upper- income poor in large numbers. As such, they continue to deserve the attention of Christian relief and development agencies and of the Christian donor community. However, as this section discusses, promoting informal finance has some potential advantages that make this approach worthy of further exploration.

MFIs often focus on providing loans,[15] and due to pressures to be financially self-sustaining,[16] there is a tendency for their loan sizes to drift upward beyond the debt capacity of the poorest households.[17] In contrast, ROSCAs and ASCAs provide the type of financial services demanded by the poorest households as they seek to reduce their vulnerability: savings and small, contingency loans. As a result, promoting informal finance has the potential to reach poorer clients than most credit-focused MFIs, a fact which has been borne out in the experiences of the promoters mentioned earlier in this chapter.

Second, most funding for MFIs comes from secular donors, who are, at best, disinterested in evangelism and discipleship activities and who, for good reason, want the MFIs to become financially self-sustaining.[18] In the presence of economies of scale in providing credit services, these priorities push MFIs to create large-scale, minimalist programs, making it difficult for Christian MFIs to include evangelism and discipleship components in their programs (Graber and Gailey, Chapter 5). Given that Christian MFIs typically desire to meet the physical *and* spiritual needs of the poor in a manner that is patterned after Christ's ministry, the pressures placed on them by secular donors can lead to significant mission drift.

Although it is possible in principle for Christian donors to complement secular funds by paying for evangelism and discipleship activities in Christian MFIs, this has proved difficult in practice. The sheer scale of operations of MFIs requires very large, *ongoing* donations from the Christian community if the evangelism and discipleship component is to be kept in balance with the financial services component. For example, one Christian MFI working in a Latin American country has over 4,000 clients scattered all over the countryside. A large church in the U.S. has paid for the salary of a single, poorly-educated pastor to perform the impossible task of providing the entire evangelism and discipleship component for these 4,000 clients. Could sufficient money be given by Christian donors to bring the "word" and "deed" aspects of this MFI into balance? Yes, in principle, but managers of MFIs rarely have either the time or the incentives to undertake such activities in the present system.[19]

In contrast, because informal savings and credit associations can be self-sustaining with only a small number of members, it is relatively easy to keep the evangelism and discipleship component in balance with the financial services component. While it is initially costly to form and train savings and credit groups, beyond some point the groups are able to operate on their own at very minimal cost to the members of the group. Furthermore, there do not appear to be significant scale economies in operating these groups, enabling them to be self-sustaining with a very small number of members. Hence, given the relative simplicity of the technology, a church, a missionary, or a typical staff member in a Christian NGO can organize ROSCAs and ASCAs *and* provide the complementary evangelism and discipleship activities.[20] Clearly, the number of "clients" served by a single church or missionary would be relatively small compared to those serviced by a MFI, so a choice may need to be made between "holistic" impact on a small number of people versus "minimalist" impact on a large number of clients.[21]

Third, the fact that these groups are user-owned and managed makes them viable even in sparsely-populated, rural areas. After the initial group formation and training, groups can maintain themselves without ongoing assistance from outsiders. In contrast, MFIs typically find it difficult if not impossible to service clients in such regions, as the perpetual costs of transportation to meet with clients is prohibitive.

Fourth, the fact that the poor themselves design and operate these groups has significant advantages over standard, one-size-fits-all programs that are designed and managed by outsiders who lack local knowledge. For example, in one of the Chalmers/FHI pilot ASCAs in the Philippines, it quickly became apparent that a subset of the group could not afford to save at the agreed-upon rate of 20 cents *per day*. Rather than simply expel these folks, the ASCA members helped the poorer members to form their own group with lower savings rates of 20 cents *per week*. This is the poor ministering to the ultra-poor without a dime's worth of outside money or influence after the initial facilitation and training.

Fifth, it is easy to integrate informal finance with other interventions that a NGO might be providing. The Chalmers/FHI ASCAs in the Philippines have largely been formed with mothers involved in FHI's child sponsorship program. As a result, these group members' families are being ministered to in range of ways—including health training and screening, educational support for children, and biblical instruction—thereby addressing more dimensions of poverty than an ASCA would on its own. Because ASCAs are user-owned and managed, there is no need for FHI to alter its management, administrative, and accounting systems in order to incorporate an informal microfinance program into its overall operations. This represents a distinct advantage over standard, credit-based, provider models, whose activities are so distinct from the other activities of their sponsoring NGOs that they typically need their own systems, thereby making integrated programs more difficult to design and implement.

Finally, an important principle of development is to build on local knowledge and institutions in order to empower local residents to be stewards of their communities. Given that informal financial mechanisms have been invented by the poor themselves, operating them successfully is within their capacity and affirms and builds upon their knowledge, skills, and resources.

Some Potential Disadvantages to Promoting Informal Finance

There are also some reasons to be cautious before deciding that promoting informal finance is a superior strategy to providing credit via MFIs.

First, the reality is that little is known about the overall economic costs of the promotion strategy. Ashe (2002) estimates that the costs incurred *by the organization* which forms and trains the savings and credit groups amount to $5–$30 per client serviced, while the start-up costs for an MFI are typically $300 per borrower.[22] While these figures suggest that the promotion strategy is cheaper for the outside development agency, they do not allow for a complete comparison of all of the costs incurred by all parties in delivering financial services to the poor under the various strategies.

Second, little is known about the relative benefits of targeting financial services to the very poor as opposed to the middle- to upper-income poor. As mentioned earlier, informal finance has the benefit of providing savings and small, contingency loans to enable very poor households to reduce their vulnerability by smoothing their consumption. However, the loans provided by MFIs to the less poor households are more likely to generate increases in income for those households, thereby contributing more to overall economic growth and potentially increasing the demand for labor, possibly even the labor of the poorest households.[23] Does targeting the financial services to the very poor yield a bigger overall benefit—even for the very poor—than targeting financial services to the less poor? Clearly, this is a very complicated empirical question to resolve, but this question must be considered in evaluating the relative merits of these different strategies.[24]

Finally, the small-scale nature of individual savings and credit associations makes them quite vulnerable to region-specific shocks. If a storm wipes out the crops in a particular village, every member of that village's ASCA might have a difficult time making their weekly pay-in, thereby placing the ASCA at considerable risk. In contrast, a MFI which services a wide geographic region might be able to continue to service this village as long as similar storms do not simultaneously hit all of the regions in which the MFI is operating.[25]

The Need for Further Collaboration Between Academics and Practitioners

Although promoting informal financial systems appears to be a promising strategy for Christians who desire to minister holistically to very poor people, there is a tremendous need for further experimentation and empirical analysis. Several key unanswered questions include:

- What is the magnitude of the impact of informal finance on a range of variables including vulnerability, income, social relations, and spiritual maturity? How do these impacts compare with those of MFIs?

- What are the total economic costs of promoting informal finance and of traditional microlending via MFIs?

- What are the most efficient methods for forming and training strong, informal savings and credit associations?

- To what extent do development practitioners need to "prescribe" the policies and procedures for savings and credit associations in a particular region, and to what extent can these decisions be left to the groups themselves? Must certain policies be prescribed while others may be left to the groups' discretion? What are the implications for developing indigenous leaders and institutions of being too prescriptive or of not being prescriptive enough?

- How well do informal savings and credit associations perform over time once the promoters' training and monitoring has ended?

- To what extent can Christian NGOs, denominations, or missions promote holistic informal savings and credit associations on a large scale?

Few promoters have either the time or the technical skill to answer most of these questions, providing a tremendous opportunity for practitioners and academics to collaborate in helping the poorest members of the global community.

References

Ashe, Jeffrey. 2002. "A Symposium on Savings Led Microfinance and the Rural Poor: Introduction," *Journal of Microfinance,* 4:2, pp. 127–35.

Ashe, Jeffrey and Lisa Parrott. 2001. "Impact Evaluation: Pact's Women's Empowerment Program in Nepal: A Savings-and-Literacy-Led Alternative to Financial Institution Building," Institute for Sustainable Development at Heller School of Brandeis University Working Paper.

Ashe, Jeffrey and Lisa Parrott. 2002. "Pact's Women's Empowerment Program in Nepal: A Savings-and Literacy-Led Alternative to Financial Institution Building," *Journal of Microfinance,* 4:2, pp. 137–62.

Donthamsetty, Smita. 2000. "God Will Supply All Your Needs from His Glorious Riches: A Widow and Her Love for the Poor," Chalmers Center for Economic Development at Covenant College Working Paper #202, http://www.chalmers.org.

Fikkert, Brian. 2003. "Christian Microfinance: Which Way Now?" Association of Christian Economists 20th Anniversary Conference Working Paper, http://www.gordon.edu/ace/devconnect/conference/authorlastname.doc

Garcia, Malu. 2003. "Light Rising in the Darkness," *Mandate,* Spring 2003, pp. 1, 7, http://www.chalmers.org.

Grant, William and Hugh Allen. 2002. "CARE's Mata Masu Dubara (Women on the Move) Program in Niger: Successful Financial Intermediation in the Rural Sahel," *Journal of Microfinance,* 4:2, pp. 189–216.

Gunderson, Jeri. 2000. "A Missionary's Journal: Bringing the Idea for a Ministry to a Church," Chalmers Center for Economic Development at Covenant College Working Paper #203, http://www.chalmers.org.

Hulme, David, and Paul Mosley. 1996. *Finance Against Poverty.* London: Routledge.

Johnson, Susan and Ben Rogaly. 1997. *Microfinance and Poverty Reduction*. United Kingdom and Ireland: Oxfam.

Rutherford, Stuart. 2000. *The Poor and Their Money*. New Delhi: Oxford University Press.

Von Pischke, J.D. 1991. *Finance at the Frontier: Debt Capacity and the Role of Credit in the Private Economy*. Washington, D.C.: The World Bank.

Notes

[1] I am extremely grateful to my colleague Russell Mask for mentoring me in the field of microfinance and for his numerous contributions to this paper. I am deeply indebted to him for all of the ways in which he has shaped my thinking in this field. I am also grateful to the editors of this book for their very helpful comments on an earlier draft. Thanks also to Ellis Chaplin, Smita Donthamsetty, Malu Garcia, and Loida Viriña for their efforts to collect and process data from the joint pilot projects of the Chalmers Center and Food for the Hungry International. I have also benefited from correspondence with Rob Gailey of World Relief's Microfinance Consulting Services. The Chalmers Center is very grateful to both Food for the Hungry International and World Relief for all of the ways in which they have shared ideas, collaborated on projects, and partnered with us in training people around the globe in church-centered microfinance. Finally, the Chalmers Center thanks the Maclellan Foundation, First Fruit Inc., and hundreds of churches and individuals whose financial support has made this research possible. Of course, all errors are solely the responsibility of the author.

[2] This story about one of the Chalmers Center's pilot projects with Food for the Hungry International in the Philippines has been copied with permission from Garcia (2003).

[3] Some MFIs are now offering savings and insurance services, implying that some of their loan funds are coming from local capital as well as from foreign donors. This approach requires considerably more technical expertise than simply lending foreign capital, and numerous legal obstacles must be overcome before MFIs are permitted to hold their clients' savings.

[4] See Fikkert (2003) for a review of the empirical evidence of the holistic impacts of microfinance programs.

[5] See Fikkert (2003) for a review of the evidence concerning households' financial service needs.

[6] See Johnson and Rogaly (1997, p. 21) and Von Pischke (1991, pp. 184–187).

[7] See Fikkert (2003) for a review of the empirical evidence on the holistic impacts of micro-credit programs on households at different income levels.

[8] Implicitly there is a negative interest rate paid on savings in a ROSCA that is equal to minus the rate of inflation. People who get the pot early in the rotation get more in real terms than people who get the pot at the end of the rotation,

implying a negative interest rate on savings. In highly inflationary environments, ROSCA contributions might be indexed to some stable commodity or currency.

[9] For an excellent discussion of ROSCAs, ASCAs, and other informal finance mechanisms, see Rutherford (2000).

[10] See footnote 2.

[11] Mata Masu Dubara is translated as "Women on the Move."

[12] "Time-bound" ASCAs have a definite end-date that is specified at the start of the ASCA. This terminal date acts as a "day of reckoning" in which all of the group's records and accounts are cleared, thereby reducing uncertainty and risk. In practice, many time-bound ASCAs go on for long periods of time, restarting over and over after expiring each period. In contrast, "non-time-bound" ASCAs are assumed to continue perpetually when they are started. See Rutherford (2000) for more information.

[13] As a result of this training, informal finance is now being initiated by a wide range of promoters—from individual missionaries to global NGOs such as Habitat for Humanity International—in quite diverse contexts including the Ivory Coast, Mexico, Uganda, the Philippines, Burundi, and Eastern Russia. While the initial reports from some of these trainees are encouraging (see, for example, Gunderson (2000)), it is simply too soon to assess their overall success.

[14] The Chalmers Center's training materials focus on group formation and group maintenance issues of mission, membership, financial policies, management and governance, and monitoring and evaluation.

[15] See footnote 3.

[16] Financial systems must be sustainable, or they will collapse. If savers perceive that a financial system might not be sustainable, they will withdraw their savings, an action which will actually cause the system to collapse. Similarly, if borrowers perceive that a financial system is not sustainable, they will have little incentive to repay their loans, thereby causing the system to collapse. In principle, sustainability can be achieved with ongoing subsidies, but since subsidies typically do not last forever, most financial systems need to become financially self-sustaining if they are to endure.

[17] See the discussion by Graber and Gailey (Chapter 5).

[18] See footnote 3.

[19] In principle, a Christian MFI could charge higher interest rates on its loans in order to cover the costs of evangelism and discipleship; however, this strategy is unlikely to work in many contexts, as increased competition from other MFIs puts downward pressure on interest rates.

[20] Donthamsetty (2000) documents how a widow in the Philippines began to promote informal finance, resulting in a church-centered microfinance program meeting the needs of hundreds of low-income persons. Gunderson (2000) describes how a Chalmers-trained missionary successfully equipped a church to use microfinance to transform a squatter community in the Philippines.

[21] As mentioned earlier, WEP has been able to reach a massive number of clients by training grassroots organizations to promote informal finance. Hence, it seems possible that a network of churches or a missions organization could also

reach a large number of people with both evangelism/discipleship and financial service components.

[22] Ashe is concerned with computing the costs to the development agency. Hence, in the case of the promotion model, he does not compute the cost of the loan capital, since this capital comes from the members of the savings and credit groups. In contrast, when he computes the costs to the MFI, he includes the cost of the loan capital, since the MFI has to raise these funds. An economic accounting of the costs of these two strategies would require all costs borne by all parties to be totaled.

[23] Although the evidence is limited, it appears that as middle- to upper-income poor receive loans from MFIs to expand their businesses, few new jobs are created for the poorest households (Hulme and Mosley 1996).

[24] I am grateful to the editors of this book for making this point to me.

[25] I am grateful to the editors of this book for making this point to me.

7

Lessons for Rural Development Practitioners from Recent Agricultural Development Economics Research

Douglas R. Brown and Christopher B. Barrett (Cornell University)

Unlike in most wealthy countries, where poverty is generally a short-lived, transitory phenomenon, long-term structural poverty is the norm in the developing world. World Bank figures show that, as of 1999, 2.8 billion people lived on less than $2/day, mostly in Asia, but with sub-Saharan Africa evincing the largest—and growing—share of its population in severe poverty (World Bank, 2002). In contrast to the United States, where the median time in poverty is 4.5 months (Naifeh, 1998), the median time in poverty in rural Bangladesh, Congo, Ethiopia, Kenya or Madagascar is one or more lifetimes. The expectation of lifetime impoverishment often fosters hopelessness. Without hope, people find it hard to contemplate or effect change. With hope, many things become possible. The Gospel message and the practical challenges of reducing persistent poverty thus go hand-in-hand with helping the downtrodden to find hope.

Seventy percent or so of the world's poor live in rural areas and work, at least part-time, in agriculture. Per the opening words of T. W. Schultz's 1979 Nobel address, "Most of the people in the world are poor, so if we knew the economics of being poor we would know much of the economics that really matters. Most of the world's poor people earn their living from agriculture, so if we knew the economics of agriculture we would know much of the economics of being poor." A few key lessons from recent agricultural development economics research must be internalized in order to achieve that goal. In this chapter, we therefore focus on

micro-level issues of immediate relevance to Christian development groups working at the grassroots level with chronically poor
or vulnerable peoples.[1]

Understanding the Goals of the Rural Poor

Perhaps the most fundamental point development practitioners and scholars must internalize is that (a few religious ascetics
excepted) no one willfully chooses to be poor. Poverty reflects the
constraints and incentives people face. This underscores the importance of taking time to understand fully the (social, economic,
ecological, and political) objectives, incentives and constraints
facing rural peoples. Behaviors sometimes appear irrational to
outsiders who do not understand sufficiently the context in which
local agents make choices, but appear quite rational once actual
local conditions are taken into account. The academic literature
demonstrates the role that incentives and constraints on labor and
other resources play in explaining phenomena such as nonpar-
ticipation in markets for inputs or outputs or cash crop production
(Fafchamps, 1992; Omamo, 1998a; 1998b), the persistent practice of shifting cultivation over other "more profitable" options
(Holden, 1993), and production within apparent cost or profit
frontiers (Barrett, 1997). Incomplete or missing markets, or high
transactions costs can mean that it is, in fact, more efficient for
small farmers to diversify production and aim for self-sufficiency
in food crops than to engage in market-oriented cash crop production (Omamo, 1998a). Shifting cultivation can be a highly efficient low-external-input technology when the constraints faced
by the typical subsistence agricultural household are considered
(Holden, 1993).

Nor are productivity and income the only goals of the poor.
Security of income and stability of production may be even more
important to the rural poor. Failure to account for other legitimate
goals can lead to intervention failure. For example, a main reason
cited for failed efforts to promote *Stylosanthes* use as a fodder
crop for improving pastures or as dry season supplemental feed in
the West African Sahel was differences in goals of livestock pro-

duction (Tarawali et al., 1999). Whereas researchers were looking for ways to improve productivity (milk, meat output), livestock owners were more interested in herd size and therefore ways to maintain an acceptable level of survival at minimum cost.

If few of the world's poor suffer because of systematic errors they make (i.e., they are doing the best they can given the constraints they face), then development agencies must address the structural causes of persistent poverty (i.e., the critical constraints) and use these as a guide to map out an effective strategy of rural poverty reduction that addresses locally limiting factors. When they are considered in light of the unique circumstances of a particular community or region they can help to identify the most relevant areas for action. Organizations working at the grassroots level are uniquely equipped to understand the exact nature and importance of these constraints and to work with local communities to assess their relative strengths and weaknesses in each of the following areas as they embark on development programming. The rest of this chapter is organized around four structural explanations for persistent poverty: (1) meager endowments of productive assets, (2) relatively unproductive technologies to generate sustainable streams of income or consumption goods from those assets, (3) poor access to markets offering remunerative returns for productive assets or one's surplus output, and (4) vulnerability to asset, yield or price shocks.

Understanding the Constraints on the Rural Poor: Meager Asset Endowments

In order to generate flows of food, services and income, people must control stocks of productive assets. In rural areas, the primary productive assets are human and natural capital.[2] An emphasis on human and natural capital is especially appropriate for Christian development organizations for concern about human beings and the earth explicitly honors the Creator by caring for His creation.

Human Capital: The principal asset of the rural poor is their labor power and intellectual ability. Health and education issues related to human capital formation are discussed elsewhere in this volume. We therefore only briefly address a few particular human capital questions of particular salience to agricultural and rural development strategies.

Christian development organizations, which have a long history of establishing and maintaining schools, clinics and hospitals, contribute immensely to education and health endowments. These matter because average adult earnings are strongly and positively correlated with educational attainment and good health. Education and skills that lead to non-farm employment may be especially important. Econometric and case study evidence from rural Africa finds a strong positive correlation between non-farm income and household welfare indicators, and, in particular, finds that greater non-farm income diversification causes more rapid growth in earnings and consumption (Barrett et al., 2001). This yields a positive feedback loop, wherein those with good education and health participate more actively in the rural non-farm economy and enjoy faster income growth, thereby providing the resources to plow back into further investment in human or natural capital, and expanded non-farm activity. Income improvements feed back into yet more investment in human and natural capital.

Local knowledge is an especially important aspect of human capital in agriculture. Too often, Christian organizations have followed the lead of development NGOs and government agents and assumed that traditional approaches are "backward," that outsiders need to "teach them how to farm" and have often attempted to introduce "modern" agricultural practices not well-adapted to the local context. Although it is important not to idealize it, development NGOs can help facilitate the preservation and transmission of valuable local knowledge to new generations and to "scientific" researchers (Peters, 2002), knowledge that has served rural households well for centuries by guiding agricultural systems that were well adapted to their ecological context. On the other hand, where circumstances are changing rapidly and the ecological balance is upset, development practitioners must work alongside local farmers to find ways to adapt to such changes in an environmentally sound and economically viable way. Human capital is not only internalized within individuals. It encompasses the broader community, the social context within which people make decisions, or what some term "social capital", a term we try to avoid.[3] Social networks—the network of social inter-relationships that define the particular societal or cultural context within which people live—matter for multiple reasons. The trust and care that members of social networks have for each other are valuable not only for their own sake, but also because they facilitate cooperation and coordination. Economists have focused especially on the role of social networks in resolving coordination failures associated with information deficiencies (e.g., social learning, contract enforcement and monitoring, reduced transactions costs) and in providing social insurance in the absence of formal insurance or credit to cushion against adverse shocks. Social networks are often the most effective and efficient means of disseminating information about new technologies or market opportunities and of providing a safety net to individuals and households who suffer misfortune. Therefore, reinforcing existing social networks that play these sorts of valuable roles needs to be a priority for organizations operating in the field. Extant networks too often get inadvertently displaced by new public services provided by governments and development agencies. Social networks also help establish and maintain individual preferences and the social norms that condition choice (Akerlof and Kranton, 2000; Platteau, 2000). Interventions that change these networks and norms thereby often have lasting effects, as has been apparent in many cases where culturally unfamiliar—but cheap—food aid has been dumped into communities, permanently changing food consumption and cooking patterns, sometimes with deleterious effects for local farmers or the natural environment (Barrett and Maxwell, forthcoming).

This is of particular concern in areas where increasing commercialization and increasing population pressure lead to increased competition for common pool resources.[4] The result can be a breakdown of essential pre-existing social networks, institutions and values that may not be adapted to the changed circumstances. For example, the commercialization of non-timber forest products may help improve households' incomes in the short term, but at a severe long run cost should it undermine effective communal systems of sustainable resource management that evolved over long periods of time.

Development practitioners need to pay attention to the social networks in the communities in which they work, taking care not to disrupt important functionings of those systems and, where possible, to add to them through the community of faith. The church functions as an important social network and source of social capital in many parts of the world (although we recognize that it is much more than this and this is not its primary role). In the Democratic Republic of Congo (DRC), for example, there are few functioning institutions apart from those established by the Christian church. Were it not for the church, there would not be an educational or health care system in the DRC today.[5]

Natural Capital: After labor, natural resources are the principal asset of the rural poor. They provide not only wealth, but power, as much local level governance in rural areas is organized around management of forest, soils, water and wildlife. Where severe inequality in access to land exists, land reform may be an essential step to reducing poverty among the mass of landless and smallholder farming households. Where smallholders have access to land, one must encourage tenurial arrangements that ensure secure access to natural resources so that people have incentives to invest in their maintenance or improvement, to care for Creation.

Land *quality* is as important an issue as land *quantity*, although it attracts considerably less attention among scholars and practitioners. Within traditional smallholder farming populations, variation in environmental production conditions may well explain most variation in yields not attributable to variation in input quantities (Sherlund et al., 2002), with water and soil nutrients commonly the limiting factors. There have been tremendous advances in recent years in practices and technologies to facilitate soil fertility improvement on small farms—improved fallows, green manure cover crops, new soil and water conservation techniques, etc.—and greater efforts need to be made to stimulate uptake of these practices (Barrett et al., 2002).

Many practitioners (implicitly) assume uniformity within the smallholder farming population in terms of natural capital endowments. Recent work in Kenya found sharp variation, however, as farmers with larger endowments were able to make the necessary investments to maintain soil quality while farmers with lower resource endowments were not able to do so (Shepherd and Soule, 1998). The poor are generally less able to invest in long fallows (Coomes et al., 2000), soil nutrient amendments (Freeman and Coe, 2002; Omamo and Mose, 2001), and other improved natural resources management practices necessary to maintain the natural capital base on which agricultural production fundamentally depends. In order to address issues of productivity, sustainability and rural poverty effectively, agricultural and natural resources management innovations and interventions therefore must target the needs of and constraints facing poor farmers. In other words, they must be doable within the set of resource constraints (available land, labor, knowledge/skills and capital) that are characteristic of the poor.

Understanding the Constraints on the Rural Poor: Unproductive Technologies

People cannot eat labor power, social networks, soil, or money. These resource stocks must be converted into flows of income or consumption goods. The "technology" available to do so dictates how much income or consumption goods farmers can derive from the resources available. For the rural poor, improvements in technology offer another source of hope for escaping poverty. While the Green Revolution, in some ways the premier example of agricultural technology improvement, successfully increased per capita food availability and ignited a period of unprecedented rapid rural income growth in Asia (Barrett, 2002), it missed Africa and the poorest in Asia, yield growth has stalled in much of Asia and Latin America, and the environmental and human health consequences have been considerable. Agricultural intensification that is part of a "doubly green revolution" (Conway, 1997)—one that is ecologically sound and environmentally sustainable—is a necessary condition for poverty reduction and economic growth in the developing world (Lee and Barrett, 2000).

The most productive and sustainable technology is useless, however, if it is not suitable to potential users. The failure of the Green Revolution to reach many offers a reminder that no single technological solution or practice will fit in all, or even most, circumstances. Labor and financial constraints and the necessity to gain practical experience with new technologies or practices make lumpy technologies difficult to adopt. For example, the labor costs associated with improved natural resource management (NRM) practices can be significantly higher than for those practices they replace. The System of Rice Intensification (SRI) has not been widely adopted by poorer households in Madagascar even though it is in many ways an "ideal" natural resource management (NRM) practice (Moser and Barrett, 2001). This is largely because of the increased labor demands at critical times of the year. Resource-constrained households are unlikely to have sufficient financial resources to hire additional labor and may have even less labor available during critical periods due to a necessity to engage in off-farm wage labor to meet basic subsistence needs (Barrett and Brown, 2002).

Fortunately, small changes in how technologies are implemented can significantly reduce labor costs and increase viability from a household perspective. This proved to be the case for the use of *sesbania sesban* in improved fallows in Eastern Zambia, for example, where farmer experience with transplanting bare-rooted seedlings reduced labor costs significantly over the method of transplanting nursery-raised seedlings in plastic bags used by researchers (Kwesiga et al., 1999).

Transition costs and associated uncertainty may be as important in adoption decisions as the actual viability of the particular practice itself, yet are rarely considered in *ex ante* evaluations of a technology (Barrett and Brown, 2002). Given the labor and capital constraints that people face and the necessity to gain practical experience with new technologies or practices, incremental adoption is easier than adoption of lumpy new technologies. It is, for example, much less risky and less expensive to plant a small portion of a field to a new variety of peanuts and thereby gain experience with its unique strengths and weaknesses than to start with one's entire crop in the first year.

It is not uncommon for development organizations to provide incentives to adoption of new practices—such as free tree seedlings, fertilizer, seed, and tools. While incentives given to offset some of the costs and encourage adoption of new management practices may speed the process, there are many examples of practices that have been employed only so long as the incentive continued. In the long run, practices that are truly viable and beneficial, as assessed by the potential adopters themselves, get adopted. The lesson to be taken from this is the importance of (1) working with farmers to identify problems and possible solutions, and (2) to develop technologies that fit the particular context of decision-making and resource constraints—i.e. which are realizable by those who need them most.

Understanding the Constraints on the Rural Poor: Poor or Costly Access to Markets

Markets are merely a technology that converts inputs (the things one sells) into outputs (the things one buys). Therefore, efficient markets, like efficient production technologies, are critical to making good use of asset endowments and, hence, to economic development. Although our knowledge of how markets function in rural areas of poor countries remains rudimentary, most empirical studies find that markets work reasonably efficiently,[6] but that transactions costs[7] are considerably greater and more volatile in rural areas of developing countries than they are elsewhere in the world.

High and volatile marketing margins impede market participation by driving down the price sellers receive for their produce and driving up the price buyers pay for inputs or—for the considerable share of small farmers who are net food buyers—for the food on which they depend. Transactions costs significantly influence behavior and livelihood strategies. For example, diversification often results from high transactions costs alone (Omamo, 1998a; b). Due to high and volatile transactions costs, smallholders face more limited options and greater uncertainty. Because deficient basic institutional and physical infrastructure remains a severe limiting factor in many places, basic infrastructure investments (e.g., roads) often offer the highest poverty reduction returns, particularly in less favored lands (Hazell and Fan, 2000).

The same principles of efficiency and security apply even when inputs are not obtained through markets. Even with traditional land tenure arrangements, where a land market does not exist, smallholder farmers need secure access to the land they use to encourage investment in sustainable and productive natural resource management strategies. Security of access is not necessarily equivalent to having formal title. Traditional systems of land tenure may be very secure and stable, rewarding those who actively manage their land with strong and secure individualized land rights under customary tenure rules (Otsuka and Place, 2001). The particular bundle of rights that goes with land tenure or access has a significant impact on land use decisions. Where exclusive rights to the product of trees standing on the plot are not included in the right of access, there may be little incentive to protect or plant trees even when tenure is otherwise secure. Without the right to alienation, land cannot serve as collateral for loans to invest in improvements. Where a woman gains use rights through her spouse and his family, she may no longer have access to productive resources should she be widowed. Finally, the choice of species for a managed fallow may depend on whether or not it gives the impression that one is claiming the right of ownership. The success or failure of development work often depends upon a good understanding of the cultural context (i.e., the distribution of rights of access and the security of land tenure) in which land use decisions are made.

The most important rural markets are arguably those for finance and labor, more so than agricultural input (e.g., land, fertilizer, and seed) and product markets. There are two main reasons for this. First, the rural non-farm economy is too often underappreciated as an engine of rural development and sustainable agricultural intensification (Haggblade et al., forthcoming). Where poverty results from meager endowments of natural and financial resources, a viable labor market provides the poor with remunerative employment opportunities that lead to income growth. Because financial capital is typically in short supply in low-income, rural areas, a viable financial market facilitates investment in the creation of profitable non-farm businesses necessary to a dynamic, diversified rural economy. As discussed elsewhere in this volume, the microfinance movement offers some promise in this regard. Second, finance and labor markets are terribly important as mechanisms to respond to shocks, our next major subtopic.

Understanding the Constraints on the Rural Poor: Shocks

People are not only born into poverty. Sometimes they fall into poverty as a result of adverse shocks associated with disease, crime, drought, floods, or other natural or human emergencies that cost them productive assets, whether directly (e.g., homes washed away or blindness) or indirectly (e.g., through distress sales as they cope with the aftermath of a shock). Safety nets—most commonly associated with food aid and public employment schemes—play a crucial role in helping people defend current consumption without having to sacrifice future opportunities through the liquidation of productive assets. The timely provision of safety nets matters as much as their availability. By the time people leave their farms and arrive at a feeding centre, for example, they may have already used up most, if not all, of their productive assets and their labor resources may be severely depleted.

Shocks are problematic not just in their realization, but also in their mere prospect because people go to great lengths to avoid potentially calamitous downside risk, especially regarding irreversible damage to health. Because livelihood security matters enormously to resource-poor farmers, (i) risk averse households are often willing to pay a premium (in the form of foregone average income) to reduce risk, and (ii) poorer households will likely be willing to pay more than richer households to avoid a risk of identical magnitude and when faced with the same production technology. Resilience in the face of stresses and shocks is of primary importance since outside of the extended family there are few, if any, sources of insurance when things go poorly. In the absence of rural financial markets, poor people reduce risk and smooth income by diversifying food (agricultural) production and into nonagricultural activities. While focusing all farming efforts on one (cash) crop may result in greater labor productivity, there is also greater risk from "putting all one's eggs in one basket". *Ex ante* smoothing of income through diversification of agricultural production and nonagricultural earnings is sometimes the only alternative when the possibility of smoothing income *ex post* through financial instruments such as crop insurance does not effectively exist. The end result may be to use more labor or to reduce output relative to choice under certainty (Antle, 1987; Barrett, 1996; Finkelshtain and Chalfant, 1991; Sandmo, 1971; Townsend, 1995), in the former case reducing leisure consumption and in the latter expected profits.

This carries important implications for adoption of new technologies since uncertainty surrounding performance, both from the biological and economic perspective, will generally limit or delay adoption. From the perspective of the subsistence householder, a known but less productive technology may be preferable to a potentially better, but very uncertain alternative, even if the system one knows is only just adequate. For this reason, it is important to clarify the particular characteristics of natural resource management and agricultural production practices in terms of their relative risk and stability.

So what can be done? Improving the capacity of the poor to anticipate—and thereby manage—changes in the environment around them is often seen as central to the strategy. This commonly underestimates the efficacy of existing information systems. For example, new climate forecasting technologies widely promoted as valuable for pastoralists subject to frequent climate shocks in the Horn of Africa have proved essentially valueless to them, most likely because the limiting factor for the poor is less the information at their disposal than their capacity to act on that information (Luseno et al., 2003). Pastoralists' livelihood strategies are typically already adapted to sporadic and dispersed rainfall patterns.

The more promising avenues revolve around improved rural financial systems and better-targeted safety nets. The economic conditions and institutional modalities under which microfinance can facilitate lasting, positive change are still not well understood (Morduch, 1999; 2000). Care needs to be taken since credit can also increase exposure to risk and break down long-established social networks. For example, credit for purchase of inputs may not be an attractive alternative in the absence of some form of accompanying crop or rainfall insurance to cover the possibility of catastrophic crop failure. New financial products such as weather insurance contracts may help improve targeting of assistance. By helping NGOs turn reasonably stable flows of contributions into large payouts on claims when the need is greatest, weather insurance could help overcome the delays and resource insufficiency that causes many safety nets to be activated too slowly or to miss many of the poor (Barrett and Brown, 2002).

Perhaps the greatest challenge to improving the targeting of assistance involves rethinking the role of food aid and public employment schemes used to absorb surplus labor. Attempts to meet both safety net and investment objectives with the same transfer programs is exceedingly difficult to do and typically leads to considerable targeting errors (Barrett et al., forthcoming). The requirements of programs designed to address these two objectives differ. The primary goal of safety net programs is conservation of productive assets, especially human capital (e.g., health, nutrition, education), the most important asset of the poor. While important, the investment value of the roads, reforestation, etc. undertaken through food-for-work programs and similar safety net schemes is almost surely less than that of human capital.

Understanding That There is No Single Solution: The Need for Specialization and Collaboration

In outlining key insights from recent research that may help in the design and evaluation of agricultural and rural development programs, we have been careful to emphasize that there are no "magic bullets" or "one-size fits all" solutions or recommendations. The rural poor are a heterogeneous lot as are their specific circumstances. Rather, we emphasize priority factors to consider when designing "best bets" in four key areas: assets, technologies, markets, and shocks.

The same observation applies on the assistance side—no one organization can do everything. Some have particular expertise and experience in emergency relief and the provision of safety nets while others have more experience in agricultural and rural development. Each organization should identify its comparative advantage, focus on that and, where needed, work in partnership with other organizations with different comparative advantage.

Finally, how one practices development is often of equal importance with what one does. It is important to work with local resources, institutions, and technologies wherever possible. This helps develop local capacity and ensures compatibility with local cultural norms and priorities, generating greater long-run returns.[8] Real development work that lasts is painfully slow and demands a lot of hard work; one needs to be in it for the long haul.[9] Christian organizations that have a long-term commitment to partner with a national organization are well placed to make the kind of contribution that is needed. Moreover, the research community can help by similarly partnering with organizations and communities to provide rigorous assessment of what works, what doesn't and why so that together we can make progress in the Gospel directive to serve God by serving the poor.

References

Akerlof, George and Rachel Kranton. 2000. "Economics and Identity," *Quarterly Journal of Economics*. 115:3, pp. 715–53.

Antle, John M. 1987. "Econometric Estimation of Producers' Risk Attitudes," *American Journal of Agricultural Economics*. 69:3, pp. 509–22.

Barrett, Christopher B. 1996. "On Price Risk and the Inverse Farm Size-Productivity Relationship," *Journal of Development Economics*. 51:2, pp. 193–215.

Barrett, Christopher B. 1997. "How Credible are Estimates of Peasant Allocative, Scale, or Scope Efficiency? A Commentary," *Journal of International Development*. 9:2, pp. 221–29.

Barrett, Christopher B. 2002. "Food Security and Food Assistance Programs," in *Handbook of Agricultural Economics*. B. L. Gardner and G. S. Rausser, eds. Amsterdam: Elsevier Science.

Barrett, Christopher B. and Douglas R. Brown. 2002. "Agriculture and Rural Development: Lessons for Christian Groups Combating Persistent Poverty." [Online]. Available by Department of Applied Economics and Management, Cornell University. Working Paper WP 2002–45, prepared for the Association of Christian Economists' conference on "Economists, Practitioners, and the Attack on Poverty: Toward Christian Collaboration," January 2003, in Washington, DC. http://aem.cornell.edu/research/researchpdf/wp0245.pdf (posted December 2002; verified 31/January/2005).

Barrett, Christopher B.; S. T. Holden, and Daniel C. Clay. Forthcoming. "Can Food-for-Work Programs Reduce Vulnerability?" in *Insurance Against Poverty*. Stephen Dercon, ed. Oxford: Oxford University Press.

Barrett, Christopher B. and Daniel G. Maxwell. Forthcoming. *Food Aid After Fifty Years: Recasting Its Role*. London: Routledge.

Barrett, Christopher B.; Frank Place, and Abdillahi A. Aboud, eds. 2002. *Natural Resources Management in African Agriculture: Understanding and Improving Current Practices*. Wallingford, UK: CAB International.

Barrett, Christopher B.; Thomas Reardon, and Patrick Webb. 2001. "Nonfarm Income Diversification and Household Livelihood Strategies in Rural Africa: Concepts, Dynamics and Policy

Implications," *Food Policy.* 26:4, pp. 315–31.

Conway, G. 1997. *The Doubly Green Revolution: Food for All in the Twenty-first Century.* London: Penguin Books.

Coomes, Oliver T.; Franque Grimard, and Graeme J. Burt. 2000. "Tropical Forests and Shifting Cultivation: Secondary Forest Fallow Dynamics among Traditional Farmers of the Peruvian Amazon," *Ecological Economics.* 32:1, pp. 109–24.

Fafchamps, F. 1992. "Cash Crop Production, Food Price Volatility, and Rural Market Integration in the Third World," *American Journal of Agricultural Economics.* 74:1, pp. 90–99.

Finkelshtain, I. and J. Chalfant. 1991. "Marketed Surplus under Risk: Do Peasants Agree with Sandmo?" *American Journal of Agricultural Economics.* 73, pp. 557–67.

Freeman, H. Ade and Richard Coe. 2002. "Smallholder Farmers' Use of Integrated Nutrient-Management Strategies: Patterns and Possibilities in Machakos District of Eastern Kenya," in *Natural Resources Management in African Agriculture: Understanding and Improving Current Practices.* Christopher B. Barrett, Frank Place and Abdillahi A. Aboud, eds. Wallingford, UK: CAB International, pp. 143–54.

Haggblade, Steven; Peter Hazell, and Thomas Reardon, eds. Forthcoming. *The Rural Nonfarm Economy.* Baltimore, MD: Johns Hopkins University Press.

Hazell, Peter and Shenggen Fan. 2000. "Balancing Regional Development Priorities to Achieve Sustainable and Equitable Agricultural Growth," in *Tradeoffs or Synergies? Agricultural Intensification, Economic Development and the Environment.* David R. Lee and Christopher B. Barrett, eds. Wallingford, UK: CAB International, pp. 151–70.

Holden, S. T. 1993. "Peasant Household Modeling: Farming Systems Evolution and Sustainability in Northern Zambia," *Agricultural Economics.* 9:3, pp. 241–67.

Krueger, Anne O.; Maurice Schiff, and Alberto Valdés. 1988. "Agricultural Incentives in Developing Countries: Measuring the Effect of Sectoral and Economywide Policies," *The World Bank Economic Review.* 2:3, pp. 255–71.

Kwesiga, F.R.; S. Franzel, F. Place, D. Phiri, and C.P. Simwanza. 1999. "Sesbania Sesban Improved Fallows in Eastern Zambia: Their

Inception, Development and Farmer Enthusiasm," *Agroforestry Systems*. 47, pp. 49–66.

Lee, David R. and Christopher B. Barrett, eds. 2000. *Tradeoffs or Synergies? Agricultural Intensification, Economic Development and the Environment*. Wallingford, UK: CAB International.

Luseno, Winnie K.; John G. McPeak, Christopher B. Barrett, Getachew Gebru, and Peter D. Little. 2003. "The Value of Climate Forecast Information for Pastoralists: Evidence from Southern Ethiopia and Northern Kenya," *World Development*. 31:9, pp. 1477–94.

Morduch, Jonathan. 1999. "The Microfinance Promise," *Journal of Economic Literature*. 37:4, pp. 1569–614.

Morduch, Jonathan. 2000. "The Microfinance Schism," *World Development*. 28:4, pp. 617–29.

Moser, Christine Michelle and Christopher B. Barrett. 2001. "The Disappointing Adoption Dynamics of a Yield-Increasing, Low External Input Technology: The case of SRI in Madagascar." Unpublished manuscript.

Naifeh, Mary. 1998. "Dynamics of Well-Being, Poverty 1993–94: Trap Door? Revolving Door? Or Both?" Current Population Reports, Household Economic Studies, U.S. Census Bureau, Washington, D.C.

Omamo, Stephen Were. 1998a. "Farm-to-market Transaction Costs and Specialisation in Small-Scale Agriculture: Explorations with a Non-separable Household Model," *The Journal of Development Studies*. 35:2, pp. 152–63.

Omamo, Stephen Were. 1998b. "Transport Costs and Smallholder Cropping Choices: an Application to Siaya District, Kenya," *American Journal of Agricultural Economics*. 80, pp. 116–23.

Omamo, Stephen Were and L. O. Mose. 2001. "Fertilizer Trade under Market Liberalization: Preliminary Evidence from Kenya," *Food Policy*. 26, pp. 1–10.

Ostrom, Elinor. 2000. "Private and Common Property Rights," in *Encyclopedia of Law and Economics, Volume II. Civil Law and Economics*. Boudewijn Bouckaert and Gerrit De Geest, eds. Cheltenham, UK: Edward Elgar, pp. 332–79.

Otsuka, Keijiro and Frank Place, eds. 2001. *Land Tenure and Natural Resource Management: A Comparative Study of Agrarian Communities in Asia and Africa*. Baltimore and London: The Johns

Hopkins University Press.

Peters, Pauline J. 2002. "The Limits of Knowledge: Securing Rural Livelihoods in a Situation of Resource Scarcity," in *Natural Resources Management in African Agriculture: Understanding and Improving Current Practices*. C.B. Barrett, F. Place and Abdillahi A. Aboud, eds. Wallingford, UK: CAB International, pp. 35–50.

Platteau, Jean-Philippe. 2000. *Institutions, Social Norms, and Economic Development*. Amsterdam: Harwood Academic Publishers.

Sandmo, Agnar. 1971. "On the Theory of the Competitive Firm under Price Uncertainty," *American Economic Review*. 61:1, pp. 65–73.

Shepherd, K. D. and M. J. Soule. 1998. "Soil Fertility Management in West Kenya: Dynamic Simulation of Productivity, Profitability and Sustainability at Different Resource Endowment levels," *Agriculture, Ecosystems and Environment*. 71, pp. 131–45.

Sherlund, Shane M.; Christopher B. Barrett, and Akinwumi A. Adesina. 2002. "Smallholder Technical Efficiency Controlling for Environmental Production Conditions," *Journal of Development Economics*. 69:1, pp. 85–101.

Tarawali, G.; V.M. Manyong, R.J. Carsky, P.V. Vissoh, P. Osei-Bonsu, and M. Galiba. 1999. "Adoption of Improved Fallows in West Africa: Lessons from Mucuna and Stylo Case Studies," *Agroforestry Systems*. 47, pp. 93–122.

Townsend, Robert M. 1995. "Financial Systems in Northern Thai Villages," *Quarterly Journal of Economics*. 110:4, pp. 1011–46.

World Bank. 2002. "Millennium Development Goals: Malnutrition and Hunger." [Online] http://www.developmentgoals.org/Poverty.htm (posted 25/11/2002; verified 31/January/2005).

Notes

[1]The macroenvironment (whether political, economic or social) within which rural poor make livelihood decisions affects the constraints and incentives they face. Problems due to changes in the macroeconomic climate (Krueger et al., 1988), persistent, institutionalized injustice, or continual insecurity arising from civil strife severely constrain the attractiveness of the options rural people face. Bad macroeconomic policy, regardless of whether it is poor policy within low-income countries or the spillover effects of the de facto protectionism of OECD countries, is responsible for a great deal of the persistent poverty in the world.

[2] By capital, we refer to resources or wealth in the most general sense. In

this context, human capital refers to the intellectual and physical resources or capabilities of people while natural capital refers to natural resources such as land, forest, etc. Using this terminology, what is often referred to simply as capital would be financial resources. We do not discount the place of financial or manmade, physical capital in agricultural and rural development. But given limited space here, we focus merely on these two primary asset classes.

[3] The Nobel Laureate Ken Arrow summarized our concern well, noting that the concept of measuring social interaction may be a snare and a delusion. Instead of thinking of more and less, it may be more fruitful to think of the existing social relations as a preexisting network into which new parts of the economy have to be fitted. (in P. Dasgupta and I. Serageldin, eds., *Social Capital*, Washington: World Bank, 2000).

[4] Common pool resources are those for which, like public goods, it is costly (through physical barriers or legal means) to exclude individuals, but for which use by some individuals reduces the benefits available to others. They are therefore subject to overuse and potential destruction in the absence of effective methods of deriving and enforcing limits on their use (Ostrom, 2000).

[5] This observation is based on ten years of personal experience in the DRC. Throughout the northern part of the country, the only functioning schools are those run by the Protestant and Catholic churches. With a few exceptions, the only affordable and reliable health care is through church-run health centers and hospitals.

[6] By efficiency, we mean that a competitive spatial equilibrium typically holds.

[7] That is, the costs of market intermediation or, in other words, the marketing margin.

[8] Although quicker results may come from drilling or digging wells for people or with only token local involvement, the results are unlikely to endure. While the alternative of going at the pace of, for example, a local village group is slower, there is a better probability of long term success. In the area of food aid that is given as a safety net in response to severe production shocks, we need to consider the impact on local markets and the risk of negative incentives to producers when we consider how to make such aid available to those who need it. Similarly, the mechanics of how we go about facilitating the marketing of produce (i.e. provision of transport or assistance to remove the barriers to those who could provide) can determine the potential for long term success. Collaboration between research and practitioners can shed light on issues such as these as well.

[9] Two-year appointments and short term missionaries are really not appropriate in this context. This time frame is only really sufficient to get one's feet wet.

8

How the Rise of Supermarkets Poses New Challenges for Christian Rural Development Organizations

Thomas Reardon (Michigan State University)

In all countries before the 1920s, traditional food retailing took place in small shops and open-air markets. Supermarkets (a term I use as shorthand for large-scale modern retail formats such as supermarkets, hypermarkets, discount stores, and so on), which now handle 70 to 80 percent of the food retail market in the United States and Western Europe, emerged in the United States in the 1920s and in Western Europe in the 1940s and 1950s. This chapter describes how the food retail sectors of developing regions have moved extremely quickly to "catch up" with this retail modernization, and describes the evolution of food procurement systems that have accompanied this transformation. The chapter then analyzes the important and very challenging implications of these changes for small farmers in developing countries, and for the Christian organizations and other actors who work with them.

The Retail Transformation in Developing Countries

Over the last decade supermarkets in developing countries have spread from their initial tiny niche among the richest urban consumers in large cities into the food markets of the urban poor and into small cities and towns. The expansion has been fuelled by rising incomes, urbanization, the liberalization of foreign direct investment (FDI) in the early- to mid-1990s in many countries, and improvements in supermarket procurement system technologies (discussed below) that vastly decreased supermarket prices and costs.

Latin America has led the way among developing regions in the growth of the supermarket sector. While a small number of supermarkets existed in most countries during and before the 1980s, they were primarily domestic-capital firms, and served at most 10 to 20 percent of the national food retail market in 1990. However, by 2000, supermarkets had risen to occupy a 50 to 60 percent share of the national food retail market. Latin America had thus seen in a single decade the same development of supermarkets that the United States experienced over five decades (Reardon and Berdegue, 2002).

The development of the supermarket sector in East and Southeast Asia is generally similar to that of Latin America. The "take-off" stage of supermarkets in Asia started, on average, some 5 to 7 years behind that of Latin America, but is registering even faster growth. Supermarkets handle on average one third of the processed and packaged food retail market in Indonesia, Malaysia and Thailand, and on the order of two-thirds in the Republic of Korea and Taiwan (ACNielsen, 2002). The supermarket sector in China is growing the fastest in the world. Starting from very little in 1991, the supermarket sector attained 71 billion dollars of sales, 30 percent of urban food retail, and growth rates of 30 to 40 percent a year by 2003 (Hu et al., 2004).

Supermarket diffusion is also occurring rapidly in Central and Eastern Europe (CEE). Within this region, the transformation has proceeded in three waves. Supermarkets in northern CEE (Czech Republic, Hungary, Poland, Slovakia) began growing in the mid-1990s, rising to handle 40 to 50 percent of the retail market. The second wave is in southern CEE (such as Croatia, Bulgaria, Romania, Slovenia) where the supermarkets handle on average 25 to 30 percent of the retail market, and where the sector is growing rapidly. The third wave seems about to take place in Eastern Europe, where income and urbanization conditions are present for a takeoff but facilitating policy reforms have lagged. The retail share of supermarkets in Russia, for example, is only 10 percent, but international retailers have identified Russia as the number one retail FDI destination (Dries et al., 2004).

The most recent[1] venue for supermarket take-off is Africa, especially in Eastern and Southern Africa. South Africa is the front-runner, with supermarkets taking 55 percent of food retail and 1700 supermarkets for 35 million persons. The great majority of that spectacular rise has come since the end of Apartheid in 1994. To put these figures in perspective, note that 1700 supermarkets are roughly equivalent to 350,000 mom and pop stores, or "spazas," in sales. Moreover, South African chains have recently invested in 13 other African countries as well as India, Australia, and the Philippines. Kenya is the other African front-runner, with 300 supermarkets and a 20 percent share of supermarkets in urban food retail (Neven and Reardon, 2004). Other African countries are starting to experience the same trends: for example, Zimbabwe and Zambia have on the order of 50 to 100 supermarkets each (Weatherspoon and Reardon, 2003).

The take-over of food retailing by supermarkets in all these regions has occurred much more rapidly in processed, dry, and packaged foods such as noodles, milk products, and grains, for which supermarkets have an advantage over mom and pop stores due to economies of scale. The supermarkets' progress in gaining control of fresh food markets has been slower, and there is greater variation across countries because of local habits and responses by wetmarkets and local shops. Despite the slower growth in the supermarkets' share of the domestic fresh produce market, the supermarket presence in markets for these products has become impossible to ignore. Reardon and Berdegué (2002) calculate that supermarkets in Latin America buy 2.5 times more fruits and vegetables from local producers than all the exports of produce from Latin America to the rest of the world.

At the same time that supermarket sectors have been expanding their reach into food retail markets in the developing world, they have also become increasingly and overwhelmingly multi-nationalized (foreign-owned) and consolidated. In Latin America, global multinational retailers constituted on average (over countries) about 3.5 of the top 5 supermarket chains. The tidal wave of FDI in retail was mainly due to the global retail multinationals, including Ahold, Carrefour, and Wal-Mart; smaller global chains such as Casino, Metro, Makro; and regional multinationals such as Dairy Farm International (Hong Kong) and Shoprite (South Africa). In some larger countries domestic chains, sometimes in joint ventures with global multinationals, have taken the fore.

The Evolution of Retail Procurement Systems in Developing Countries

The heart of the impact of the retail transformation on farmers arises out of the evolution of the food retail sector's procurement system, especially since 2000. Through most of the 1990s, traditional retailers and emerging supermarket chains tended to obtain farm produce on a store-by-store basis, through interactions with local producers and wholesalers. They relied heavily on traditional wholesale markets, on immediate "spot-market" transactions, and on existing public standards of quality and safety. In the past several years the leading supermarket chains in most countries have made deep changes in procurement systems. The following paragraphs discuss "four pillars" of these changes (Reardon et al., 2003).

The first pillar of change is the centralization of procurement. As the number of stores in a given supermarket chain grows, chains tend to shift from per-store procurement to the use of a distribution center serving multiple stores in a given zone, district, country or even region. Regional chains (over several countries) are increasingly procuring products in one country for sale by supermarkets in another country. This is accompanied by fewer procurement officers and increased use of centralized warehouses. Centralization increases the efficiency of procurement by reducing coordination and other transaction costs—by some estimates reducing costs by 30 to 40 percent, although it may increase transport costs by increasing the total distances over which products move.

The second pillar of change in the procurement system is a shift from use of traditional wholesalers to specialized or dedicated wholesalers as agents of procurement for the supermarket. As supermarket sector development proceeds, supermarkets tend to shift toward buying through the supermarkets' own procurement departments, or through a "channel captain" (supplier or wholesaler) with whom the supermarket has a special relationship. The channel captain organizes supply in a given category of products. For example, it is increasingly common for supermarket chains to buy fruit from a wholesaler who specializes in fruit and who works almost entirely with supermarkets (and possibly exporters), rather than from traditional, less specialized wholesalers.

The third pillar of change is the shift from use of spot markets (in which buyers and sellers undertake individual and immediate transactions without any longer-term relationship) to the use of implicit contracts with preferred supplier systems. Through specialized wholesalers (acting on their behalf) or their own procurement offices, supermarkets establish contracts (usually implicit) with a list of producers, specifying volumes, quality, timing, and price for future produce deliveries. Being included on the supermarket's list is attractive to suppliers, because it reduces market risk and often offers higher producer prices. Increasingly such contracts also include credit to facilitate the purchase of inputs. Even when contracts do not provide credit directly, they encourage lending by other parties by providing a collateral substitute. As a result of all these advantages to listing, the threat of being "de-listed" is useful for enforcing procurement standards. Establishment of longer-term contracts also provides incentives for investment in assets (such as learning and equipment) required for meeting specific producers' procurement specifications.

The fourth pillar of change is the establishment of much more stringent and uniform private standards regarding product quality and food safety. While food retailing in these regions previously operated in the informal market, with little use of certification and standards, supermarkets are now moving increasingly toward the imposition of uniform and fairly stringent quality standards. Supermarkets impose standards as they seek to differentiate their products, establish reputations and gain market share. It is possible to impose these standards only because of the concomitant development of specialized wholesalers and preferred supplier relationships.

Implications for Processors, Wholesalers, and Farmers

The four pillars of change in food procurement associated with the rise of supermarkets are reshaping agricultural markets, creating new opportunities for some farmers and food processors, while threatening to drive other farmers and food processors out of business. The changes imply that individual suppliers are competing with other suppliers over larger and larger geographic areas, and that suppliers who can deliver large volumes on a consistent basis, and who can upgrade their pre- and post-harvest technologies and commercial practices, are enjoying increasing advantages.

The changes are increasing the hurdles that small farmers must overcome for commercial success. The preferred supplier system now constitutes a toll gate through which producers must pass to gain access to consumer markets. As supermarkets take over dynamic urban markets, access to those markets is available only to producers that are able to meet the transactional and technological requirements implied by the retailer's requirements. Those requirements are embodied in standing orders to those on the list, and those orders require meeting private standards of quality, safety, volume and consistency. These can be daunting to small producers.

For example, the leading supermarket chain in Kenya, Uchumi, requires its preferred suppliers to meet "private" (specified by the chain, not the government) quality standards for fruits and vegetables, focused on appearance (color, size, blemishes, etc.). Tomato standards consist of 20 specifications for cleanliness, size, shape, weight, variety, and so on. Produce not meeting the quality standards is rejected. About 10 percent of fruit and vegetables received by Uchumi are rejected, of which 45 percent comes from small farmers, 45 percent comes from brokers (buying mainly from small farmers), and only 10 percent comes from medium farmers. In addition, Uchumi enforces requirements regarding minimum volumes and consistency of deliveries over several seasons per year. These requirements and standards necessitate substantial investment at the farm level (in irrigation assets and sometimes greenhouses) and for post-harvest activities (in such assets as sheds and trucks)—which is challenging for small farmers to undertake (Neven and Reardon, 2004).

At the same time, the changes are increasing the opportunities available to some producers. Supermarkets represent efficient and powerful "market motors" to diversify products, reduce costs to consumers, and extend modern markets. They thus help producers, as a group, to have bigger and more diversified markets. Moreover, supermarkets directly, or more commonly through their specialized or dedicated wholesalers or processors, can improve the returns and lower the risk to farming—through better prices, through contracts, through technical assistance, sometimes through credit, and often through transport.

As an example of the opportunity for transformation offered by supermarket development, consider the Yogyakarta region of Indonesia. The supermarket chain Carrefour wanted to supply several Southeast Asian urban markets with a distinctive black melon (small in size and seedless), but did not find ready suppliers. They asked the specialized wholesaler, Bimandiri, to find or create a source of supply. Bimandiri, in turn, contacted the Makarbuah small farmer association in Yogyakarta. Entry into production of specialized and high value commodities like the black melon had been beyond the reach of these farmers, in part because credit (for drip irrigation and improved seeds) and extension services were lacking in the region. Bimandiri brought in a fourth partner, Syngenta, a large multinational agribusiness firm that provides seeds, other inputs and technical expertise to groups entering new higher value markets around the world. Through the four-way partnership catalyzed by the supermarket chain, many small farmers of Yogakarta were able to become listed black melon suppliers, doubling net incomes per hectare. Though a tremendous success story, this episode is not without its qualifications. The partnership had to exercise a selective approach in determining which farmers would be given the opportunity to make the transition, because not all farmers were equally capable of becoming competitive. Only about half the farmers made a successful transition (Reardon, 2004).

Implications for Development Programs

Supermarkets are rapidly taking over urban markets in developing regions: they are becoming the gatekeepers to these markets. Access to dynamic urban markets is crucial to poverty alleviation among small farmers; selling to poor, mainly stagnant rural markets is usually not a door out of poverty. Exporting is also an option for poverty alleviation in theory, but in practice exports are a tiny fraction of the size of the urban food market, and the tough requirements of highly contested export markets tend to limit participation to large producers, with some exceptions. Thus, NGOs, donors, and governments concerned with improving the economic well-being of small farm households must shape their programs in the light of this on-going transformation in food procurement. In regions where the transformation is yet in its early stages, it may be difficult to perceive the pressures that farmers will soon begin to face. But the rise of supermarkets and the transformation of procurement systems appears inevitable. If small farmers are to profit from the changes, rather than being impoverished by them, they must be assisted in taking actions that will help them surmount the challenges and take advantage of the opportunities that supermarket expansion brings.

If development organizations are to help small farmers gain or retain access to modern urban markets, they must possess—and have the capacity to convey to farmers—a much higher level of business savvy and understanding of legal and contractual issues than has historically been the case. Conveying these skills to farmers may first require substantial investments in basic education. Developing and conveying these skills will certainly require NGOs to expand the range of actors and institutions with which they have vital relationships. They must study the procurement systems of the supermarket chains in their region, developing good working relationships with their procurement officers or channel captains. They should consider creating alliances with business school faculty and other researchers, who could help them understand market developments, develop business negotiation skills and perhaps facilitate communication with supermarket representatives, who are more comfortable conversing with people trained in business than with small farmers and grass roots organizations. The Mennonite Economic Development Association is making a good effort to draw in people with expertise in dealing with supermarkets as it builds ways for small farmers to enter new markets (www.meda.org).

Without substantial investments in skills for assessing markets and operating within a contractual framework, NGOs run the risk of leading small farmers to disaster. For example, some NGOs have encouraged farmers to make costly investments to enter production of organic foods, giving farmers the impression that as long as their motivation is correct they will be able to sell whatever they produce. In some cases farmers were unable to meet organic certification and supermarket quality standards, were de-listed by the only potential supermarket buyers, and were unable even to dump the specialized produce onto local markets. In other cases farmers were tempted to sell contracted produce to independent intermediaries at higher prices, not understanding the implications for their reputation and future opportunities of breaking contracts.

The rapid changes in procurement that have taken place to date appear to be only the beginning of on-going change. If development organizations are to help the farmers they work with to ride the waves of opportunity, they must try to anticipate the way procurement will be changing. Thus their interactions with a new range of partners—including academics, business experts and multinational firms—must be on-going, collaborative and forward-looking.

Development organizations must furthermore study carefully the assets required for success in selling to supermarkets, and must design programs that help farmers with the potential for success to achieve it through appropriate investments (Berdegué et al. 2003). Farmers must acquire the equipment necessary for meeting volume, consistency, quality and safety standards (such as better irrigation, and equipment to wash, weigh and bag produce). Organizations might encourage such investments through provision of cash or low-interest loans that can be used to purchase assets. Even better, organizations might attempt to increase lending by third parties through the development of imaginative partnerships with banks, suppliers, and supermarkets, perhaps offering credit guarantees as a collateral substitute. Finding effective ways to encourage successful investments will require some carefully studied experimentation.

In light of the recent popularity of microfinance, it is useful to point out that the capital requirements for success in selling to supermarkets are likely to be much larger than the size of typical microloans. Detailed research seeking to identify these requirements specifically is still lacking, but even a few simple observations make clear that lending on larger scale, perhaps to well-organized and large organizations of small farmers, are likely to be much more helpful than a comparable quantity of finance distributed in microloans. Most obviously, necessary investments in packaging and storage facilities make more sense when done on a scale to serve 100 farmers rather than individual farmers. But even at the individual level, significant investments are required to get quality and safety up to minimum certification standards. Berdegué (et al., 2004) estimate that costs per hectare for certified, higher value production are 10 to 50 percent higher in Central America than for traditional production, and are associated with high up front investments. Even putting in place a single sanitary toilet to meet work standards can cost on the order of 1000 dollars. Irrigation and greenhouse investments are, of course, far more substantial.

Scale issues also matter in production and delivery. Development organizations seeking to help small farmers meet supermarket requirements must recognize the role of scale and organization in rendering small farmers competitive. Sufficient scale of production is required to render investment in some packaging and processing equipment economical, for achieving the delivery volume requirements specified by supermarkets, and for improving bargaining power vis-à-vis the procurement officers. It may be possible to enjoy such advantages of scale through the formation of producer market organizations (PMOs), as have arisen in the Czech Republic, Chile, Indonesia, and Guatemala, among other places.

Simply banding together in producer organizations is not, however, enough to guarantee success for small farmers. A recent study in Chile showed that 80 percent of PMOs are now failing (Berdegué, 2001). While sufficient conditions for success are not yet fully understood, some requirements are readily apparent. Farmer organizations need help in learning how to monitor market conditions, develop partnerships with supermarket officers, specialized wholesalers and seed and input suppliers, understand contractual relationships, manage consistent deliveries, and provide all members of the organization with incentives to share the burden of meeting new requirements. Organizations must be given not only a first opportunity to gain access to modern urban markets; they must be encouraged to invest in the capacity that will allow them to survive and thrive in these dynamic markets. Again, on-going experimentation will be required to determine what is required for success.

The food retail transformation also calls into question another popular trend in grassroots rural development work. With food retail markets evolving so rapidly, it may be very difficult for farmers themselves, and even for the development organizations working with them, to anticipate and understand technological requirements. Thus popular efforts to allow small farmers or their communities to "take ownership" and chart their own course for development may not make sense in this environment. Information about evolving changes must be sought from outside and adapted to local circumstances by organizations with multiple links, to the grassroots, to modern market actors, and to researchers in various disciplines.

Given that farmers and development organizations are moving into uncharted territory, and given the wide-ranging requirements for success, development organizations must be increasingly flexible about partnering with a wide variety of individuals and organizations. As examples have already highlighted, they need to work with supermarkets, wholesalers and agribusinesses dealing in seeds and inputs. Beyond this, they must work with packer/shippers and a variety of specialized service providers that are emerging in markets related to high value agricultural commodities. NGOs may have important roles to play, not only as matchmakers between farmers and firms providing required services, but also as advocates with government extension agencies, seeking to identify and fill the gaps that might otherwise prevent profitable partnerships from emerging.

Unfortunately, for some farmers who are poorly located and who are endowed with poor production conditions, even top-notch programs and substantial investments may prove insufficient for success in the new world of food retail. In yet another story of (mixed) success, many Guatemalan farmers who entered the lettuce market were able to triple net incomes (Flores, 2004), but only the upper tier of farmers in the region enjoyed this success. For the rest, upgrading attempts would have failed, and in some cases did fail. Organizations may find it necessary to engage in explicit triage exercises, in which they attempt to distinguish farmers who can and cannot become successful in the evolving food retail markets. For NGOs employing scarce resources, it may make most sense to develop explicitly differentiated strategies. Farmers with the greatest capacity can be encouraged to enter the highest value supermarket segments (as in the case of black melons for large urban market in Indonesia). Other farmers may be better directed toward somewhat less lucrative, but still advantageous new crops (such as cantaloupes for the local market). (Again, MEDA is an example of an organization attempting to develop a differentiated strategy.) Yet others may not have the capacity to become competitive in any higher value market. For those who will not become successful, it may make the most sense to encourage a transition into non-agricultural pursuits. For some who will find it very difficult, if not impossible, to make such transitions, organizations—in collaboration with researchers and others—must seek to design appropriate safety nets, so that they will not be left destitute by on-going agricultural transformation. Differentiated strategies of the sort sketched here may be beyond the reach of many small grassroots organizations. The need for differentiation then suggests that continued expansion of consultation and collaboration among such organizations is called for. Together the organizations seeking to improve economic circumstances of small farm households in a region can develop a differentiated strategy and then implement it in a coordinated fashion.

References

ACNielsen. 2002. "Modern Trade (Self-Service)—Share of Trade," powerpoint presentation by Peter Gale, ACNielsen Asia-Pacific Office.

Berdegué, Julio A. 2001. *Cooperating to Compete. Peasant Associative Business Firms in Chile*. Ph.D Thesis, Wageningen University and Research Centre, Department of Social Sciences, Communication and Innovation Group. Wageningen, The Netherlands.

Berdegué, Julio A.; Thomas Reardon, and C. Peter Timmer. 2003. "Rural Development Policy in an Age of Supermarkets," powerpoint presentation at the United Nations Food and Agriculture Organization (FAO) Scientific Workshop on "Globalization, Urbanization and the Food Systems of Developing Countries: Assessing the Impacts on Poverty, Food and Nutrition Security." October 8–10, Rome.

Dries, Liesbeth; Thomas Reardon, and Johan F. M. Swinnen. 2004. "The Rapid Rise of Supermarkets in Central and Eastern Europe: Implications for the Agrifood Sector and Rural Development," *Development Policy Review*. 22:5, pp. 525–56.

Flores, Luis. 2004. *Small Lettuce Farmers' Access to Dynamic Markets in Guatemala*. Unpublished masters thesis, Michigan State University.

Hu, Dinghuan; Thomas Reardon, Scott Rozelle, Peter Timmer, and

Honglin Wang. 2004. "The Emergence of Supermarkets with Chinese Characteristics: Challenges and Opportunities for China's Agricultural Development," *Development Policy Review*. 22:4, pp. 557–86.

Neven, David and Thomas Reardon. 2004. "The Rise of Kenyan Supermarkets and Evolution of their Horticulture Product Procurement Systems," *Development Policy Review*. 22:6, pp. 669–699.

Reardon, Thomas. 2004. "Supermarkets and Agricultural Development in Indonesia: First Impressions." FPSA Consultancy Report.

Reardon, Thomas and Julio A. Berdegué. 2002. The Rapid Rise of Supermarkets in Latin America: Challenges and Opportunities for Development," *Development Policy Review*. 20:4, pp. 317–34.

Reardon, Thomas; C.Peter Timmer, Christopher B. Barrett and Julio Berdegue. 2003. "The Rise of Supermarkets in Africa, Asia, and Latin America," *American Journal of Agricultural Economics*. 85: 5, pp. 1140–1146.

Weatherspoon, David D. and Thomas Reardon. 2003. "The Rise of Supermarkets in Africa: Implications for Agrifood Systems and the Rural Poor," *Development Policy Review*. 21:3, pp. 333–355.

Notes

[1] South Asia is poised at the edge of a take-off, with the share of supermarkets in India at 5 percent, but identified as number 2 in the top 10 destinations for retail FDI today.

9

Meeting Local Education Needs

Diana Dahlin Weber (SIL International)

Investment in all of a country's people is no longer a luxury. Not only is education a basic human right, necessary for human dignity and good citizenship; it is also vital for achieving economic and social development. (K. Asmal, 2002)

Literacy is of great importance to individuals, and high literacy rates are of great importance to countries seeking to develop. But a large fraction of the world's population remains illiterate. Christian organizations have a heritage of educating the world's poor. They now face a wide range of choices about how to do this. This paper describes the range of choices they must make, emphasizes the importance of involving the local populations they seek to serve in making these decisions, and notes the ways that academic researchers might help them in making good program design choices.

Diversity of Literacy Activities by Christian Development Organizations

Christian organizations may employ a wide range of models for literacy education. Which model will work best varies from circumstance to circumstance. The first step toward making wise choices is to spell out the range of choices available. This section describes the dimensions along which choices must be made.

First or Second Language. In 26 countries, more than 90 percent of the population speaks a lesser-known language. Speakers of lesser-known languages are also disproportionately illiterate. In fact, of the world's non-literate population, approximately half of them—or an estimated 476 million—are speakers of lesser-known languages (http://www.sil.org/literacy/index.htm). Among speakers of less-known languages multilingualism is the linguistic reality. The potential beneficiaries of literacy programs speak the mother tongue at home, but may need to speak other languages in the market place, in government offices, and in interchange with people from other regions or countries. As a result, the designers of literacy programs must make the important and difficult choice regarding whether to help participants become literate in their mother tongue, in a second language, or in both.

Notion of Literacy Pursued. Closely related to the choice regarding language is the choice of the activities for which readers are to be equipped through literacy training. Programs may aim simply to equip readers to take advantage of health, social or government services, by providing them with skills for understanding a limited range of printed materials. Programs may aim at a somewhat broader notion of functional literacy and numeracy, equipping learners for acquisition of more varied social and vocational skills. Some programs aim as well at preparing individuals to enter the formal education system.. Even more ambitious literacy programs aim to equip readers for critical thinking, problem identification, and problem solving.

Groups to be Served: Literacy programs are often shaped with particular demographic groups in mind. Programs might be aimed at adults or children, at specific ethnic or cultural minorities or more mixed groups, and at church members or entire communities. Literacy needs in all these groups are great. According to UNESCO (1998), in the world today there are about 1 billion non-literate adults. That represents approximately 26 percent of the world's adult population. Women make up two-thirds of all non-literates. In all developing countries, the percentage of children aged 6–11 not attending school is 15 percent. In the least developed countries, it is 45 percent (http://www.sil.org/literacy/index.htm).

Modes of Delivery. Literacy programs carried out by Christian organizations cross the continuum from formal to nonformal to informal education, including school-based bilingual education, church-based adult literacy, one-on-one tutoring, and television and radio literacy programs.

Staffing and Training. When creating guidelines for the selection of instructors, literacy programs make choices regarding desired credentials and experience, gender, age, ethnicity, and whether candidates must have local ties or may be brought in from other regions. In conjunction with such choices, programs must also determine what sort of training, oversight and backstopping will be provided for instructors. The range of options varies from place to place. In some communities unemployed government-trained teachers would be glad for a job, while in other communities it is difficult to find candidates with even minimally adequate preparation, until the program produces graduates that may be apprenticed. In one bilingual program, no licensed teacher spoke the language of the region. The solution came via a bilingual high school graduate who received training as a bilingual teaching instructor and whose salary was paid by a Christian organization. In other settings parents or older members of the community have been a solution for staffing.

Materials. Written materials for teachers and learners play an important role in shaping literacy programs. Materials are a much smaller problem now than they were twenty years ago, for two reasons. First, with improved desktop publishing, easier reproduction with copy machines and silkscreen technologies, and easier dissemination via the Internet, materials have become cheaper and more widely available. Second, a change in the understanding of the reading and writing process has increased the role played by printed materials that are not specifically designed for literacy programs. Reading theory has shown how important student writing is to the acquisition of reading. When new readers write their world, and express creatively their observations, reading becomes an interaction with the author of the text. Literacy programs might then want participants to draw their inspiration from the books of the church or vocational materials. Teachers and participants may also create their own materials, drawing each other into greater understanding.

The choice of materials is closely tied to choices regarding the language in which literacy is to be achieved and the notion of literacy that shapes the program. When working in languages for which many materials are available, programs must make choices between materials with varying content and pedagogic structure. When working in lesser-known languages, the choices may be more limited. For some languages no written materials at all may be available. When the nature of literacy envisioned for graduates involves primarily the ability to access social services or understand public health materials, pamphlets on problems such as AIDS, leprosy, teen pregnancy or the acquisition of land titles may be prominent among program materials. Programs aiming at the development of critical thinking skills will naturally require quite different materials.

The choice of materials will also reflect the broader goals of the program. If there is a goal to maintain cultural integrity within the community, program materials will use local language and local cultural content, and will exhibit sensitivity to local learning and teaching styles. If a primary or secondary goal is to transition the community to the global culture there may be more translated materials, content may present foreign ideas and values, and the teaching and learning activities may be modeled after the global society. If the organization's primary goal is evangelization through the reading of the Bible, the content of the materials will likely be Bible texts.

Partnerships. Christian literacy specialists may partner with governmental agencies, multilateral organizations, universities, churches, and other non-governmental organizations (NGOs). Literacy specialists in Christian organizations may play roles ranging from those of consultants, program designers, material developers, teacher trainers and evaluators, to those of instructors.

Local Involvement in Assessing Needs and Designing Programs

When making choices about the literacy program design features discussed in the previous section, Christian organizations must attempt to do the best they can at achieving goals given local constraints. If they are to create programs that become self-sustaining and have long-lasting impact, they must involve local communities in defining the goals and identifying the constraints that shape their choices. Studies suggest that literacy programs fail to become self-sustaining when outside program designers fail to elicit local input in the assessment of needs, devote insufficient time to appreciating local culture, and devote insufficient energy to listening to the weak voices of those with greatest needs (Collins and Blot, 2003; Malone and Arnove, 1998; Wagner, 1987).

Spending time listening is crucial for identifying goals, because the goals that Christian organizations would tend to identify before consulting local communities may well differ from the goals of the communities themselves. Consider, for example, goals regarding the language in which literacy is to be achieved. Choosing to pursue literacy in a second language that is more widely used than the local mother tongue may be seen as attractive to an outside organization, because it means access to a broader array of printed materials and pedagogies, and because it is thought to provide readers with access to more job opportunities and with greater power to improve their relative position within society. On the other hand, communities may place more weight on the potential for such programs to promote loss of first language and weaken local culture, and may be willing to sacrifice some pedagogic and economic gains in order to prevent such harms. Christian organizations may also differ from local communities in the priority they place on achieving broader notions of literacy. Literacy for democratic action, which emphasizes critical thinking and problem solving, may be perceived as valuable by the community but less important to church-based aid.

In an effort to ensure that the people who are being "helped" are the ones deciding what help is needed, Christian organizations are increasingly adopting the learner-centered or participatory approach, involving on-going dialogue between teacher and learner, to determining the learning objectives and content of literacy programs. The participatory approach advocates literacy as a vehicle for personal transformation and social change. One of the first steps is to have communities share past experiences, describing problems experienced and inviting suggestions for possible changes. This is often accomplished through multiple meetings. Implementing such an approach in a truly representative way can be a challenge, because some cultural groups might shy away from participation and decision-making. One successful practice in Africa has been to have the community select representatives to visit other literacy programs, talk with other nationals and then return home with a report. A visit from members of another program to talk about their own program is also helpful. Both types of visits have been inspiring and decisive in new efforts. Other strategies for developing participatory literacy programs can be found at Actionaid (www.actionaid.org) in the "Reflect, Mother-Manual" and at PLAN:NET LIMITED (www.plannet.ca) where the reader can find detailed steps for community-based projects.

Christian organizations can take steps to increase the likelihood of success in achieving true participation in needs assessment and decision making. They can choose program developers who are known and trusted by local leaders as their interfaces in the community. They can model open and reciprocal communication about goals and felt needs. They can model commitment to finishing what they begin, even when economic and policy changes make that difficult, and they can remain flexible in response to changes in local circumstances.

In directing their efforts to understand local priorities, Christian organizations must not mistake government goals for the goals of the communities they serve. Some governments seek economic development—for those in power—by having a better-trained workforce, while the non-literate workers' goal is to help their children do school work.

Imposing the developers' perception of needs follows quite naturally from the cynical—but too often accurate—definition of development as "seeking to reshape the other in the image of one's self." In this line, perhaps a Christian definition of development could be defined as "seeking to provide options that allow the other the choice to be reshaped into the image of God."

Local Involvement in Implementation

The importance of local involvement in management and evaluation of programs is seen throughout the life of literacy programs. A professor in a bilingual education course once said: "Unless the parents and community are fully behind the program, it will fail." I have never forgotten those words as I have visited both successful and failing programs. When communities felt that their desires were understood and respected, and that they had a voice in the development of curricula and in evaluations, the program went ahead. Usually when a program was designed, managed and funded from without, the program ended when the outsider was gone.

The potential value of participation may be seen in three successful programs with local management and evaluation taken from SIL's files. First is the result of a literacy effort by the Ghana Institute of Linguistics, Literacy and Bible Translation (GILLBT), an SIL partner. The energy behind the program came from Grace Paltuu, who herself first learned to read—first in Frafra (her mother tongue) and then in English (Ghana's national language)—through a women's evening literacy class. In her twenties, Grace returned to formal school, but poverty forced her to end her education in middle school. As a result, Ms. Paltuu determined to make sure other women did not suffer the same fate. Working with GILLBT, Ms. Paltuu is now in charge of the women's activities in the Frafra Language Project. She mobilizes rural, illiterate women into groups to learn to read and write Frafra. She initiates programs to help women acquire skills to manage rural micro-economic businesses, raise income, and receive education on public health and environmental hygiene. Over the years, Ms. Paltuu has become a role model for girls and women in her community. The local Frafra people elected Ms. Paltuu to the District Assembly in The Nabdan Constituency where she served two consecutive two-year terms. In 2003, she strengthened and increased women's literacy groups, wrote funding proposals for exporting products from women's cottage industries, and promoted the construction of a dam to improve the area's agriculture. Ms. Paltuu, together with the Frafra Language Project and GILLBT, hold the conviction that literacy is the foundation for all sustainable development, and poverty reduction. (For more details, see http://www.sil.org/literacy/Literacy_Builds_Hope.htm.)

Second, the Kabiye Women's Project, (Togo, Africa) or AFASA, was founded through a partnership between the Kabiye community and SIL. Its primary goal was to train local people to be effective project leaders, managing operations and funding. AFASA pursues women's development in health, literacy and sustainable income-generation. Through various programs and workshops, from chicken raising and malaria prevention, to marketing and leadership seminars, AFASA encourages women to build on new ideas and skills. An important part of the instruction is learning from both failure and success. The leaders are trained to help village women discover possibilities for increasing their families' incomes. (For more details, see http://www.sil.org/literacy/atamon.htm)

Third, the Ngbaka program (Democratic Republic of Congo), which began in 1983, has since been the vehicle through which over 200,000 adults have learned to read and write in their mother tongue. As people became literate, their confidence empowered them to start their own NGO and income-generation projects. In 1994, the Ngbaka NGO "Sukisa Boyinga" (End Ignorance) was formed to represent all areas of the adult literacy program and administer its partnership with SIL, educational authorities, and local Protestant and Catholic Churches. It provides teacher training and coordinates outside training in subjects such as accounting and English. (See http://www.sil.org/literacy/ngbaka.htm)

Each of these programs was characterized by intentional partnering, intentional training of local leaders and teachers, intentional training of managers, and efforts to find culturally appropriate ways to evaluate the programs. And most important, the communities decided how they wanted to use their newly acquired literacy skills.

Without a doubt there were many challenges for all parties involved. One challenge is to open the door to local involvement without opening the door to corruption. In some communities, putting local people in charge of money (and thus giving them access to money) exposes them to pressures to divert money, because culture obliges them to give when needy family members ask. An individual who has access to money but does not give is seen as evil. Programs must tread carefully, then, in shaping local involvement in the financial management of a project.

Another cultural norm that causes stress in educational programs under local management (funded from outside) is the allocation of personnel on the basis of status (family, friends, social obligations) rather than ability. The answer to these and many other problems are often unique to the community and emerge over time.

Potential Contributions from Academic Research

While community participation is valuable for defining goals and identifying local constraints, it does not provide program designers with all the information they might like to make wise choices. Good decisions require careful assessment not only of values and priorities, but also of facts, many of which can be revealed only by careful evaluation research for a variety of literacy programs. When choosing between program designs, for example, it is useful to know how successful each design tends to be at retaining students and achieving the notions of literacy at which they aim. It is also useful to know how much each model tends to cost, what staffing problems tend to be encountered in each model, how useful the differing skills conferred on program graduates tend to be in the labor market and in social and political activities, and more.

Organizations like SIL that are involved with literacy training have a lot of people on the ground, who are keenly interested in doing their job well, and who are in a position to collect data. Working together with academic researchers, who could offer methodological guidance and access to outside funding, they are thus in a position to undertake evaluation research of great value for many organizations undertaking literacy programs. Academic research might also contribute to the growth and development of Christian literacy programs by simply documenting how much Christian organizations have done to provide literacy programs and materials. Further, by developing accounting programs that are easily learned and maintained, they could improve the flow of information to program funders and to the local community. Finally, by developing management models that allow local participation while resisting pressures for corrupt or inefficient practices, they could encourage the use of participatory approaches.

References

Asmal, Kader. 2002. "Education is the Key," *OECD Observer*. June 25.

Collins, James and Richard Blot. 2003. *Literacy and Literacies: Texts, Power, and Identity*. New York: Cambridge University Press.

Malone, Susan and Robert Arnove. 1998. *Planning Learner-Centred Adult Literacy Programmes*. Paris: UNESCO.

UNESCO. 2002. "Education Goals Remain Elusive in More than 70 Countries," press release no. 2002–86, November 13.

Wagner, Daniel, ed. 1987. *The Future of Literacy in a Changing World*. New York: Pergamon.

World Bank. 2000. *World Development Report 2000/2001*. Washington, D.C.: World Bank.

10

Academic Research and Education Projects: Determining What Schools Need

Paul Glewwe (Department of Applied Economics, University of Minnesota)[1]

Many Christian aid agencies assist schools in developing countries. They make many project choices as they seek to use wisely their limited resources. At the same time, many Christian academic economists conduct research on education in developing countries. Both groups have the same goal, improving education in developing countries, but there has been little interaction between these two groups. Common sense suggests that collaboration could lead to more useful research and, ultimately, better projects.

This paper examines two practical questions that aid practitioners face when they design education projects in developing countries: (1) What school characteristics and policies are most effective in promoting learning and reducing dropout rates? (2) What payments, if any, should be required of students and their families? The paper ends with a proposal for collaboration among Christian economists and Christian aid organizations.

What School Characteristics and Policies Are Most Effective?

Almost all observers agree that primary schools in developing countries should provide students with basic literacy and numeracy skills, and virtually all Christian aid organizations that assist primary schools in those countries share that goal. Yet achieving this goal is not a simple matter; many decisions must be made in implementing any project. In most communities, existing schools have a wide variety of needs, and building a new school in an area currently without one raises even more questions regarding what to do. Resource constraints force Christian organizations to choose only some of the many possible options for assistance. Each option will have a different impact on literacy and numeracy, both directly and indirectly through its impact on dropout rates. Aid organizations should choose the options that are most effective, but does that mean that a particular school should be provided with new textbooks or with other instructional materials? Or should funds be spent on hiring new teachers to reduce class size? Or should they be spent on training existing teachers?

These are the crucial questions faced by Christian aid organizations. Ideally, for each type of school characteristic or policy, they would like to know how much it contributes to learning and how much it costs, in order to see which options increase learning at the lowest cost. In principle, academic economists and other social scientists should be able to supply this information because they have been conducting research for many years to understand what school characteristics and policies increase basic literacy and numeracy skills.

While cost data are relatively easy to collect, accurate estimates of learning impacts are much harder to obtain. Indeed, based on my own research in Ghana, Jamaica, Kenya, the Philippines, and Vietnam, and my reading of others' research, I have reluctantly concluded that surprisingly little has been learned thus far on the impact of school characteristics and policies on learning.[2] In retrospect, this is not entirely surprising because teaching and learning are complicated processes, which greatly increases the difficulties in conducting such research. Schools and students vary in many ways, and it is far from clear what it is about "good" schools that make them good. At first glance, one characteristic of a good school may appear to be the key to its success, but it is possible that the correlation between measures of success and that characteristic is just picking up the effects of other characteristics of schools, and of the students in them (and their families), that are just as important or even more important and also happen to be correlated with the characteristic thought to be key.

The most common research methodology used to estimate the impact of school and student characteristics on learning is multiple regression analysis applied to "non-experimental data." Non-experimental data are data collected from the "real world" in which school and student characteristics are not controlled in any way by the researcher. Multiple regression analysis is a statistical method to estimate the β coefficients in an equation such as:

Test Score = β_0 + $\beta_1 \times$School_Characteristic$_1$ + $\beta_2 \times$School_ Characteristic$_2$ + ...
+$\beta_6 \times$Student_Characteristic$_1$ + $\beta_7 \times$Student_Characteristic$_2$ + ...etc.

This method requires data on students' test scores and on all "important" school and student characteristics (or at least requires that any important characteristics not in the data be uncorrelated with those that are in the data). If this requirement is met, the method uses the data to obtain statistically unbiased estimates of the β's, which show how each of the associated school and student characteristics affects students' test scores.

A critical problem of multiple regression analysis is that one almost *never* has data on *all* of the important school and child characteristics, and incomplete data often lead to biased estimates of the β's. A simple intuitive example is that, in many countries, students in private schools score higher than students in public schools on academic tests. Part or all of this difference reflects differences in child characteristics, such as their parents' income and education levels, across the two types of schools. But if there are no data on those characteristics, regression analysis will assign all of the difference in the test scores of children in public and private schools to the variable indicating which schools are private. Even within public schools, a similar type of bias can occur. In communities where parents strongly support education, parents usually not only finance (through taxes) a variety of school improvements (such as new textbooks, better educated teachers, or computers for students' use) but also encourage their children to study. If data are available only on the school improvements, and not on parental encouragement, regression analysis will assign all effects to the observed variables and thus will overestimate the impact of the school improvements on learning.

The simplest solution to this problem of incomplete data is to collect data on *all* child, family and school factors that are "important." Yet in practice this is very difficult because schools and children vary in so many ways, and some data are sensitive and thus may not be reported accurately (such as teacher absences or how much parents help their children with schoolwork). This problem affects education research not only in developing countries but also in developed countries; to date education research has generated more heat than light concerning the debates in the U.S. and Europe on how to make schools more effective.

An alternative research methodology to multiple regression analysis is randomized trials, also known as "experiments." For a particular policy option of interest, one begins with a large number of schools and randomly draws some for which the policy will be implemented (the "treatment group"), while those not chosen serve as the "control group." Random selection is key because it ensures that *all* other school characteristics, and *all* characteristics of students and their parents are, on average, the same for both groups, which implies that any statistically significant difference in students' test scores or dropout rates across the two groups measures the impact of the policy.

In theory, randomized trials can provide very useful information for Christian (and other) aid organizations facing decisions about the kind of educational assistance to provide; yet several problems can arise in practice. One is that teachers, administrators, parents and students may change their behavior in response to the new policy. For example, a policy that makes the treatment schools more attractive may sharply increase student enrollment in those schools, and the higher class size could reduce children's test scores and thus underestimate the "pure" effect of the policy. Similarly, even if no new students enter treatment schools, parents in those schools may reduce the time they spend helping their children with schoolwork or their cash donations to the school, again underestimating the impact of the policy on students' academic achievement. Yet since such behavioral responses can happen in the real world it may be that the overall ("net") effect, which includes such behavioral responses, is what one really wants to know.

Another disadvantage of randomized trials is that they examine only one policy at a time, and often only in a limited geographic area. Strictly speaking, the results apply only to that precise policy and only to that geographic area. Small policy changes (for example, the precise textbook provided) could make a big difference, and what works in one area may not work in another. Thus randomized evaluations provide general lessons only when a particular policy has been tried in many places, so that a "probability of success" (perhaps varying according to local circumstances) can be calculated. Accumulating general lessons in this way could be a slow process, and it will be effective only if the lessons learned are widely disseminated.

The above assessment of what has been learned from research on education in developing countries may seem quite pessimistic, but in fact several studies conducted in recent years have shed some light on the impact of a number of policies and programs in specific contexts. Indeed, a few lessons have been learned using extremely simple data and methods. The best example of such a lesson is that the existence of a nearby school does not guarantee that a child will enroll. The case of India is illustrative; the primary school completion rate in India was 76 percent in 1999, even though 94 percent of the rural population lived within one kilometer of a primary school (PROBE Team, 1999). Yet other lessons are more difficult to ascertain, especially with respect to specific education programs or policies. The following paragraphs describe a few of the best studies that are based on non-experimental data, after which results from recent randomized studies will be briefly discussed.

Most parents, and indeed most teachers, are likely to agree that a good way to increase learning in the classroom is to lower class size. Thus most would be surprised that analysis of non-experimental data from developing countries has not, on average, supported this widely held view (Hanushek, 1995). Yet almost all of these studies used data sets that were missing one or more of the factors thought to be "important" determinants of learning. A much better recent study of class size is that of Angrist and Lavy (1999), who exploit an ancient Talmudic rule used in Israel that limits class sizes to 40 or fewer students. The authors, using variation in class size caused by adherance to this rule, find a significantly negative impact of larger class size on the reading and mathematics scores of fifth graders and on the reading (but not mathematics) scores of fourth graders, but find no significant impacts for third graders. Yet Israel is arguably a developed country, so it is unclear whether this result applies to developing countries. The discussion of experimental studies below offers some additional evidence from a much poorer country.

Recent research using non-experimental data has provided fairly strong support for the hypothesis that children who are better nourished in the first one or two years of life are more successful students. While this may also seem to be an obvious point, and data from almost any developing country show that nutritional status and school outcomes are positively correlated, correlation does not necessarily imply causation. For example, one could argue that poor households are less able to provide both health care and education for their children, so that most or perhaps even all of the above correlation may be due to the causal impact of household income on both health and education outcomes. There are many potential problems in estimating the causal impact of child health on schooling, but a careful analysis by Glewwe, Jacoby and King (2001) that compares Filipino children within the same family finds a causal impact of poor nutrition in early childhood on subsequent learning, age of enrollment and grade repetition.

A final study based on nonexperimental data sheds light on a potential problem faced by school feeding programs, which is that parents may reduce food given to children when they are at home if a school feeding program is implemented at their children's school. Jacoby (2002) uses the same data from the Philppines to investigate this issue, taking advantage of the fact that feeding programs are sometimes limited to certain grades or certain days of the week. He finds, contrary to what most economists would expect, that parents in the Philippines do not reduce the amount of food they give to their children at home in response to the availability of a feeding program at their children's school.

In the last 5 to 10 years, a large number of experimental studies have been undertaken in several different developing countries. For a detailed description, see Glewwe and Kremer (2003). The following paragraphs summarize the most important results.

Experimental evidence has shown that there are policies that can increase enrollment, attendance and grade attainment of children from developing countries. Research in Honduras, Kenya, Mexico and Nicaragua has shown that reducing the cost of schooling, such as providing payments to parents whose children are enrolled in primary school, can lead to large increases in enrollment, attendance and grade attainment. Similar results have been shown for a program that provided deworming medicine to children in areas of Kenya where intestinal worm infections (hookworm, roundworm, whipworm, and schistosomiasis) are common. The studies from Kenya are particularly interesting because they have shown that providing deworming medicine is a much less expensive way to increase enrollment and attendance than providing textbooks and school uniforms (another way to reduce the cost of schooling).

The experimental evidence on which policies increase learning, as measured by performance on academic tests, is less encouraging but still very useful. An early study in Nicaragua showed that radio education programs led to very large increases in learning among primary school children, but somewhat surprisingly this finding has had little effect on education policies in developing countries. Evidence on textbooks and workbooks is mixed in that there seem to be strong impacts in some countries (Nicaragua and the Philippines) but not in another (Kenya); this suggests that some textbooks may be more effective than others.

Other studies from Kenya find little impact on learning from lowering class size, providing flip charts, rewarding teachers for student performance and administering deworming medicine, although school meals were found to have positive impacts when teachers are well-trained. Finally, a computer-assisted learning program in India suggests that such programs have potential in developing countries. Obviously, there is much more to be learned. Fortunantely, there are several more randomized studies currently underway in Africa, Asia and Latin America, and the results should be available within one to two years.

To summarize this section, much remains to be learned regarding the impact of various school policies on student learning. Given this situation, Christian aid organizations, as well as other organizations and Ministries of Education, must make decisions based on educated guesses and "instinct." There is ample evidence from developing countries that many education policies and projects have not worked well (see Glewwe, 2002), which implies that better knowledge of the impact of those policies and projects could lead to better education outcomes in those countries. One particularly promising avenue for future research is to examine the incentives faced by teachers under different institutional arrangements for schools; the effects of providing materials and other assistance to schools is likely to vary widely depending on how schools are organized and the extent to which local communities have some influence on how they are run. Given that much remains to be learned, the last section below offers a proposal to improve this situation, but first another important issue requires some discussion.

Should Students (and Their Families) Pay for Schooling?

A second issue faced by Christian aid organizations concerns the contributions, if any, of a project's beneficiaries. Some organizations, such as Internationaal Christelijk Steunfonds (ICS), a Christian non-governmental organization (NGO) based in the Netherlands, usually require in-kind or monetary assistance from the communities they serve to ensure each community's commitment to the project. Yet this may clash with the desire to help the poorest if poor communities cannot provide even a small contribution. On the other hand, requiring contributions from students, their families, and/or the local community increases the resources available to the aid organization.

Cost sharing for school and education projects can take three forms. First, the local community could be asked to contribute labor, materials and/or funds to get the project started. Second, "cost recovery" could be implemented by charging fees to some or all of the children enrolled in schools assisted by the project. A third, relatively rare option is to establish a student loan program that enables students' families to send them to school at no cost (or at least at a reduced cost) today in return for payments in future years (at which point, hopefully, the students have higher incomes due to their higher skills).

Proposals to recover costs must be planned very carefully because such efforts could reduce the benefits to the project's intended beneficiaries. Conversely, rejecting cost recovery as a matter of principle is likely to reduce the total resources available to the aid organization. Key questions are: Who can afford to make a contribution? How many children would drop out of school if a contribution were required? Is it possible to require contributions of better-off families while exempting the poorest families? How much money can be raised from different kinds of cost recovery mechanisms?

These questions are difficult to answer. Economists have attempted to answer some of them using non-experimental data—for example, see Gertler and Glewwe (1990) for an attempt to estimate willingness to pay for education in Peru—but their efforts have not always been successful. It may be that randomized experiments are best able to answer these questions for different cost recovery schemes.

Christian Aid Organizations and Christian Economists: A Proposal for Collaboration

I claimed above that much remains to be learned about the impact on learning of different kinds of school characteristics and education policies, and that the research methodology most commonly used, multiple regression analysis with non-experimental data, may not be able to shed much light on the effectiveness of different education projects. What can be done? In my opinion, the best way to learn which projects and policies are most effective in raising literacy and numeracy, and reducing dropout rates, is to institute a rigorous program of randomized trials and to disseminate the results to all organizations and government agencies that assist schools in developing countries. This would be a major undertaking, but the importance of this issue to Christian aid organizations implies that the time has come to devote serious amounts of time and financial resources to such an endeavor. This section lays out a broad strategy.

An Example. In 1995, I began collaborating with Michael Kremer, a professor of economics at Harvard University, and other researchers on a series of randomized studies of schools in Kenya. We doubted that the Kenyan government would agree to conduct randomized trials. Fortunately, Michael (who had taught secondary school for one year in rural Kenya) persuaded ICS, the Dutch NGO mentioned above, to participate in randomized trials. Since 1995, we have evaluated several different types of projects: ICS's standard package of assistance, textbooks, flip charts (sets of classroom posters), grants that could be spent on whatever the school chooses, deworming medicine, a teacher incentives program, and a package of assistance to preschools.

The evaluations of these randomized trials have taken longer to complete than initially expected and, to our dismay, most of the interventions seem to have had little or no effect on students' literacy and numeracy skills. Yet several papers are now available (see Glewwe, et al., 2004; Glewwe, Ilias, and Kremer, 2003; and, Miguel and Kremer, 2004), and much has been learned even though many of the projects appear to have had little impact. This is a first modest step toward providing practical information on how specific kinds of school policies affect learning in developing countries. Many more studies of this type are needed to develop a "data bank" of the likely impacts of different education policies on learning.

Possible Objections. Although randomized trials are common in the analysis of health issues, they are rare in education research. Some may argue that they are unethical because they treat children as experimental subjects. Yet the same is true for randomized trials of new medicines, and in response medical researchers have established clear procedures that satisfy strict ethical standards, which could be adapted to education research. Moreover, most education projects seem much less dangerous than medical trials that evaluate a new drug or medical treatment.

Another objection is that randomized trials are unfair because the schools or students assigned to the control group are denied the potentially important benefits received by the treatment schools or students. This objective is less compelling because the policy being evaluated may be ineffective. Moreover, the limited resources of governments and aid agencies imply that most projects cannot be implemented everywhere, so some schools or students are already being left out; the issue is whether such "rationing" can be done in a way that provides information about the effectiveness of different education policies. Finally, denial of treatment to any school or student will not continue forever but instead will last at most a few years. Any policy found to be unusually effective can be implemented in all schools, subject to the usual financial constraints of governments and aid agencies. Indeed, a careful study showing that a project works could be a good fund-raising tool for Christian aid organizations.

A final problem is that teachers, school principals and Ministry of Education officials may be cool, if not directly opposed, to randomized trials. For example, teachers may feel that they are being judged. Most policies being evaluated are not closely related to teachers' performance, so teachers can be assured that the results cannot be used against them. This may take time to explain, but cooperation of all school and education professionals is essential for a rigorous evaluation.

Next Steps. If Christian aid organizations that assist schools are willing to conduct randomized trials, much planning and hard work is required to ensure their success. A handbook is needed that thoroughly describes how to implement randomized trials; some already exist, but it would be best to write one specifically for education projects. Academic economists and other professional researchers must make long-term commitments, including travel to the countries, to ensure that evaluations are being done according to the highest standards. An archive, perhaps based at a college or university, is needed to store and disseminate the results of the studies. Finally, a steering committee of academic researchers and staff from aid organizations should be established to coordinate plans for new studies in order to avoid duplication and ensure that the most promising policies are the first to be evaluated.

References

Angrist, Joshua and Victor Lavy. 1999. "Using Maimonides' Rule to Estimate the Effect of Class Size on Children's Academic Achievement," *Quarterly Journal of Economics.* 114:2, pp. 533–576.

Gertler, Paul, and Paul Glewwe. 1990. "The Willingness to Pay for Education in Developing Countries: Evidence from Peru," *Journal of Public Economics.* 42:3, pp. 251–275.

Glewwe, Paul. 2002. "Schools and Skills in Developing Countries: Education Policies and Socioeconomic Outcomes," *Journal of Economic Literature.* 40:2, pp.436–482.

Glewwe, Paul, Nauman Ilias and Michael Kremer. 2003. "Teacher Incentives," National Bureau of Economic Research, Working Paper No. 9671.

Glewwe, Paul, Hanan Jacoby, and Elizabeth King. 2001. "Early Childhood Nutrition and Academic Achievment: A Longitudinal Analysis," *Journal of Public Economics.* 81:3, pp.345–368.

Glewwe, Paul, and Michael Kremer. 2003. "Schools, Teachers, and

Education Outcomes in Developing Countries," forthcoming in *Handbook of the Economics of Education*. E. Hanushek and F. Welch, eds.. Amsterdam: North Holland.

Glewwe, Paul; Michael Kremer, Sylvie Moulin and Eric Zitzewitz. 2004. "Retrospective vs. Prospective Analyses of School Inputs: The Case of Flip Charts in Kenya," *Journal of Development Economics*. 74:1, pp.251–268.

Hanushek, Eric. 1995. "Interpreting Recent Research on Schooling in Developing Countries," *World Bank Research Observer*. 10:2, pp.227–246.

Jacoby, Hanan. 2002. "Is There an Intrahousehold Flypaper Effect? Evidence from a School Feeding Program," *Economic Journal*. 112:476, pp.196–221.

Miguel, Ted, and Michael Kremer. 2004. "Worms: Identifying Impacts on Education and Health in the Presence of Treatment Externalities," *Econometrica*. 72:1, pp.159–217.

PROBE Team. 1999. *Public Report on Basic Education in India*, New Delhi: Oxford University Press.

Notes

[1] I would like to thank Julie Schaffner, Judy Dean, and Stephen Smith for comments on previous versions of this chapter.

[2] For a detailed discussion, written for economists, see Glewwe (2002).

11

Health Economics and Health Practice

Paul E. McNamara (University of Illinois at Urbana–Champaign)[1]

For a Christian health economist, motivated by the biblical themes of justice, solidarity with the poor, and the welfare of all people, the international health programs of Christian non-governmental organizations (NGOs) present a wonderful challenge: how can health economics inform and assist in the design, implementation, and evaluation of international health programs that are distinctively Christian? To the health economist, the answer might appear patently obvious as health economics provides a theory and a body of empirical research explaining the demand for health and health inputs (like vaccinations, nutrition, and curative medical services), the supply of health care, and analytic tools such as benefit-cost analysis and cost-effectiveness analysis. However, to the health program manager operating in the context of an NGO, the answer might just as clearly be that no role exists for health economics in this endeavor, because every human being has a right to access to health and health care and poor people should not be forced in the market to trade-off their health for their shelter and food.

This chapter develops the notion that the analytical tools provided by health economics can be used to make valuable contributions to the health programs of international Christian NGOs, provided that care is taken in building fruitful collaborations between academic health economists and NGO managers and staff. Particularly useful tools for health programs are "burden of disease analysis" and cost-benefit analysis (and its cousins, cost-effectiveness and cost-utility analysis), but economists have more to offer. The economic thinking around the relationships between income and health, education and health, and insurance and health care, have important implications for the design of NGO health programs. Additionally, economic methods of policy analysis and statistical analysis apply directly to NGO program design questions. Health economics also can contribute to the health programs of NGOs when they venture into discussions of poverty reduction strategies at the national level. Indeed, a significant contribution of health economics relates to its emphasis on health systems, and this emphasis raises a challenge to NGOs to include building the national health infrastructure explicitly into their program objectives.

The Diversity of Christian NGO Programs in International Health

To develop an understanding of where and how health economics can make a contribution to Christian NGO international health efforts, we must first appreciate the goals, objectives, program designs and areas of operation of these programs. Christian NGO efforts in the area of international health address myriad issues and utilize a variety of program strategies to reach their multiple goals. Today, Christian NGO international health programs range from running hospitals in Zimbabwe, to implementing community-based health education efforts to confront HIV/AIDS in West Africa, to child survival programs in Asia and Africa, to providing care to AIDS orphans in Brazil, and to training pastors throughout the world about HIV/AIDS in order to craft a Christian response to the epidemic. An appreciation for the diverse programs makes a starting point for helping these organizations apply health economics methods to generate the greatest health impact possible with limited programmatic resources.

The range of approaches and project designs in Christian efforts in international health is striking. The programs and projects differ along numerous dimensions, including the program objectives, the size and scope of the program (in terms of budget, staff, geographic area), the formal role of the church in the project or program's implementation, the definition of the target audience and the role of the community or program participants in shaping and controlling the program, the extent of bilateral or multilateral development agency funding, and the role of formal evaluation systems in the program or project design. With respect to the health objective and the project or program design, we see variety ranging from health education and prevention approaches (particularly common in the HIV/AIDS area) to projects that provide access to primary medical care through clinics and hospitals. Other Christian health projects integrate health components with an economic development or economic security dimension, such as the case of credit groups that also serve as a delivery channel for health and nutrition education messages. With respect to partnerships and funding arrangements, some Christian health NGOs develop collaborations and partnerships across denominational lines, while others partner with local government (Ministry of Health or other agency) or international development agencies (bilateral or multilateral). Some rely entirely on outside donor funding, while other mobilize local resources (beyond in-kind contributions of time). Certainly differences in funding sources and partnerships drive differences in the constraints that shape their objectives and choices.

NGO health efforts also vary in the role of formal mechanisms for monitoring and evaluating the project impact and program outcomes. While many, if not most, of the large NGO projects have specific project outcomes or indicators to measure the project impact, some projects, particularly those of smaller organizations, may not have a formal evaluation strategy or set of measurable project outcomes. Furthermore, many projects involve community health development interventions, which do not have a firm basis in terms of evidence in the public health literature concerning their effectiveness.

Health economics tools have the potential to expand the contribution of Christian health NGOs in varying ways. The organizations with the largest programs (in terms of budget and staff), and who tend to work under contract with USAID and other multilateral and bilateral aid agencies, have the capacity to engage in strong evaluation and monitoring shaped by health economic methods, and thus have the potential to improve their impact by modifying their programs in light of what they learn about how best to achieve their objectives. An increasing number of NGOs are developing explicit goals of shaping public health policy at a national level, and some are well placed to have an important influence. Health economics reasoning will be useful in framing issues and communicating positions in debates with a broad range of actors. Finally, health economics research methods may help some NGOs demonstrate their institutional comparative advantage in delivering health services—as evidenced by indicators such as available medicines in clinics, trained staff on duty, up-to-date record keeping, and others—creating opportunities for them to play new roles in the implementation of national health policy strategies.

Four Contributions of Health Economics

Health economics is the branch of economics that studies the production, demand, supply, organization and distribution, and financing of health and health-related services and products. The press for evidence-based medicine, where the evaluation of medical and public health treatments considers the effectiveness of treatments and programs in producing the desired health outcomes in a cost-effective manner has helped spark the growth of this discipline. In this role health economics can assist policy makers in allocating limited health care budgets to the most productive uses and, thereby, increase overall population health (Kindig, 1997). The World Bank and the World Health Organization and their partner institutions across the globe lead the movement to bring economic tools to the analysis of international health projects and programs. While much of the attention of this movement has been at the level of national health policy setting, health economics provides ways of thinking and analyses that may improve the programs of Christian NGOs operating in the international development context. Four key insights from health economics for these NGOs come in the form of the concept of the burden of disease, the theory of health investment and the demand for health, the tools of economic measurement, and the economic evaluation tools of cost-effectiveness analysis and cost-benefit analysis.

The Burden of Disease Concept—A Useful Method for Guiding Program Priorities

An important methodology to help in targeting health resources and health programming efforts is the notion of the burden of disease. The World Health Organization, the World Bank, and others (including academic health economists) have led important efforts in developing the burden of disease methodology, conducting studies, and disseminating results to affect policy and planning (see, for example, WHO's The World Health Report, 2002). The burden of disease approach seeks to determine the magnitude and relative contribution of specific diseases and health practices (health behaviors, environmental health factors, and injury-types) to the overall amount of illness and disease (measured in morbidity and mortality terms) observed in a country or region. Ezzati and co-authors (2002) present a global analysis of health risks and the burden of disease with direct implications for the design and implementation of NGO health projects. They considered 26 major health risks, including being underweight or Vitamin A deficient, having high BMI, practicing unsafe sex, using tobacco, alcohol or illicit drugs, and being exposed to air pollution and occupational health risks. Using Disbility Adjusted Life Years (DALYs) for their outcome measure, they found that in the set of countries with high mortality rates (including all of Sub-Saharan Africa and countries like Egypt, India, Afghanistan, Bolivia, Haiti, and Peru), being underweight (15 percent), and practicing unsafe sex (10 percent) were the risk factors that contributed the most (about 25 percent of DALY in the region combined) to the overall burden of disease. Obtaining an overall ranking of the relative contribution of disease risk factors to the overall level of morbidity and mortality is one step towards efficient allocation of health resources.

One NGO (the International Development Research Center, IDRC, based in Canada) has partnered with the Tanzanian Ministry of Health (MOH) to apply the burden of disease concept to health program targeting (The Economist, 2002). The Tanzania Essential Health Interventions Project (TEHIP) operates in two rural districts (Morogoro and Rufiji) and the basic thrust of the project was that IDRC would augment MOH spending in the districts if the health ministry would align health spending and programs to address the relative burden of diseases in the district. To achieve this goal of better matching of resources to health burdens, the project conducted a door-to-door survey (not an inspection of clinic records or disease registries) to find out whether anyone had died or been sick and obtain a description of the symptoms. This allowed the construction of district-wide burden of disease estimates and a comparison with the health budgets identified major discrepancies between disease burdens and resource allocation. For example, prior to the project, malaria accounted for 30 percent of the disease burden in Morogoro, but health spending was only 5 percent of the 1996 budget. In addition, some diseases attracted more spending than the burden indicated, with tuberculosis at 4 percent of life years lost and 22 percent of spending providing one example. The project used this information to reshape the budget somewhat, with the additional funding from IDRC allocated to neglected diseases where cost-effective interventions were available. This is one example of how the burden of disease concept could be applied to help better target health problems in developing countries. Another use for the burden of disease concept would be in national-level health planning discussions where NGOs might work with the MOH to make sure that overall health resources (private sector, including NGOs, and public sector) match the burden of disease.

The Economic Determinants of Health—A Source of Program Design Guidance

Economists generally credit Michael Grossman (1972), with developing an economic approach to the production of health and the demand for health inputs within a household context. This economic theory of the demand for health and production of health capital has spawned a research literature that has focused on exploring the economic role of improved health in generating wealth and income, the role of education and health knowledge in producing improved health status, and the link between income and improved health status. Furthermore, the demand for health research has examined the impact of user fees on consumer welfare and helped inform policy makers and managers about the limits and benefits of user fees as a means to mobilize finances to support health programs and services. Cross-country comparisons of health status measures, such as infant mortality or life expectancy, portray a strong income gradient with respect to health indicators. Consider, for example, World Bank data on human health from countries around the world, which shows a strong correlation between a country's Gross Domestic Product and basic health status variables, such as the infant mortality rate (IMR). In 1999 the country with the highest IMR (Sierra Leone) had a rate roughly 20 times higher than the high income countries such as the U.S., Japan, and Switzerland. Interpretation of simple correlations like this is controversial, but a careful study of cross-country data by Pritchett and Summers (1996) suggests that in 1990, if developing country incomes were 1 percent higher, 33,000 infant deaths and 53,000 child deaths would have been prevented. One implication these results holds for Christian NGOs in the health arena is the need to participate in the coalitions that advocate for improved policies to help developing country economies (including fair trade policies, well-crafted debt relief programs, effective microenterprise and microfinance programs, and, investments in agriculture and other productive sectors). For Christian NGOs operating in developing countries, this evidence demonstrates the need to support and push for effective national-level economic development policies and excellent governance of the essential government services, as well as well-designed NGO projects and programs aimed at strengthening incomes, especially incomes of the poorest people.

Economists also have focused on the important contribution of health to economic growth and raising incomes, what Grossman (1972) labeled the investment effect of health. This investment effect highlights the central role that health capital formation can play in increasing national incomes. The economic impact of the HIV/AIDS epidemic provides evidence of the opposite effect, where neglected health investments or where significant health shocks reduce national income. Haacker (2002) reports on an economic analysis of HIV/AIDS on the economies of Southern Africa that finds that the long-run impact of the HIV/AIDS epidemic on per capita GDP ranges from between a 1.2 percent decline in Mozambique to a decline of 3.2 percent in Botswana. The differing impacts arise from different HIV/AIDS infection rates and from the differing prevalence of the disease across types of workers. In Haacker's analysis, most of the decline in national income due to HIV/AIDS is due to increased mortality of workers in their productive years, which results in the costs of training new workers and productivity declines from lowered levels of experience in the workforce. NGOs have played a central role in addressing the HIV/AIDS epidemic through prevention, treatment, and outreach and care programs. The economic evidence, along with the realization of the crushing human burden of the disease, highlights the importance for research that documents the effectiveness of NGO efforts in the area of preventing new cases of the disease.

The demand for health capital framework also raises the possibility that education or knowledge might affect the demand for health inputs, as well as the productivity of health capital production. The strong correlations between health measures and education have generated a large economic literature about the role of education in health production, with a particular emphasis on maternal education and child health. Behrman and Deolalikar (1988) and Behrman (1990) survey a number of studies on the effect of maternal education and children's health, which tend to show positive correlations between the years of maternal education and decreased child mortality. Though in general difficult econometric problems render it difficult to conclude that higher maternal education truly *causes* reduced child mortality, some studies establish relationships with practical implications for health practitioners. For example, Glewwe (1999) finds that the most important contribution of mother's schooling on health is an indirect effect that acts through specific health knowledge. The literacy and numeracy skills obtained in formal school affect the mother's ability to acquire health knowledge, and the specific health knowledge itself that improves child health. This implies, first, the need to teach health in schools. It also implies the need to increase schooling for girls, to provide health education programs for women of child-bearing age, and to improve school quality so that schools impart literacy and numeracy skills.

Despite the contention of some that prices do not constrain the demand for health and health care, health economics researchers—careful to measure the full cost of seeking health care and to control for the quality of health service provided—find convincing empirical evidence that prices play an important role in determining the demand for health care in developing countries, with higher prices playing an especially strong role in reducing health care demand by the poor. Gertler and van der Gaag (1990) examined the demand for health care using a provider choice models for rural people in Peru and the Côte d'Ivoire. The demand elasticities from their models imply that compared to free care (which still imposes time costs on consumers) a system of across the board user charges will be regressive. That is, poor peoples' demand for care will be reduced much more than the rationing effect experienced by wealthier households. Moreover, they also find that the price elasticity for children exceeds that of adults, implying that user fees disproportionately reduce the utilization of health care by children. This result argues for the geographic targeting of health care services to where poor people live, if equitable access to health care is a policy or program goal. In addition, targeting user fees may be one means of avoiding the regressive impact of health care user fees.

Research also suggests that even the poor are willing to pay more for a guarantee of higher quality care. Leonard (2002) provides a theoretical framework and empirical evidence supporting the argument that African health care NGOs do a better job than government providers in providing quality care, because of their greater ability to create well-tailored and trusted agreements regarding the quality of care with their patients. The NGOs under consideration by Leonard often charge more than government providers for the same service, but they offer greater consistency on quality dimensions such as available pharmaceuticals and staff performance. Leonard's analysis supports the contention that NGOs offer at least a partial solution to the improvement of African health care systems, because their institutional form allows them to overcome some of the difficulties (including informational asymmetries in health care markets and pernicious rent-seeking behaviors) found in these health care markets.

Empirical Tools for Assessing Impact

For managers in NGOs with international health programs, a significant challenge is to muster and interpret evidence on the effectiveness of the NGO's health programs. This chapter is not the forum to delve into technical details concerning econometric issues, however, program managers should realize that health economists have a background and training in addressing these sorts of statistical issues. In addition, program managers can be aware of the statistical issues posed in an effort to demonstrate the effectiveness of a public health or health care program. Mullahy and Manning (1995) describe the statistical issues faced in conducting a cost-effectiveness analysis for a health care treatment. Achieving meaningful assessments of program impact, based on some sort of comparison of a treatment group to a control group, can be difficult for a variety of reasons, related to such problems as: selection of a treatment group predisposed to above or below average health; the drop out of some members of the treatment group who may have been experiencing below-average impact; difficulties in obtaining accurate measures of desired health outcomes or control variables, and the inability to control for some factors likely to play an important role in shaping health. The point here is that in order to demonstrate the effectiveness of an NGO's international health program to many audiences, the standard of evidence is quite high. It is the standard of evidence familiar to academics, who face these standards when publishing in scientific journals in public health and international development. Academics thus have much to offer in helping program managers make choices regarding research design and data analysis.

Tools for Thinking about Cost-Effectiveness

Knowledge of the burden of disease is not sufficient to ensure an efficient allocation of health spending. Depending on the availability of effective interventions and their costs, it may make economic sense to forgo treating or preventing some diseases with a high burden in order to focus resources on diseases with a lower burden with an inexpensive and effective treatment or prevention strategy. Cost-effectiveness analysis and cost-benefit analysis represent two common ways for health economists to compare alternative health projects or interventions and assist decision-makers with making an efficient use of their limited budgetary resources. Both cost-effectiveness analysis (CEA) and cost-benefit analysis (CBA) take the societal perspective in considering the relevant costs and benefits for inclusion in the analysis. The societal perspective is consistent with the public health perspective of population health. In addition, CEA and CBA are the analytic methods used (along with expert reviews and meta-analyses) for evidence-based public health (Brownson, Gurney, and Land, 1999; Brownson, et al., 2003). Evidence-based public health is a best practice for public health agencies and organizations, where the design of major programs rest upon scientific analyses that demonstrate the effectiveness of the program at producing outcomes in a manner that is consistent with resources used to deliver the program.

In CEA the analysis aims at comparing the costs of a health care intervention with its outcomes. Alternative methods of producing the same outcomes (i.e., discounted life years saved) can be compared to find which method is the most efficient way to produce population health given a limited budget. CBA analyzes the costs of a health program with an economic measure of the program's entire impact, where the impact is measured in money terms. The impacts captured in a CBA may be broader than in a CEA, since impacts like improved labor productivity can be valued in money terms. For example Kim and Benton (1995) use a CBA approach to value the West African onchocerciasis control program (OCP), which provided health benefits to rural West Africans and opened up previously oncho-infested land areas to agricultural production.

International public health examples of the CEA include Jha, Ranson, and Bobadilla (1996). They calculate the burden of disease for Guinea and then conduct a CEA of forty selected health interventions in use at clinics and hospitals. Conducting a CEA requires estimates of the efficacy or treatment effect of the selected interventions, as well as information on the average number of life years lost to each treated disease or risk to health. In addition, information is required about the pre- and post-intervention coverage for the treatment. Once the cost structure of the intervention is known, then a calculation of the CEA can be made. A table that compares CEA results for a set of interventions is called a league table, and such a table allows the selection of the most efficient measures to produce additional life years at the societal level. Jha, Ranson, and Bobadilla (1996) provide a ranking of all forty interventions and they find that the three most effective ways to produce additional life years include (1) treatment of children with pneumonia at health center ($3/life year saved), (2) rehydration therapy at health center ($7/life year saved) (3) rehydration therapy at health post ($8/life year saved). A cost-effectiveness analysis such as Jha, Ranson, and Bobadilla (1996) provides an easy to understand research result useful for targeting program budgets and health interventions. In addition, the analytic framework highlights some addition questions for anyone in health program design: what is the efficacy of the program's treatment? How effective is the program in terms of producing public health or clinical outcomes?

The World Bank has developed a decision-making tool based on CEA called the ABC (Allocation by Cost-Effectiveness) Model (World Bank, 2002). While designed for allocating HIV

Prevention resources, the framework could easily be extended to other prevention or treatment arenas. The model provides a set of Excel-based spreadsheets that can be used to compare alternative HIV Prevention programming strategies to find out which programs should receive the limited funds from an HIV Prevention budget.

This section has surveyed some of the main tools of health economics with an eye towards their potential contribution in designing, implementing, and evaluating the international health projects and programs of Christian NGOs. Readily applicable examples exist of tools and methods that might help NGOs hone project designs for greater effectiveness. For example, the economic research on the contribution of education to health status suggests that NGO programs doing health education and prevention education might consider building in specific attention to literacy and numeracy skills needed to produce health. These economic methods can also be used to shape project monitoring instruments and to conduct evaluations. While health economics has a potential contribution to make to the work of international NGOs, thinking about the context and operational issues faced by the health programs of Christian NGOs might also contribute to the work of an academic researcher.

The Promise and Challenge of Collaboration

In many parts of the developing world, certainly in many parts of the poorest countries, NGOs represent the most effective organizations on the ground with a capability of delivering health programs. Interacting with these programs, either formally in a cooperative-research capacity or less formally, offers an economist researcher a real-world problem with potential significance for research literatures on international health and public health. However, sincere engagement or interaction with NGOs will challenge economists not only because of the quick pace of the NGO world, but also because of the clear statements of mission and purpose of the Christian NGOs.

In my conversations with NGO managers, they repeatedly

mention the desire for economists to contribute to discussions and analyses of health equity concerns across countries. Their concern is rooted in the fact that $1000 dollars spent in Sierra Leone on bednets for malaria prevention or rehydration therapy at a health center, for instance, can produce many more additional years of life than that same sum used here in the U.S. Sincere engagement with international public health raises the extreme differences in net benefits in terms of life years saved or QALYs obtained per dollar of health spending across rich and poor countries. How do economists respond to this enormous variation? Are we willing to raise our voices in our churches and in communities to ensure that people are aware of the enormous inequities in health spending at the present time? Do our lives reflect a Christian commitment to live in solidarity with the poor?

Another area where the NGOs and their health programs raise questions for health economists is with respect to the church. Some Christian NGOs strikingly assert the church's ability to be one of the most effective institutions to effect behavioral change with respect to health behaviors. However, few development economists or health economists have seriously entertained this question in the published literature. Does this assertion hold up to the evidence-based public health criteria? Do development economists interested in health have an economic theory that might explain this effect, such as Leonard's institutional solution to a contracting problem approach?

What are some practical ways to facilitate the incorporation of health economics into the design, implementation and management, and evaluation of international public health programs of faith-based NGOs? For economics to contribute to the health programs of NGOs, academic economists are going to have think a bit outside the box and work on doing research and teaching activities in concert with NGOs and in collaboration with them. Christian professors at major universities that allow consulting days might consider donating some consulting days directly to an NGO. One very practical step would be to assist with staff in-services, training workshops, and distance education training for NGO staff and for field practitioners. A simple email-based course of readings and facilitated discussion might be a useful place to start. A second starting point might be collaborative research. However, as James Garrett from the International Food Policy Research Center has noted (2002), a number of issues arise in doing collaborative research with NGOs. Garrett notes that there are conflicting perceptions, with some people feeling that researchers are too theoretical, slow, expensive, and ignorant of the real world, while others perceive NGOs as too grassroots, ideological, small to affect real change, and slipshod. He points out that for such research collaborations to work the focus must be on commonalities, where differences are agreed upon and acknowledged. Researchers do things like produce information, analyze policies, evaluate programs, and think at a general level with an audience of research peers and policy makers. NGOs use information to deliver programs and to advocate, work within a policy framework, and target households and individuals. Garrett states that NGOs desire information that is practical and that adds value to their programs, such as stating how to design or deliver a given program. The benefit of acting on the information should be readily apparent and the information should assist the NGO in advancing its agenda. Another way for researchers to contribute would be to focus on research of direct relevance to the NGOs and agencies like USAID through research into questions such as the economics of the church in developing countries as a social network for changing health behaviors or the optimal geographic targeting of spending on HIV/AIDS. The academic training of key staff offers a further means to contribute to NGOs and their programming.

As Garrett (2002) notes, engagement and collaboration with NGOs requires commitment from the researcher but also has great potential for benefit. Researchers ought to consider carefully the need and opportunity of speaking and writing about these issues as engagement with NGOs might challenge a researcher's viewpoint of detachment.

Conclusion

This chapter has argued that economics has a role to play in helping NGOs make their health programs more effective. However, that contribution may be modest and it certainly is tempered by the operational environment of NGOs, where deadlines, project schedules, and funding agency requirements play prominent roles. In the area of health programming, the burden of disease approach and the cost-effectiveness approach to targeting health programs offer immediate ways to incorporate economic ideas into health programs. To increase the usefulness of the contribution of economics in the health program of NGOs internationally, collaborative relationships will need to be fashioned that take into account the realities of the NGO operating environment.

References

Behrman, Jere R. 1990. "The Action of Human Resources and Poverty on One Another: What We Have Yet to Learn," LSMS Working Paper No. 74. Washington D.C.: World Bank.

Behrman, Jere R. and Anil B. Deolalikar. 1988. "Health and Nutrition," in *Handbook of Development Economics*, Vol. 1. Hollis Chenery and T.N. Srinivasan, eds. New York: North Holland, pp. 631–711.

Brownson, RC; J.G. Gurney, and G.H. Land. 1999. "Evidence-Based Decision-Making in Public Health," *Journal of Public Health Management Practice*. 5:5, pp. 86–9.

Brownson, Ross C.; Elizabeth A. Baker, Terry L. Leet, and Kathleen N. Gillespie. 2003. *Evidence-Based Public Health*. New York: Oxford University Press.

Ezzati, Majid; Alan D. Lopez, Anthony Rodgers, Stephen Vander Hoorn, Christopher J. L. Murray, and the Comparative Risk Assessment Collaborating Group. 2002. "Selected Major Risk Factors and Global and Regional Burden of Disease," *The Lancet*. 360:9343, pp. 1347–60.

Garrett, James. 2002. "Considerations on Urban Research: Priorities and Partnerships." Presentation at the World Bank Urban Research Symposium held at the World Bank, Washington D.C., December 11.

Gertler, Paul, and Jacques van der Gaag. 1990. *The Willingness to Pay for Medical Care: Evidence from Two Developing Countries.* Baltimore: Johns Hopkins University Press for the World Bank.

Glewwe, Paul. 1999. "Why Does Mother's Schooling Raise Child Health in Developing Countries? Evidence from Morocco," *The Journal of Human Resources.* 34:1, pp. 124–59.

Grossman, Michael. 1972. "On the Concept of Health Capital and the Demand for Health," *Journal of Political Economy.* 80:2, pp. 223–55.

Haacker, Markus. 2002. "The Economic Consequences of HIV/AIDS in Southern Africa," IMF Working Paper WP/02/38. Washington DC: International Monetary Fund.

Jha, Prabhat; Kent Ranson, and Jose Luis Bobadilla. 1996. "Measuring the Burden of Disease and the Cost-Effectiveness of Health Interventions: A Case Study in Guinea." World Bank Technical Paper No. 333.

Kim, Aehyung, and Bruce Benton. 1995. "Cost-benefit Analysis of the Onchocerciasis Control Program." World Bank Technical Paper No. WTP 282.

Kindig, David. 1997. *Purchasing Population Health.* Ann Arbor, MI: The University of Michigan Press.

Leonard, Kenneth L. 2002. "When Both States and Markets Fail: Asymmetric Information and the Role of NGOs in African Health Care," *International Review of Law and Economics.* 22, pp. 61–80.

Mullahy, John, and Willard Manning. 1995. "Statistical Issues in Cost-Effectiveness Analysis," in *Valuing Health Care.* Frank A. Sloan, ed. New York: Cambridge University Press, pp. 149–84.

Pritchett, Lant, and Lawrence H. Summers. 1996. "Wealthier is Healthier," *The Journal of Human Resources.* 31:4, pp. 841–68.

The Economist. 2002. "For 80 cents more," August 17, pp. 20–2.

World Bank. 2002. "Optimizing the Allocation of Resources for HIV Prevention: The Allocation by Cost-Effectiveness (ABC) Model." Accessed at http://www.worldbank.org/lachealth/ on December 10, 2002.

World Health Organization. 2002. *The World Health Report 2002: Reducing Risks, Promoting Healthy Life.* Geneva: The World Health Organization.

Notes

[1] The author appreciates the comments of the editors and the attendees of the Association of Christian Economists conference titled "Economists, Practitioners and the Attack on Poverty: Toward Christian Collaboration," which was held in Washington, D.C. in January 2003. A more detailed paper surveying the work of Christian NGOs in international health is available at http://www.gordon.edu/ace/mcnamara.pdf.

12

Faith Communities as Partners in Holistic Health

Ndunge Kiiti (MAP International)
Claire Boswell (Plan International)
James Oehrig (MAP International)

Political turmoil, social disintegration and economic disaster confront the world with a challenge of catastrophic proportions. The tragic specter of hunger, disease, cultural disintegration and spiritual poverty has mobilized non-governmental organizations (NGOs) around the world to address the problem of human suffering. Some of these are faith-based organizations (FBOs), mainly Christian organizations. But in spite of good intentions, many NGOs may be doing more harm than good. They lack the vision, commitment, and intellectual resources to effect lasting or meaningful change.

Ondeng (2003), in his book, *Africa's Harvest: Sowing the Seeds of Hope,* states that few people would dispute the assertion that the so-called development effort has failed. From his perspective, the failure emanates from a flawed concept of development: that an outsider can somehow transform the lives of insiders without actually understanding and appreciating the context. Sometimes this failure erodes any sense of hope and sustainability that NGOs may have cultivated among the people they have come to serve. Donors become skeptical. Indeed, development organizations are at crossroads as increasing numbers of development workers from both the South and North lose faith in their own solutions and question the paradigms that undergird their program planning and anticipated results.

This paper argues that Christian development organizations must continue to rethink and alter their development paradigms if they are to improve their impact on health. The paradigm of a top-down, narrow approach must increasingly give way to a bottom-up, holistic approach, if they are to achieve appropriate, sustainable solutions for communities. The paper suggests that strong partnerships between NGOs and academic institutions and professionals involved in health can help facilitate the integration of relevant research, knowledge and policy to strengthen health programs.

Defining Health

> The Church has a vision of health that goes beyond the mere absence of disease, a vision that cannot be confined to the narrow views of physiological mechanisms, as important as they are, or reduced to numbing statistics of rates, proportions, and risk factors. Because it is a vision of wholeness, because it is a vision of hope, and because it is a vision of holiness, it is a vision of grace. And because it is of grace, it makes us whole and hopeful. (Robert Mckeown, quotes in Centers for Disease Control and Prevention, 1999:5)

Whether the decision is conscious or unconscious, every organization grounds itself in a theoretical framework or ideology of what health is and what it means to the poor of our world. The definition they choose has important implications for the work that they do and the approach that they take. Both Christian and secular organizations would likely agree that health is much more than a biological state. WHO defines health as "a state of complete physical, mental, and social well-being, and not merely the absence of disease" (www.who.net). In its mission, MAP International, a global health development agency, reiterates the same definition and refers to it as "total health." Plan International works towards "realizing full potential."

The communities with which we work also have their own definitions of and perspectives on health. Through community participation, these perspectives must be tapped, understood and allowed to influence the definition of health. This is a challenge.

Although such participation is well-embedded in the international development discourse, the short timeframes of externally funded projects and the emphasis on tangible or measurable outcomes often become impediments to its realization (Jacobs and Price, 2003). Thus, it is important that we learn what these perspectives are, who is involved in the health process, how the process can put theory into practice, and what lessons have been learned to date. Failure to ask these questions, specifically, failure to tap and understand local perspectives in defining program objectives, often leads to limited impact and sustainability.

Theoretical Framework: A Bottom-up, Holistic Approach to Better Health

Development is a process by which the members of a society increase their personal and institutional capacities to mobilize and manage resources to produce sustainable and justly distributed improvements in their quality of life consistent with their own aspirations. (Korten, 1990)

The work of Paulo Freire has had a profound impact on the evolution of health programs and health processes in spite of the fact that it originated in the field of education (more specifically, adult literacy). Freire (1984) challenged that, if holistic development is to be achieved, the poor must be able to critically analyze their situations, understand their own context and outline solutions to solve their problems. He argued that creating an environment of open dialogue helped achieve self-awareness and increased participation in molding and improving the society in which they live. Freire's arguments have led development organizations to carefully examine who is determining the agenda in their programs, both in health and in other sectors.

The starting point of any health development program has to be the knowledge and resources in the communities in which we work (Kiiti, 2002). Influenced by Freire, Robert Chambers's recognition of "indigenous technical knowledge" and his work in empowerment through participatory appraisal, learning, and action has also evoked the question of *whom*, and has promoted the "social health" of the poor as not just a process, but as an end in itself. Chambers (1994b) describes how methods used to facilitate agricultural programs have since been applied to health, and how what was originally a means to extract information has now become a means by which the poor take the lead in problem analysis, planning, and action. This focus on indigenous knowledge should challenge Christians and Christian organizations to ask the question, "What assets already exist within the community that we can build on to help address health?"

An asset that we sometimes ignore is the spiritual one. For example, many African and Latin American communities, for different reasons, may be poor in material resources but wealthy in the spiritual dimension. In the midst of poverty, these communities demonstrate healthy lives through their loving relationships and support for one another while among the world's affluent, many are chronically ill. Medical science has begun to affirm the roles of beliefs and values as tools of healing while unresolved guilt, anger and resentment are suppressors of the body's immune system (The Christian Medical Commission, 1990). Wilkinson (1996) argues that "the social links between health and inequality draw attention to the fact that social, rather than material, factors are now the limiting component in the quality of life in developed societies."

It is increasingly clear that one must recognize the unity of mind, body, and spirit to address modern health problems. Although medicines are needed, they are not the sole solution for communities. Many of the health problems treated by medicines have their root in socio-economic, spiritual, and psychological causes. These aspects must be part of the strategy in addressing health in these communities. This recognition was the turning point of MAP International from a relief and development organization that merely shipped and distributed medicines to an agency that also facilitated change for improved health from a holistic approach. If health problems are perceived and addressed only from a narrow and limited approach, they will continue to be cyclical, and rarely be resolved.

Ultimately, this means we are challenged to recognize that each person is a part of God's creation, unique and yet shaped by the community of which he/she is a part. Thus, the individual and community are inseparably linked in our understanding of health. This must be our beginning point in establishing and strengthening better health programs: to tap knowledge and build understanding to facilitate dialogue and processes that lead to a better holistic health for individuals, families and communities. Ram (1995) explains it explicitly, "Health is based on harmony with one's self, with one's neighbors, with nature and with God. It depends on one's physical, mental, spiritual, economic, political, and social well-being."

Achieving Health: Roles and Responsibilities

When people and local organizations engage in dialogue and critical reflection, they not only learn new ways of thinking but also solve local problems in ways that produce sustainable change. The shift from individually-based, instrumental learning to locally situated, collective learning and action provides both a tool for analysis and a mechanism for community transformation. (Ewert and Grace, 2000:328)

Setting the Agenda in Health Programming. If we adhere to the approaches developed by Freire and Chambers, we recognize that the community must drive the setting of priorities and problem identification in order for the effects to reach beyond physical health. This methodology gives outside organizations the role of catalyst or facilitator, instead of doer. Even if the identified problem *is* physical health, the process of participatory learning, decision-making, and leadership by those in need addresses other components of health, particularly social health, by empowering people to determine their own health. Chambers' (1994a) work suggests that without the contribution of indigenous knowledge and resources, program design will often fail to achieve maximum effectiveness because it does not incorporate fully the community's reality in terms of culture, practices, assets, constraints,

geography, and climate. Furthermore, if driven by the poor themselves, real change can be lasting, whereas outsider agendas are
often short-lived and rarely address structural issues of justice and
power/resource distribution.

For development organizations working in health, one of the
practical challenges to this approach is the very real possibility
that the community prioritizes its needs much differently than do
outsiders. A health organization may view malaria as the primary
problem to be addressed due to its impact on mortality and morbidity. However, the community may see lack of roads and transport to facilitate sale of their crops as the priority issue. One factor
that explains this divergence in priorities may be the *capacity of
the organization* itself. If it works primarily in health, the organizational knowledge may not include technical aspects of road
building. If the organization does both health and infrastructure
development, the problem may be *funding*. Many health programs
are relatively inexpensive (in donor terms), whereas infrastructure
projects require greater amounts of resources. Another factor may
be *foreign policies* of governments and the macroobjectives of
large agencies and NGOs. A national government may determine
that immunization is a top priority, due to pressure from the international community to eradicate specific diseases. NGOs may
then be motivated to contribute to the effort.

One obvious solution to this dilemma is negotiation with the
community to include both external and internal priorities in programming ("piggybacking"). Another is the formation of partnerships among organizations with differing areas of capacity and
funding. This includes the academic community. Health economists often have access to research opportunities, information and
knowledge that can help guide NGOs in health programming and
a better understanding of health policy issues. According to Elisa
Weiss (2002) and her colleagues, these creative partnerships can
create synergy by: combining the perspectives, knowledge, and
skills of diverse partners in a way that enables the partnership to
(1) think in a new and better way about how it can achieve its
goals; (2) plan more comprehensive, integrated programs; and (3)

strengthen its relationship to the broader community. For example, a sound well-balanced, multi-disciplinary needs assessment process is necessary before initiating a program. Health economists can be instrumental in collecting and analyzing data to help determine the underlying causes of health issues, their consequences, and the effectiveness of different solutions in addressing them. *Finding the Unique Role of Christian NGOs.* The role of FBOs in health has been debated for years. Critics argue FBOs do more harm than good, while supporters believe they are foundational to any health program. In the book *Faith in Development*, Wolfensohn, President of the World Bank and Carey, Archbishop of Canterbury, state that faith communities offer health services, education and shelter to the vulnerable and disadvantaged. They suggest that faith communities are close to the poor and are among their most trusted representatives so they become key partners for the larger institutions (Wolfensohn and Carey, 2001). The issues surrounding the argument are not as black or white as the debate seems to present them. In developing countries, many health programs were products of missionary theological traditions where the focus was on development activities such as education, hospitals and agriculture. But churches and FBOs are no longer the sole players in these development activities, and in some cases may not be the best-qualified to carry out health initiatives. Governments, international, national, and local organizations are positioned to address health irrespective of religious or political affiliation (Tsele, 2001).

FBOs must demonstrate that they bring something substantive to health. Tsele makes a case for the church's authenticity in health when he states:

> I argue that it is only by reintroducing faith-inspired motives in development, which seek to restore the dignity of our work and which in turn make people subjects in their own human restoration project, that the Church's development enterprise can become authentic. We are not saviors of the poor. We are servants, vulnerable and fallible, yet convinced that it is not the fate of the poor to remain in poverty, nor is

it their fault. In other words, to the extent that development does not seek transformation and liberation of the poor from conditions of dependency and structures of oppression, it is ideological and thus its authenticity is in doubt. Thus, redefinition of the content and goals of development is itself part of the task of defining the role of faith in development (Tsele, 2001:209).

Despite the debate and struggle for identity, the role of FBOs in health is critical. They are grassroots organizations, found in every community whether urban or rural. When properly supported, they fill a strategic niche in addressing health issues, building on their established tradition of involvement in community development. As part of their mandate to serve the underserved and marginalized, the faith community becomes a healing community, touching people in a holistic way—physical, spiritual, emotional and psychological.

Determining Responsibility for Financing. In recent years, the development community has embraced the concepts of cost sharing (Bamako Initiative) coupled with exploration of health as micro-enterprise through the sale of services, drugs, contraceptives, and mosquito nets, among other products. Experience with the Bamako Initiative has shown that it only works if the community itself gives high priority to the service or product. This has interesting financial implications for the theories of Chambers and Freire. The results of a community-driven program might well be commitment on the part of the community members to provide available resources, including their time, materials, and money. More significantly, a mobilized community with a voice increases the potential for the commitment of outside resources. Involvement of all sectors in the democratic process and the determination and empowerment of the poor to demand their rights lead to a more equitable distribution of power, which ultimately leads to a more equitable distribution of resources. Here again, health economists can play a role in helping to evaluate the effectiveness of programs that include cost sharing and health as microenterprise in achieving these various objectives.

Developing an Exit Strategy. Development organizations must design exit strategies from the inception of the program. Organizations that have failed to see themselves as mere facilitators of a process "owned and driven by the community" often fall into the trap of "holding on to power." Rather than relinquishing and sharing power with the community, these organizations often feel threatened by the democratic process required for genuine community empowerment and development. To avoid this problem, development agencies must discuss and plan their exit strategies with the communities where they work to ensure effective capacity building and mutual learning.

As part of the data collection process, health economists can help ask the appropriate questions to guide the overall program and to facilitate smooth exit strategies (Holloway, 1997). For example, needs are often identified in the area of training and access to health information and education. Health economists can provide training to build capacity and facilitate the design of appropriate tools with local counterpart organization staff, which helps NGOs and community members in the process of overall program development, growth and transition.

Turning Theory into Practice

To be able to walk the talk we must honestly try. (White, 1999)

Sector Integration. The variety and complexity of factors affecting health suggests that we make greater attempts to integrate our sectors of programming. Health organizations must make greater efforts to collaborate with experts in sectors such as agriculture, microenterprise, water and sanitation, and education. Health economists and other development specialists within academic institutions can play a key role in identifying, linking and building the right coalitions for an effective response. As Rev. Joan Brown-Campbell, former General Secretary of the National Council of Churches, stated in an address for the American Public Health Association,

. . . to change our present reality, we need allies from all sectors of society. We need holistic thinking that recognizes the caring for the soul. Caring for the spiritual life of a person cannot be the sole and exclusive responsibility of the school, and caring for the body cannot be the special preview of the health professional. We need people who understand their task, to be the integration of body, mind and soul. And this is at the heart of it all. (Interfaith Health Program: http: //www.ihpnet.org/alphatxt.htm)

Experience has already shown us that all of these areas have a profound impact on health and could have a longer lasting effect than simple physical health interventions. Integration can also help us to address root causes rather than merely symptoms of poor health.

Many countries and organizations are experimenting with various models of consortia, forums, and networks to achieve better complementarity of programs. Though such collaboration is often difficult, we have seen some success stories. For instance, in Uganda a concerted multi-sectoral response to the AIDS epidemic has been credited in reducing the HIV prevalence. Early commitment and responses to the epidemic helped create the multi-sectoral Uganda AIDS Commission, which enlisted a wide variety of national participants and sectors in the "war" against the decimating disease. The strong partnership and collaboration between the government, NGOs and FBOs has helped reduce the prevalence rate in the country (Hogle, 2002:3–4).

Effective Collaboration and Partnership. The magnitude and impact of health issues in developing countries requires a forging of partnerships and collaborations in areas and communities that were once incomprehensible. For instance, in Kenya, the Kenya AIDS NGO Consortium was established to bring NGOs, FBOs, government, donors, academic institutions and communities together in response to the HIV/AIDS epidemic. Within the East and Southern Africa region, the Pan African Christian AIDS Network (PACANET) links churches, Christian organizations, and networks to enhance their HIV/AIDS responses. The Emory

Interfaith Health Program and School of Public Health have established a coalition of NGOs, FBOs and other academic institutions to help research and identify the health assets and resources available in Africa. Building these stronger collaborations with communities, academic institutions and other NGOs will ensure the development of a sustainable health education and service delivery system, and will provide a public health model for faith communities' programs.

Mission Driven Programs. Many development organizations, seeking money to continue their work, will follow the money rather than the vision. This can be a dangerous strategy for an organization, and a death sentence to community-driven development and social change. The difficulty in resisting this temptation is to submit our organizational loyalties and identities to the voice of the communities with which we work. Being true to the vision and mission of a particular organization must begin in the fund-raising, taking care not to exchange accountability to God and to the poor for accountability to a certain donor. As Korten (1990) reminds us, organizational commitment must be to serve the people, not the donor.

The Goal: Sustainable Health Development using Effective Leadership

It depends on a belief in the dignity of human life and making decisions that are consistent from the micro (personal) level through to the macro (structural) level of society. There are no halfway choices. Either we help change happen, or we help maintain the 2/3-World as it is. (O'Gorman, 1992)

Korten's work challenges us to make special efforts in our health work, to move beyond relief, and even local development, to development of sustainable systems and on to social movements. Although local development can and frequently does have a positive impact on several aspects of health, the approach may still be driven by an outsider agenda, may not bring about lasting change, and may create dependency on external intervention. Sustainable systems development challenges structures that maintain current balances of power and distribution of resources. Korten (1990) asserts that for this change to take place, the outside organizations must serve as facilitators in a dialogue between the community and the powerful leadership. The community members must be empowered to make demands on the system and, simultaneously, dialogue and interaction must be held with top-level policy makers so they create an environment that is responsive to the needs of the people.

For the most part, the world has operated on a leadership paradigm that perpetuates more power for the powerful and less voice for the voiceless. Health in this leadership paradigm is viewed as something that is "given" or "provided" by those in power rather then a process of developing people's capabilities to build healthy environments and behaviors. The damage this paradigm has done has penetrated all spheres of society, creating dysfunctional ways of exercising power where a few people or institutions control resources, information, knowledge management, and technology. This control often leads to abuses that hinder health.

It is urgent that we foster new organizational and educational paradigms that promote a more participatory and just society. This is where the Church can play an effective role. In their book, *Beyond Poverty and Affluence: Toward an Economy of Care,* Goudzwaard and Lange argue that the Christian church must have a sense of social responsibility that challenges and compels the broader society to set the course of economic life toward meeting basic human needs. This is an ethic of responsibility that seeks to pursue the interests of others rather than self-interest. At the heart of this ethic is the scriptural command that is central to the Gospel—to love God and your neighbor. Those who love God and neighbor seek justice. It is this perspective that the global Church needs, to provide leadership in the redefinition of global responsibility and a renewed economic paradigm.

Summary: A Way Forward

What is clear is that those working in development must take the journey which empowers both individuals and communities to find their voice, and move toward enhanced autonomy and sustainable actions which can be supported in the future. (Kiiti and Nielsen, 1999)

In recent years, many lessons have been learned through health efforts, in particular, HIV/AIDS programs, in developing countries. Uganda, Senegal and Thailand are often highlighted as the "success stories." What we've learned in all these experiences is that effective responses and impact require honest individual, institutional and national commitment. In their book, *We Make the Road by Walking*, Horton and Freire (1990) challenge us to help design the path of sustainable development and to walk it. Kamla Bhasin (1992), a program officer at the FAO in India, suggests we must begin with ourselves.

First, we must promote democracy and self-reliance in skills, knowledge, and information, so that we reduce dependence and build stronger communities. Second, development organizations must seek greater collaboration with governments and local authorities (particularly the Ministry of Health), which have an important role in long-term provision of health services. In addition, NGOs must work with academic institutions, specifically health economists and other health experts, to make sustainable, participatory health development a key part of academic curriculums, policy development processes, internship opportunities, case study forums for learning, and research agendas of universities.

Third, we must seek out the voice, participation, and leadership of community members. Addressing behavioral issues from a knowledge perspective, requires those working in health to understand that human behavior is much more complex than simply access to or lack of information. Programs must look deeper at the cultural, political, economical, social, and emotional barriers that prevent acceptance of healthy behaviors and working with communities to find ways around these barriers. Thus, health initiatives must be developed and strengthened using a "total health" approach to problems and solutions.

Finally development organizations must improve in documenting their successes and failures in an attempt to share lessons learned and best practices with others. Academic institutions are key resources in this process. They have the resources, knowledge and manpower to help NGOs systematically collect and analyze data from health programs, to help guide policy and programs. Relatively slow uptake of effective monitoring and evaluation, particularly by Christian organizations, has impeded effective collaboration. Yet these are vital to determining whether an approach or strategy is worth pursuing, and to ensuring that health programs achieve the highest quality possible.

In summary, we must engage in a process of self-reflection. We must partner and build coalitions that encourage and promote justice, ethics, morality, and the values that bring back the human face to development. In essence, we must play our role in facilitating a vision for a better world and better communities.

References

Bhasin, Kamla. 1992. "Alternative and Sustainable Development," *Convergence*. 15:2, pp. 26–35.

Chambers, Robert. 1994a. "The Origins and Practice of Participatory Rural Appraisal," *World Development*. 22:7, pp. 953–969.

Chambers, Robert. 1994b. "Participatory Rural Appraisal (PRA): Analysis of Experience," *World Development*. 22:9, pp. 1253–1268.

The Christian Medical Commission-Churches' Action of Health. 1990. *Healing and Wholeness: The Churches' Role in Health*. Geneva: World Council of Churches.

Ewert, D. M. and K. A. Grace. 2000. "Adult Education for Community Action" in *Handbook of Adult and Continuing Education, New Edition*. Arthur L. Wilson and Elisabeth R. Hayes, eds. San Francisco: Jossey-Bass.

Freire, Paulo. 1984. *Pedagogy of the Oppressed*. New York: Continuum.

Goudzwaard, Bob and Harry de Lange. 1995. *Beyond Poverty and Affluence: Toward an Economy of Care*. Grand Rapids, MI: Eerdmans.

Hogle, Jan A. 2002. *What Happened in Uganda?: Declining HIV Prevalence, Behavior Change, and the National Response*. Washington, D.C.: USAID.

Holloway, Richard. 1997. *Exit Strategies: Transitioning from International to Local NGO Leadership*. Washington, D.C.: PACT.

Horten, Myles and Paulo Freire. 1990. *We Make the Road by Walking*. Philadelphia: Temple University Press.

Interfaith Health Program. *Expanding the Public Health Envelope Through Faith Community-Public Health Partnerships*. http://www.ihpnet.org/alphatxt.htm.

Jacobs, Bart and Neil Price. 2003. "Community Participation in Externally Funded Health Projects: Lessons from Cambodia," *Health Policy and Planning*. 18:4, pp. 399–410.

Kiiti, Ndunge. 2002. *The Role of Indigenous Knowledge in HIV/AIDS Communication and Education in Eastern Kenya: A Perspective from the Kamba Community*. Doctoral Dissertation, Cornell University.

Kiiti, Ndunge and Nielsen, Erik. 1999. "Facilitator or Advocate: What's the Difference?" in *The Art of Facilitating Participation: Releasing the Power of Grassroots Communication*. Shirley A. White, ed. New Delhi: Sage Publications.

Korten, David C. 1990. *Getting to the 21st Century: Voluntary Action and the Global Agenda*. West Hartford, CT: Kumarian Press.

Mckeown, Robert. 1999. *Engaging Faith Communities as Partners in Improving Community Health*, Center for Disease Control and the Carter Center Report, CDC/ATSDR Forum. Atlanta: CDC.

O'Gorman, Frances. 1992. *Charity and Change: From Bandaid to Beacon*. Melbourne: World Vision Australia.

Ondeng, Pete. 2003. *Africa's Harvest: Sowing the Seeds of Hope*. Tarentum: World Association.

Ram, Eric. 1995. *Transforming Health: Christian Approaches to Healing and Wholeness*. Monrovia, CA: MARC Publications.

Tsele, Molefe. 2001. "The Role of the Christian Faith in Development," in *Faith in Development*. Derrick Belshaw and Robert Calderisi, eds. Washington, D. C.: World Bank and Oxford: Regnum Books.

Weiss, Elisa S.; Rebecca M. Anderson and Roz D. Lasker. 2002. "Making the Most of Collaboration: Exploring the Relationship Between Partnership Synergy and Partnership Functioning," *Health Education & Behavior*. 29:6.

White, Shirley A. 1999. *The Art of Facilitating Participation: Releasing the Power of Grassroots Communication*. New Delhi: Sage Publications.

Wilkinson, Richard G. 1996. *Unhealthy Societies: The Afflictions of Inequality*. London: Routledge.

Wolfensohn, James D. and George Carey. 2001. "Foreword," in *Faith in Development*. Derrick Belshaw and Robert Calderisi, eds. Washington, D.C.: World Bank and Oxford: Regnum Books.

13

Partnering with Local Organizations in Poverty Reduction Efforts

Roland Hoksbergen (Calvin College)[1]

In their efforts to fight Third World poverty, many northern NGOs (NNGOs) opt to work in partnerships with Southern NGOs (SNGOs). Partnerships are so much in vogue these days that Alan Fowler says that "today's rule of thumb in international development is that everybody wants to be a partner with everyone on everything, everywhere" (2000:3). Recent studies, however, have shown that few, if any, organizations have achieved what Fowler refers to as "authentic partnerships" (1998:144). Instead, the word "partnership" is used with such abandon in describing almost any working relationship that Eade and Ligteringen conclude that it has "become devalued through uncritical overuse, often to mask paternalistic practices on the part of NGOs" (2001:15). North-South organizational relationships, they argue, are still dominated by traditional patron-client relationships associated with development contracting. Development programming decisions are still made largely in the North and the direction of influence remains North to South.

In spite of the failure to achieve authentic partnerships, there are good reasons, especially for Christian NGOs, to work harder at building strong partnerships. Foremost among these is increased effectiveness in reducing local poverty, but another, less acknowledged, reason is that partnerships help build the Kingdom community. Fortunately, where there's a will, there's a way; building authentic partnerships is certainly possible. It helps that most theorists and practitioners already believe that working in partnership is the right way to do development work. Where it gets difficult is in the actual working practices, where funding and longstanding Northern domination of North-South relationships continue to undermine the authenticity of the partnerships. In this chapter I will explore the reasons why partnerships are important in development, what authentic partnerships actually look like, and some practical steps toward achieving them. Many of these practical guidelines were gleaned from my year-long study of the Christian Reformed World Relief Committee (CRWRC), an NNGO that has been working in partnerships with SNGOs, and struggling to improve these partnerships, for some 30 years.

Why Should NNGOs Partner with SNGOs?

The most commonly accepted rationale for NNGO-SNGO partnerships is increased efficiency in achieving impacts in such areas as agricultural output, health, income, and literacy. Reasons for efficiency gains include that local organizations know the local culture better, SNGO labor costs are lower, SNGOs and their staff have more longevity than NNGOs and their staff, and partnerships take advantage of complementary strengths (see Penrose, 2000:243 and Mancuso-Brehm, 2001:24).

A second reason for working in partnership is the importance of strengthening local organizations that form part of the nation's civil society. Civil society organizations provide channels through which local people participate in, direct, and thus own the development programs that affect them. Civil society also provides one means by which citizens can participate in political and legal processes and thus both influence policy and hold governments accountable. In authentic partnerships, NNGOs do not dominate, but facilitate and catalyze local processes, thus strengthening local civil society.

A third reason for working in partnership is that the scope of development is bigger than what occurs just in the South. Global issues like climate change, terrorism, AIDS, ocean fishing, drug and arms trafficking, and international debt call for global solutions that require North and South to listen to each other, learn from each other, and work together. If people in the South are to own the solutions and be committed to them, their voices must be heard and they must contribute to the decisions and programs just as much as people in the North. The way to achieve this is in partnership. Unilateral decision-making on the part of the North, even if successful at achieving targeted short run goals, will likely fail in the long run. For example, Bolivian campaigns to reduce coca production resulted mostly from Northern pressure. Bolivian farmers were hardly consulted. In reaction to that pressure, and as economic times got difficult, Bolivian farmers willingly returned to coca cultivation, joined anti-American protests, and helped to overthrow their government (Zurita-Vargas).

Fourth, global development is about more than just solving problems and tackling global issues; it is also about forming global community. It is not only the impacts we achieve, or the problems we solve, but the relationship itself that has value. Andrew Gwairangmin, director of CRUDAN, a CRWRC partner in Nigeria, says "we need each other. Partnership is like being a friend. We work together to grow and change." Karl Westerhof of CRWRC says that "partnership is about living in community with one another, which is how God created us to live. We must work together to overcome the world's brokenness, to build communities in which we can serve each other and learn together" (2002). CRWRC colleague Tom Post says "partnerships of mutual respect build each other up and enrich each other, and so give us a sense of life in the Kingdom of God" (2002). Partnerships are thus one form of the Pentecost vision of people from every tribe and nation joining together in life and in worship.

Toward Authentic Partnership

In recent years the partnership ideal has gained widespread approval, but organizations desiring to develop authentic partnerships struggle to overcome longstanding habits and practices. Presently, many of the existing relationships among NGOs, though often loosely referred to as partnerships, are little more than donor-recipient, or patron-client, relationships in which the

SNGO follows the dictates of the development contract offered to it by the NNGO. In turn, the NNGO is often itself under contract to a large official donor like USAID or CIDA, forming what some call "the aid chain." Such a hierarchical structure forces local organizations to cope "with the whims, fancies and inefficiencies of those above (them) in the chain who can give, and stop giving their resources or services without being accountable in any way to the ultimate recipients" (Taylor, Marais, and Heyns, 1998:15). Many dangers lurk in this sort of structure, including the fairly common outcome that as soon as Northern organizations withdraw, development projects flounder and die. Among the most horrific outcomes of the top-down aid chain was what happened in Rwanda, where prior to the genocide Northern organizations enlisted local partners to carry out their development plans. In a sobering analysis, Peter Uvin points out that the newly forming local "civil society" fell apart as soon as the genocide began. Uvin suggests that local organizations were not really owned by Rwandans, but were instead bought and paid for by Northern donors. Even more serious, Uvin argues that by sticking to their narrow development projects and to the goals and working practices developed in the North, Northern organizations actually helped to prepare the way for the days of slaughter by not confronting the real problems (Uvin, 1998)

Authentic partnerships are characterized by "mutually enabling, inter-dependent interaction with shared intentions," and with "a joint commitment to long-term interaction, shared responsibility for achievement, reciprocal obligation, equality, mutuality and balance of power" (Fowler, 1998:144 and 2000: 3). In authentic partnerships, autonomous self-standing organizations work together from a foundation of common vision, values and sense of purpose. They articulate joint goals clearly and contribute complementary strengths in their efforts to achieve them. Responsibility is shared, roles are clearly understood, and a sense of equality prevails. Partners listen to each other, learn from each other, plan together, and work through conflicts and disagreements constructively. Decisions are made jointly in an authentic partnership, with staff from both organizations working together to carry them out. Partners are accountable to each other for the work they do and the results achieved. Communication is open, frequent, and transparent. Finally, authentic partners share a clear understanding about the future of the partnership (Lister, 2000).

This is obviously a challenging set of standards, and one that is not being met in most NNGO-SNGO working relationships. Fowler says that many of the relationships referred to as partnerships tend to "slide toward patron-client relationships associated with contracting" (1998:140). Kilalo and Johnson, studying a partnership in Uganda made up of World Neighbors, the UN, and the government of Uganda, expected to find a relationship of "mutual respect and exchange," but discovered instead that SNGOs were really doing little more than "delivery of public goods and services" (1999:457). This and other recent research has found that partnership rhetoric is much stronger than the reality. Fortunately, the challenges of bringing the reality in line with the rhetoric and building authentic partnerships can be met, and the practical guidelines of the next section are intended to help point the way.

Steps Toward Creating Productive and Satisfying Partnerships

Building authentic partnerships is not so hard if both organizations are committed to it, but there are pressures on both sides that must be overcome. NNGOs bear the burdens of financial, political, and technological power, and imposition and domination are ever-present temptations. For SNGOs there is the temptation to acquiesce to Northern dominance and just to play along, to avoid the hard work of building locally owned and supported organizations, and to get what they can along the way. But these temptations can be overcome, and for those NGOs in North and South that are serious about building authentic partnerships, the following practical guidelines will help form, maintain, and strengthen their partnerships.

Choose the Right Relational Model. A first step is to be sure an authentic partnership is the best relationship. Authentic partnerships should be reserved for organizations that have deep similarities in identity, underlying values, belief systems, and sense of mission; diaconal offices of two churches for example, or two Christian community development NGOs. In some cases, alternative forms of collaboration are more appropriate. For example, some CRWRC partners speak of "strategic partnerships," which tend to be short term and have lower expectations about the depth of the relationship. Such a partnership might link a broad-based community development SNGO with an organization that provides microfinance support and capital. Compatibility of identity and underlying beliefs is less important in such a relationship, and short term, business-like contracts might well be the appropriate model. Other relationships might properly be identified as collaborations, alliances, consortia, networks, or joint ventures, which differ from authentic partnership in longevity, scope of collaboration, and/or nature of the bond. For example, a relationship among a large international donor, an NNGO, an SNGO, and a local government body to bring potable water to a region, might better be thought of as a cooperative venture than as a partnership, because it has a fixed term, a single tangible purpose, and doesn't require deep levels of compatibility in overall mission and vision.

Partner with Locally Rooted Organizations. When CRWRC began its move toward working in partnership with SNGOs back in the 1970s, it believed it could hire people, train them, give birth to local organizations, and then withdraw as these new organizations matured. This strategy hasn't worked. As CRWRC withdrew, most daughter organizations disintegrated; the few that survived did so by attracting operational funds from other Northern donors. Not one such organization has developed into a firmly rooted, locally owned and supported membership organization. Among CRWRC's strongest partners today, however, are those founded by local people with their own vision, who put in large amounts of volunteer time, and who inspire others in their country to join them. These organizations have joined in partnership with CRWRC from a position of strength, with a strong sense of their own identity and mission. Nicaragua's Acción Médica Cristiana (AMC) is one such organization. It began in the early 1980s when university students in various health professions assembled to study Scripture and to engage in volunteer efforts among the poor. Their dedication and competence led outside organizations to take notice and now AMC works in collaboration with many Northern organizations. Some it refers to as donors, others as partners.

The great advantage of locally rooted SNGOs is that they enjoy the commitment of their members and are well positioned to avoid the mercenary participation that comes when NNGOs call the shots, hire SNGO staff, and pay the bills. Members participate primarily to carry out a mission, not just to get a pay check. Local accountability and good organizational structure are thus more likely, because there is a foundation of local people who witnessed and felt the pangs of birth, who believe in the organization, and who keep watch over it.

Make Covenants, Not Contracts. Like other NNGOs, CRWRC has typically signed contracts with its partners, but it is gradually supplanting this practice with more general, longer-term agreements. In Uganda, for example, CRWRC staff speak of partnership covenants, which are formed after an initial courting period when the two organizations discuss their identity, their values, and their vision and mission. They also do some preliminary community work together. The resulting covenant, developed through mutual discussion and negotiation, establishes the two organizations as partners and assumes a high level of mutual commitment. Detailed working plans are then discussed, agreed upon, and put into action. Secure in the knowledge that their partnership is deeper than a short-term contract, the partners continually monitor, evaluate, and adjust their joint work in response to changing conditions and circumstances.

Really Work Together. In most NNGO-SNGO working relationships the NNGO provides funds and training and the SNGO does the work. The NNGO assesses project or program proposals, provides funds and training, receives reports, and evaluates the work via reports and periodic site visits. In an authentic partnership, however, one "partner" doesn't just supervise the other; they actually work together. Over the years, CRWRC has developed a liaison, or accompaniment, model of partnership, which typically assigns a team of two or three staff persons to reside in the field and work with five or six partner organizations in a given country. CRWRC staff are thus engaged in frequent consulting and planning with partners. Community visits, annual planning, various types of training at both organizational and community levels, and evaluations are done in close collaboration. There is no predetermined model of how CRWRC and partner staff will work together. Depending on the needs and strengths of communities and partner organizations, as well as on the needs and strengths of CRWRC and its staff, the contributions and involvement of each are largely determined in joint planning sessions. Davis Omanyo from Kenya says that "with other (Northern) partners, it is grant writing, funding, reporting, and evaluations." Omanyo, familiar and comfortable with this style of work, eventually discovered how rewarding working together could be. CRWRC staff, he says, "became workmates and friends, and a good level of trust was built up through this frequent interaction." One drawback of this practice is the high cost of maintaining field staff. Surprisingly, when given the option of more money, 90 percent of SNGO personnel interviewed preferred to maintain the close working relationship.

Match Funds. The international development community, along with its Christian subset, is torn by two contradictory principles regarding development assistance. On one hand, it is clear that the wealthy ought to help the poor. It is this principle that often leads people to lament decreases in North to South development assistance. On the other hand, Northern funding, accompanied by an insistence on accountability, inhibits development processes that foster local ownership, control, and organizational integrity. In keeping with these two conflicting principles, some believe that all funding for SNGO work should come from the North, while others believe that a good local development organization must become completely financially self-sustaining.

In some fields, CRWRC has worked with the well-known, but little practiced, compromise strategy of matching funds, which allows for a continued flow of assistance from the North, while not undermining local commitment and ownership. To encourage good local development, two guidelines are in order: First, SNGOs should pay salaries and start-up costs with resources raised from its own membership and local donor base. Second, once in partnership, both SNGO and NNGO should finance jointly created programs in keeping with their capabilities. The extent to which the membership of each organization contributes should be a matter of periodic joint evaluation.

Work Toward a Relationship of Equality. Money is among the main forces that corrupt authentic partnership. Firoze Manji takes the pessimistic position that "no matter how good the personal relationship between the Northern NGO and the Southern NGO, the latter must accept the humiliation of being the receiver of charity. Perforce, there is a relationship of unequals" (Manji 2000:78).

In spite of the pressures imposed by the flow of money, most of CRWRC's partners actually profess to a sense of equality with CRWRC. Partner responses to detailed questions provide helpful hints for developing practices that foster a relationship of equality. SNGO staff feel "more" equal the less direct funding there is from CRWRC, the less dependency there is on CRWRC funding, the more funds the partner raises by itself from local sources, the more CRWRC listens to its partners, the greater the role partners play in decision-making, the more trust and mutual respect has grown, the more frequent and transparent is the communication, the higher is the education level, competency and self-confidence of the partners, and the more partners lead training sessions.

Phase Out Phase Out. One striking finding from the CRWRC interviews is that partners are unanimously opposed to the idea of the NNGO phasing out of the relationship, and not only out of a concern for funding. They see the partnership itself both as part of the development process and as a step on the way toward building up global community. Like their SNGO partners, CRWRC staff also have become increasingly disenchanted with phase out, mostly because they do not think they should withdraw from a partnership when good development work is being done. Both these views counter the prevailing assumption in development thinking that phase out is a necessary part of good development work. If, however, development is not only about improvements in the local standard of living, but also about the growth of civil society, the ability to adequately address global problems, and building global community, then it makes little sense to phase out of authentic partnerships. Under this broader understanding of development, partners should continue to work together into the indefinite future, changing and evolving as times and needs call for. For its part, CRWRC has heard the call of its partners and its own field staff, and is now moving away from embedding withdrawal plans into its partnership agreements. Instead, CRWRC and its partners are searching for, and creating, new models of evolving partnerships.

Evaluate the Partnership. Even though CRWRC has worked with SNGOs for thirty years, puts a lot of value on partnering in and of itself, and has developed many practices for working together and listening to partners, it has not been careful about evaluating partnerships. Instead, CRWRC and partners formally evaluate community impacts and SNGO capacity development, and are just beginning to think about evaluating the working relationship itself. Few, if any, models exist for such evaluations, but if CRWRC and other NNGOs are serious about building authentic partnerships, then that will have to change. Partners should continue to evaluate what they achieve in traditional program areas, but they must also begin to evaluate the quality of partnership agreements, how well they work together, how sound mutual accountability structures are, and how helpful plans for the future of the relationship are.

Patron-client relationships, even if we call them partnerships, are much easier to set up and maintain than authentic partnerships, but they have neither the local impact nor the long-term value. If NGOs, hopefully led by Christian NGOs who know the importance of deep commitments, exhibit the will and the effort to build authentic partnerships, the results in overcoming poverty and promoting broad-based human development will be profound.

References

Eade, Deborah and Ernst Ligteringen, eds. 2001. *Debating Development: NGOs and the Future.* Oxford: Oxfam.

Fowler, Alan. 1998. "Authentic NGDO Partnerships in the New Policy Agenda for International Aid: Dead End or Light Ahead?" *Development and Change.* 29:1, pp.137–59.

Fowler, Alan. 2000. "Beyond Partnership: Getting Real About NGO Relationships in the Aid System," *IDS Bulletin.* 31:3, pp. 1–13.

Gwairangmin, Andrew. 2001. Personal interview, December 11.

Kilalo, Christine and Johnson, Deb. 1999. "Mission Impossible? Creating Partnerships Among NGOs, Governments, and Donors," *Development in Practice.* 9:4, pp. 456–461.

Lister, Sarah. 2000. "Power in Partnership? An Analysis of an NGO's Relationship with its Partners," *Journal of International Development.* 12, pp. 227–239.

Mancuso Brehm, Vicky. 2001. "Promoting Effective North-South NGO Partnerships: A Comparative Study of 10 European NGOs," INTRAC Occasional Papers Series. No. 35.

Taylor, James; Dirk Marais and Stephen Heyns, eds. 1998. *Community Participation & Financial Sustainability: Action-learning Series: Case Studies and Lessons from Development Practice.* Cape Town: Juta.

Manji, Firoze. 2000. "Collaboration with the South: Agents of Aid or Solidarity?" in *Development, NGOs, and Civil Society: Selected Essays from Development in Practice.* Deborah Eade, ed. Oxford: Oxfam, pp. 75–79.

Penrose, Angela. 2000. "Partnership," in *Managing Development: Understanding Inter-Organizational Relationships.* Dorcas Robinson, Tom Hewitt, and John Harriss, eds. Thousand Oaks, CA: Sage Publications, pp.243–260.

Post, Tom. 2002. Personal interview, March 28

Uvin, Peter. 1998. *Aiding Violence: The Development Enterprise in*

Rwanda. New Hartford, CT: Kumarian.

Westerhof, Karl. 2002. Personal interview, March 26.

Zurita-Vargas, Leonida. 2003. "Coca Culture," *The New York Times*. October 15.

Notes

[1] The author wishes to thank CRWRC for giving him the opportunity to do a year-long study of its partnership work. He also wishes to state that CRWRC bears no responsibility for the analysis and views expressed herein. For a more complete version of this paper, please see www.gordon.edu/ace/devconnect/ conference/ hoksbergen.doc.

Section III

The Evaluation of Christian Development Efforts

14

Impact Assessment
for Christian Development Organizations

Julie Schaffner (The Fletcher School, Tufts University)[1]

Impact assessment seems like a good idea to most development professionals, at least in principle. The problems of world poverty, malnutrition, disease, exclusion, and despair are vast, while the resources available for attacking these problems are few. It makes sense to study the effectiveness of programs for combating ills, and to respond to the lessons learned in ways that increase the good achieved. At a practical level, however, practitioners have very mixed feelings about impact assessment.[2] While it may increase the good achieved in the future, it also pulls scarce resources away from poverty reduction today, seems to carry more risk than reward to individual development organizations, and can be technically and logistically daunting.

This paper offers an economist's vision of impact assessment that makes practical sense for Christian development organizations. The paper's aim is twofold. First, it seeks to motivate greater enthusiasm and boldness on the part of Christian practitioners, by suggesting that good impact assessment can be more valuable and less costly than they might think. Second, it highlights the ways in which collaboration with Christian academic economists—who are eager to get involved and offer service—can make impact assessment even more beneficial and less costly.

Two Examples

Examples will be helpful for motivating and describing good impact assessment. Here are two fictitious programs for which impact assessments must be designed, which will be employed throughout the text:

Example 1: Micro Lending Program. Grace Lending International (GLI) runs a microlending program targeting women in rural communities. GLI encourages borrowers to save and reinvest profits from their microenterprises, in the hope of achieving expanded and more sustained improvements in future living standards. Because domestic violence toward women is widely believed to have increased in communities served by another microlending program in the region, GLI makes a point of involving the husbands of married borrowers in program activities and promoting teamwork within borrowing households.

Example 2: Education Matching Grant Program. Kindness Education Assistance (KEA) runs a program through which communities may obtain technical assistance and funding for small projects aimed at increasing enrollment rates at the primary school level. KEA believes firmly in equipping community members to work together for mutual benefit. They offer communities technical assistance for assessing local barriers to school attendance and for designing projects to reduce the barriers. Community projects are diverse, from repairing school buildings to organizing cooperative daycare centers. KEA provides partial funding for materials, but requires the community to contribute labor and a fraction of funding for other materials.

A General Definition of Impact Assessment

Impact assessment can be defined as the collection, analysis and interpretation of information regarding the effects of a well-defined set of actions on a set of outcomes for a set of target groups. For NGOs, the actions are typically projects, programs or program changes undertaken by their organizations. The outcomes are important features of the economic and social landscape (e.g., income levels, degree of peace between ethnic groups) that may be changed as a result of introducing programs or program changes. The target groups are the sets of individuals, communities or organizations for which the NGO hopes to induce change. Within this broad definition, there is room for a great deal of variation and choice.

The Importance of Purposeful Design

Whether they do it explicitly or not, organizations like GLI and KEA make many specific design choices when they undertake impact assessment. Not only must they choose which actions, outcomes and target groups to study, they must also choose what kinds of information to collect and which methods to use in identifying the impact of actions on outcomes, as well as whom to involve in the assessment, when to undertake it, how the results will be disseminated, and more. Each of these choices affects the character, cost, and ultimate impact of the assessment.

Impact assessments will make sense for organizations like GLI and KEA only when the organizations recognize the need to engage in purposeful design. That is, they must identify the effect they hope to achieve through engaging in impact assessment, and then make each design choice in a way that contributes to the achievement of this effect, while prudently balancing the future benefits against the present costs of their efforts.

Internal Motivation for Impact Assessment

The most obvious potential effect that organizations might hope to achieve through impact assessment is improved resource use within the organization. Impact assessments may serve to identify bottlenecks in the delivery of benefits, draw attention to overlooked concerns of stakeholders, or uncover unintended side effects, offering a focus for future efforts to improve the organization's performance. Assessments can go even further in providing direct evidence on the likely benefits and costs of specific program modifications. Well-designed assessments will also motivate staff, by recognizing their accomplishments and demonstrating commitment to help them meet their challenges.

A second effect of impact assessment is improvement in the organization's ability to engage in debates and consultations with donors, the government and other organizations. Through careful assessment research and thoughtful writing of assessment documents, GLI and KEA can communicate to other actors not only a measure of their success in achieving objectives, but also:

1) What kinds of impacts they believe are important for the populations they serve

2) What they have learned about how to deliver these impacts effectively

3) What they have learned about the systemic barriers to better performance (with implications for policies of governments and other organizations)

4) Their commitment to continuous improvement

5) Their willingness to put the concerns of other interested parties on the table for the sake of productive conversation

In what follows, this chapter discusses how to make specific impact assessment design choices with an eye to producing these intended impacts.[3]

Choosing Outcomes and Target Groups

Assessments will be narrow and misleading, unless organizations like GLI and KEA take the lead in defining the outcomes for their assessments.[4] Household per capita consumption expenditure is often considered an excellent summary measure of households' (current) level of material well-being, but if GLI adopts an assessment template in which this is the main outcome of study, the assessment may miss the point of GLI's activities. If GLI is successful in encouraging its borrowers to reinvest rather than consume profits, then current consumption may increase little, even though GLI may be highly successful at increasing incomes and future consumption levels. Similarly, if KEA examines the impact of its grant program only on primary school enrollments, it may appear to produce much less impact per dollar spent than other organizations working toward the same objective. The narrow assessment misses the point that KEA is devoting resources not only to increasing primary school enrollment, but also to the development of community institutions, through which a wide range of additional development benefits may emerge.

How, then, should an organization go about choosing which outcomes to analyze? First, it should articulate carefully the objectives of the programs for which assessments are being conducted. GLI needs to articulate its emphasis on improvement in future living standards, and select a set of outcomes (including household saving or wealth) that capture impact in this area. KEA needs to articulate its multiple objectives, and to identify outcomes related to the development of community institutions as well as to primary schooling outcomes. Second, the organization should identify additional outcomes of concern to the organization, its donors, and other actors with whom it wishes to engage in productive conversation, including outcomes that may be made worse as unintended consequences of program activities. Even though GLI feels it has eliminated the potential for microlending to increase domestic violence, it may want to include the nature of relationships between husbands and wives among its outcomes, in order to communicate its awareness of the problem and gather evidence on the effectiveness of its approach to preventing the problem.

When defining outcomes, organizations must be careful to include the outcomes of ultimate concern, and not mere program "outputs." GLI will find it useful to study microlending program outputs such as numbers of borrowers, loan sizes and repayment rates. But the ultimate aim of the program is not merely to stimulate borrowing. The loans are a means to more intrinsically valuable ends: improved material well-being of the poor, whether now or in the future, and perhaps increased self-esteem of women, greater hope and more. The link between outputs and outcomes may be very loose. Households may obtain loans, and work very hard to repay them, but not end up much better off; and some households may be prevented from falling into destitution even when they cannot fully repay. An organization using scarce resources to achieve good ends must take an interest in understanding impacts on ends as well as means, and in communicating the importance of its ultimate goals to other actors.

While measures for some outcomes are well-developed, measures for others will have to be invented and tested. But this should not stop an organization from defining the terms of its own impact assessment. If GLI's priority is to instill hope in a situation of despair, then to do its job increasingly well, it must devise ways of studying the impact of its activities on hope. Creating new indicators for objectives (like hope) that have not traditionally figured prominently in development discussions may be important, not only for rendering the assessment more useful to the organization itself, but also for enriching and redirecting broader debates among other implementing NGOs, donors, and governments. "Vulnerabilty," for example, has entered the mainstream of thinking about poverty reduction and economic development policies, in large part because efforts have been made to define, measure and study it.

Care must also be exercised in choosing the target groups of relevance to the assessment. To GLI it may seem most natural to pose the question: What is the impact of the program on the wealth of borrowers? This focuses attention narrowly on the impacts within the group of individuals who choose to participate in the program, rather than on the group GLI was hoping to reach. Framing impact questions instead around an explicitly defined target group (e.g., poor households in a particular region) would allow GLI to answer two questions that are not addressed when it examines impacts on borrowers only. First, how well did GLI do at reaching its target group? It may have attracted many borrowers, but only a small share of the poorest households in the community, for which it was most concerned. Second, is it possible that the GLI program has helped (or hurt) members of the target group indirectly? The poorest households may not have become borrowers, but perhaps their well-being improved anyway because those who did borrow created jobs and strengthened local labor markets. Careful identification of target groups may also be of great importance in communicating about the program. GLI may have lower repayment rates, or may charge interest rates that cover a lower fraction of costs, compared with other microfinance organizations, but they may be highly successful at bringing hope to a much poorer target group.

Seeking Program Improvement

There is no reason why impact assessments must produce only terse verdicts on whether or not programs have achieved significant impact. Impact assessments may be designed to shed light on why impacts are low or high, and on the likely benefits and costs of well-defined program modifications.[5] In the interest of understanding why impacts are high or low, an organization can identify the full set of links in the logical chain between program and impact, and examine impacts on intermediate outcomes all along the chain. For example, when examining KEA's impact on primary school enrollment rates, it can examine not only the bottom line impact on enrollment rates, but also a range of intermediate outcomes answering such questions as:

- How many (and which) communities were aware of the grant program?

- How many communities offered proposals, and which did not, either because they could not convene a functioning group or because they could not afford to make the required community contributions?

- Which communities received grants?

- How effectively did community groups engage in assessing local barriers to primary school enrollment?

- How effectively did they design projects appropriate for reducing those barriers?

- What kinds of projects were financed?

- Which of these projects were ultimately completed, and what prevented completion of others?

- How well did the projects address local barriers to enrollment?

- Which households within the communities are aware of the new facilities or services created by the project?

- For which households do the new facilities or services change their behavior so that they begin sending children to school, or keeping children in school longer?

- How did the awareness, use, and impact of the new facilities or services vary across project types?

- What has been the resulting impact on school enrollment rates?

Examining this chain (using a mixture of the empirical methods described below) provides the organization with an opportunity to identify specific features of the program—publicity, matching fund requirements, technical assistance, range of encouraged project types, logistics of money transmittal—where study and experimentation are most likely to produce improved impact in the future.

In the interest of illuminating potential program modifications, the organization can furthermore build into the assessment a study of the costs and benefits of a well-defined "design change." That is, instead of examining only the overall impacts of the microlending program (relative to having no program operating in the community at all), GLI could explicitly examine the impact of increasing the interest rate on microloans, increasing loan sizes, or lending to individuals rather than groups. If GLI is willing to experiment with different loan terms in some communities, then such questions can be answered in a more direct (and probably more accurate) way than the larger question about overall program impact. Answers to such questions may be of great practical value. GLI might learn, for example, that while increases in the interest rate leave repayments high and increase "sustainability," they also lead large numbers of the poorest borrowers to drop out of the program. Such evidence would shed important light on practical choices about interest rates to be made by decision makers within GLI.

The Right Mix of Quantitative and Qualitative Research Methods

If impact assessments are to uncover real lessons and communicate persuasively, then they must employ research methods that inspire confidence. A first methodological choice has to do with the appropriate mix of so-called *qualitative* and *quantitative* research methods. The distinction relates not to the nature of the outcomes studied, but to the way in which information on the outcomes is collected and analyzed. Methods are labeled quantitative if they involve the application of statistical methods to information that has been collected in comparable fashion from a random sample of informants.[6] Often this means statistical analysis of the data produced by a household survey, in which an identical questionnaire has been administered to all respondents in a sample. Quantitative methods may be used even to study qualitative (i.e., non-numeric) outcomes like church attendance, knowledge about AIDS transmission, and degree of agreement with the statement "it is acceptable for men to beat their wives if they burn the cooking." Qualitative methods include focus group discussions, key informant interviews, participant observations and other methods that typically do not involve the use of random samples, and typically involve smaller numbers of informants and more open-ended and flexible methods of eliciting information.[7]

Quantitative methods provide the skeleton around which most good impact assessments are built, because they offer the potential to generalize results from the specific individuals interviewed to the larger target groups of concern, and because they allow assessment of the confidence that it is reasonable to place in the research findings.[8] When small focus groups are formed without the use of random sampling, or when inferences are drawn from a few household case studies or anecdotes alone, there is much greater chance of drawing skewed conclusions without realizing it. If GLI's microlending project, were very small and unlikely to be expanded or replicated, then generalization may be of little interest and formal quantitative research methods may be unnecessary. But if the population GLI deals with is large and diverse, then quantitative methods will be crucial for deriving results that can be generalized and defended.

Quantitative methods provide only the skeleton of good impact assessments. Rich qualitative research is required as well. Often the quantitative methods will be directed toward measuring the net impact of the program on the ultimate outcomes (e.g., household income, savings, hope, or school enrollment), and perhaps a few key intermediate outcomes (e.g., knowledge of program, use of new facilities), while qualitative research will be used to flesh out answers to question about program implementation and perhaps to measure impacts on a wider range of secondary outcomes. The flexibility and speed of qualitative methods also render them useful for identifying the outcomes that are of most concern to stakeholders, for designing standardized questions that do a good job of eliciting the desired information, and for identifying possible explanations for surprising or disappointing results of quantitative research.

Sample Sizes

Some readers may be put off by the need to use quantitative methods, because high profile quantitative impact assessments employ data from household surveys administered to many thousands of households. But even modest data collection efforts have the potential to offer significant contributions to understanding.[9] In some cases, simple surveys administered to 80 or 100 randomly selected households in each of several carefully selected communities (with communities similar in many respects, but differing in the presence or absence of GLI, or in the interest rate GLI charges on micro loans) could shed important new light on micro lending effectiveness or design choices. Surveys administered to key community informants in 80 or 100 communities that differ in their relationship to KEA's program may shed useful light on the nature and extent of the program's impact on community institutions. While these are not trivial undertakings, they could be orchestrated by a graduate student during a several month internship, provided that the student, a faculty advisor and program officials have made preparation ahead of time and maintain frequent communication during data collection.

Choosing Research Designs for Inferring True Impact

Quantitative research methods may be used in straightforward ways to measure outcomes for a target group in the presence of the program. GLI or KEA simply draws a random sample from the target group exposed to the program—subsequently referred to as the "intervention group" (to distinguish it both from a possible comparison group not exposed to the program and from itself prior to the program)—and collect information from each sampled individual or household on the outcomes of interest. To measure the impact of a program or program modification, however, more is required. GLI and KEA must collect additional information with an eye to estimating the counterfactual outcomes that the intervention group would have experienced had it faced economic and social circumstances that were in every way the same, except that the program was absent or modified in some specific way. To assess its impact on school enrollment, KEA would like to compare current school enrollment rates for a sample of households in KEA communities to what enrollments would have been had the program not been introduced, but other salient economic and social circumstances had evolved in the same way. In a study of the impact of increasing interest rates, GLI would like to compare income, wealth and other outcomes in program communities where interest rates are low to what the outcomes would have been in those same communities had interest rates been higher.

By definition, it is impossible to observe counter-to-fact outcomes directly. It is, however, often possible to produce good estimates of them. An ideal estimate of counterfactual outcomes would involve sampling from a group that is identical to the intervention group in individual and household characteristics, and that faces identical community, regional and macroeconomic and social circumstances. That is, the ideal research design would allow for a comparison in which two groups are exposed to differing program conditions, but in which all the other characteristics and circumstances are "held constant." Failing to hold some of these characteristics and circumstances constant opens the door to misleading inferences about program impact. If, for example, GLI compared current outcomes for its intervention group to outcomes for a group that was not exposed to the GLI program, but in which average business experience, land holdings, or education levels were higher, then the GLI incomes might appear little better than the estimated counterfactual incomes, even when the true impact of the GLI program on incomes is high, because the estimate of the counterfactual income is too high. The households that received the GLI intervention would have done worse in the absence of the program than did the imperfect comparison group; household characteristics were not held constant in the comparison.

Four main approaches are taken to estimating the counterfactual.[10] They differ in the sets of characteristics and circumstances that they are best suited to hold constant. They thus build in differing safeguards against misleading inferences about program impact. The choice of approach must be made on a case by case basis, taking into account not only the costs and feasibility of the various approaches, but also the greatest risks of misleading inferences.

After-the-fact Comparison of Intervention Group to Control Group. The first approach to learning about the counterfactual is to sample from a comparison group that is similar to the intervention group but faces either no program or a modified program. For example, GLI might compare outcomes for the target group in communities in which it operates to comparable target groups in communities where it does not operate, or where it offers a somewhat modified program. Because both intervention and comparison groups are sampled at the same time, they tend to be subject to the same macro conditions (provided they both derive from localities subject to the same macro circumstances). The main potential for error in this approach arises because intervention and comparison groups may differ in individual and community characteristics. The potential for such errors may be great, as a result of the process of *selection* that determines which communities and individuals become participants in a program. If GLI officers tend to give program benefits to households in especially grave circumstances, then the communities and households not exposed to the program will tend to have better inherent abilities to generate income than will GLI communities and households. If instead GLI officers tend to pick communities and households that they expect to perform especially well, or if only relatively well-off households expect to profit from participation in GLI programs, then the communities and households not involved with GLI will tend to have inferior inherent abilities to generate income.

Baseline—Follow-up Comparison for Intervention Group Only. The second approach to learning about the counterfactual is to measure outcomes for the intervention group itself before the intervention took place. This is best done by collecting *baseline* data in the intervention groups before the intervention takes place. For example, KEA might collect data on school enrollment rates and a measure of community collaboration prior to commencement of its activities in the community, and then collect the same information again after the program has been in place long enough to have an impact. In some cases, and for some outcomes that are easy to remember or for which good records are kept, it may be possible to measure these "before" outcomes by asking *retrospective* questions after the intervention has taken place. The strength of this approach is that, because the intervention and comparison groups involve the same people or communities (just sampled at different times), many characteristics (those that do not change over time) are identical in the two groups. The weakness lies in the possibility that the mere passage of time may cause some individual and household characteristics to change (as a result, for example, of aging) and will tend to bring changes in community and macro circumstances. Enrollment rates, for example, may have increased over time in KEA communities in part as a result of improvements in agricultural incomes or the activities of the government or other NGOs.

Baseline—Follow-up Comparison for Both Intervention and Control Groups. The third approach to learning about the counterfactual involves collection of data on both intervention and comparison groups, both before and after the intervention. GLI might collect baseline data in two sets of communities, one of which is about to begin participation in its program, while the other is not. It later returns to the same two sets of communities to collect follow-up data. GLI analysts recognize that the before-after change for the intervention embodies both program impact and the effects of other changes that have unrolled over time. They may use the before-after change for the control group to assess the effect on outcomes of these other changes that have unrolled over time, because the control group was exposed to these changes while not being exposed to the introduction of the program. They then estimate program impact by examining the extent to which the before-after change for the intervention group exceeds the before-after change for the control group. The strength of this "difference in differences" approach lies in the potential to hold constant characteristics that do not change over time for individuals and households (by employing samples from exactly the same individuals and households under two sets of program conditions) and to hold constant macro and other circumstances that change over time in the same way for intervention and comparison groups (by subtracting away an estimate of the effect of changes in these circumstances). The potential weakness lies in the possibility that the effects of aging and changing macroconditions on the intervention group were greater (smaller) than the effects of aging and changing macroconditions on the comparison group, rendering the estimate of program impact too high (too low).[11]

Experimental Comparison of Intervention and Control Groups. A fourth approach to learning about the counterfactual involves orchestrating a true *policy experiment,* in which communities or individuals that are equally eligible for the program are divided randomly into "treatment" and "control" groups exposed to differing program conditions, and in which data are collected for both groups. For example, GLI might randomly assign communities into groups that are and are not given access to the program in the current year (perhaps promising to introduce the program one or two years down the road in the communities that do not receive the program now), or into groups that face higher and lower interest rates on GLI loans. If the samples are large enough and if the random assignment is effective, then even though the two groups are not literally identical, they should be "as good as identical," exhibiting very similar averages and distributions of individual, household, community and macrocircumstances. The strength of the approach lies in the potential to generate comparisons in which individual, community and macrocircumstances are all very similar. But even this approach may not be perfect. Small sample sizes and other problems may cause the randomization to fail in generating identical groups.

Choosing one or more of these approaches to inferring impact is unavoidable, because good impact assessments must move beyond mere description of outcomes in the target population to estimation of impact. In choosing among the approaches, it is useful to weigh the benefits and costs of moving up from the cheapest and most feasible quantitative methods (often involving small samples and the use of the first or second approaches described above) to the methods that build in more safeguards against misleading inferences (tending to employ larger samples, and the third or fourth approaches). For some organizations the obvious "next step" in development of research methods might involve taking a first and modest foray into the use of quantitative survey methods or a first attempt to gather data on a comparison group in addition to the treatment group, while for others it would involve increasing sample sizes, planning ahead and gathering baseline data, or even planning a randomized trial of well-defined modifications to the usual program. Each such step builds in more safeguards against drawing misleading inferences and increases the precision with which specific impacts may be measured. These improvements tend also to increase the rhetorical value of the reports when used in poverty reduction strategy consultations. Thus it is useful to exercise boldness in looking for next steps in improving research methods.

In a few cases good arguments could be made that the expense and difficulty of taking the obvious "next step" are not justified, because the benefits are likely to be small. For example, where economic and social conditions other than program activities are largely stagnant, simple before-after comparisons are likely to provide quite good estimates of program impacts. In many cases, however the dual problems of selection—which produces important differences between participant and non-participant groups—and macroeconomic and other fluctuations—which produce important differences between groups observed at different times—are likely to be important. Especially when selection processes and unfolding macroevents are complicated and subtle, rendering it difficult to guess the likely direction of the biases they introduce into simple comparisons, the more costly and difficult research methods may be crucial for obtaining believable estimates of impact.

Fortunately, close examination will sometimes reveal that the cost of taking "next steps" in improving research methods is lower than expected. For example, it may be possible to study a control group without having to undertake an independent survey of non-participants, by making careful use of publicly available data from censuses or surveys in the relevant region. It may be possible to collect data in a comparison community not exposed to the program without creating animosity (among people who must answer a survey but who expect to get nothing in return), because it may make great sense to choose for comparison a community that is on a waiting list to receive program services in the near future. (Such communities are likely to be very similar to communities already accepted into the program, thus they serve as particularly good controls.) In the initial year such data allow a simple comparison, but they also become baseline data, allowing a transition toward difference in difference methods (i.e., the third approach described above) in the future. Randomized trials may be more feasible than is sometimes thought, and may even be desirable. Where resources are limited and programs cannot reach an entire population in the first year, selecting which communities to serve first "by lot" may be as fair a means of proceeding as any other.

And where the organization does not know which of two specific program designs will work the best, it may again be acceptable to randomly divide communities into groups that will be served by different designs.

Making the Most of Any Research Design

Detailed choices regarding how to implement a basic research design, and how to analyze and interpret the data produced by the basic research design, are at least as important as the choice of research design itself. Both implementation and analysis must be guided by deep understanding of both the research methods and the economic and social context in which data are collected. When choosing a comparison group for a simple contemporaneous comparison study of the impact of GLI on its target group, for example, researchers should recognize the potential for differences in individual and community characteristics between the intervention and comparison groups to bias the comparison. If they seek to measure impact on household incomes, then they must identify the household and community characteristics that play the greatest roles in determining income in the local environment, and seek to choose a comparison group in which those key characteristics are as similar as possible to the intervention group. Similarly, when KEA has collected baseline data on school enrollment and wishes to collect follow-up data for use in a simple before-after comparison study, it must recognize the potential for aging, and for changing regional conditions, to bias the comparison. They should look at complete community enrollment rates or enrollment rates in fresh random samples of children in the same age ranges in both baseline and follow-up years, rather than following a sample of children who are aging, and they should pick a follow-up year in which the regional economic conditions with the biggest impact on enrollment rates (e.g., strength of agricultural demand for child labor) are as similar as possible to those of the baseline year.

Even when care is exercised in selecting comparison groups, they are likely to differ from the intervention groups in some respects, rendering simple comparisons of outcomes across groups flawed as estimates of program impact. It will often be possible to improve the estimation of program impact by employing multiple regression methods and related econometric techniques.[12] Multiple regression methods allow the analyst to study simultaneously the roles played by the program and by individual and community characteristics in determining the outcomes of concern. Even though individual and community characteristics were not held constant by the research design, the analyst may use the results of multiple regression analysis to construct estimates of program impact in which individual and community characteristics are "held constant" hypothetically. To produce good estimates of program impact in this way, however, two conditions must be satisfied. First, data must have been collected on the important individual and community characteristics that may differ across individuals and groups in ways that bias the impact estimate. Second, the data must be incorporated into well-formulated regressions. (Poorly formulated regressions can easily make impact estimates worse rather than better!) Thus the quality of impact assessments tends to be improved by planning ahead and by involving people with expertise in data analysis at all stages.

Sometimes, even when research design and estimation methods are highly imperfect, it will still be possible to draw strong conclusions about impact, as long as the results are interpreted in the light of supplementary knowledge about the economic and social circumstances. For example, if incomes and wealth are higher in GLI communities than in other communities, even though known but unmeasured differences in community infrastructure would tend to render outcomes worse in GLI communities than in the others, then it is reasonable too conclude that the program produced an impact *at least as great* as the observed difference. Similarly, if outcomes improved from baseline to follow-up surveys, despite a known but unmeasured deterioration in the village economy as a result of non-program factors, it is reasonable to conclude that the program produced an impact *at least as big* as the observed improvement. Again, involvement of specialists who understand both poverty and data analysis is useful for making the most of such results.

Communicating the Results of Impact Assessments

If an important goal of impact assessment is to improve resource use within the organization, then designers of impact assessments must concern themselves with how the impact assessment results will be communicated and how decision makers at various levels within the organization will be given incentive to act on what is learned. Plans should be in place from the beginning not only to communicate the results to relevant staff in a timely and easily digestible fashion, but also to involve them in the design of the assessment itself, so that the assessment answers the practical questions with which they wrestle on a daily basis.

If an important goal of impact assessment is to facilitate the organization's involvement in consultations and debates about government and non-governmental approaches to poverty reduction and economic development, then the reports must translate the organization's broad and deep concerns, and the findings of its research, into a language that is intelligible to other organizations, including the large, secular organizations. This will often require clear articulation (without apology) of program goals, a detailed program description that illuminates all the salient choices that shape its character and impact, a precise statement of the research questions posed and the research methods employed, and an even-handed and intuitive discussion of the conclusions that can (and cannot) be drawn from analysis of the information collected.

Perhaps even more important than how the assessment documents are written is the question of where and how the documents will be made available to the larger development community. From an economist's perspective, there is currently far too little sharing of the results of impact assessments. It is likely that many other organizations are using methods similar to those of GLI and KEA to achieve similar goals. The impact of GLI's and KEA's impact assessments could thus be greatly multiplied if documents describing the assessments were disseminated broadly within the development community, allowing many organizations to improve their performance on the basis of the findings in a single study. The ideal solution to the problem of broad dissemination of impact assessment results will probably require collective action among many development actors in the creation of a new institution: a global clearinghouse of impact assessment documents, where development actors worldwide could easily learn about the range of program designs currently in operation, impact assessment designs and costs, and the lessons learned from impact assessments. Perhaps Christian development organizations (or their umbrella groups) should be among the first to take steps in this direction. In the meantime, however, they should at least demonstrate more eagerness to publish what they are learning. (Extensive web searches produce precious few non-governmental organizations that include any discussion at all of impact assessment in their web pages.)

The Potential Benefits of Collaborating with Christian Economists and Other Academics

Many Christian academic economists (and other academics) are eager to contribute their time, energy, and skills to impact assessment work of importance to their practitioner brothers and sisters. We are trained (and inclined by personality) to ask questions, help articulate objectives and targets, recognize as choices what others see as givens, identify logical links between actions and impacts, weigh benefits and costs (even of possible improvements in research methodology), articulate precise research questions, devise justifiable methods for answering the questions, exercise care in the interpretation of research findings, and communicate research findings to various audiences. We thus have some hope of being useful to Christian NGOs in most of the impact assessment design and implementation activities discussed in this chapter.

NGOs may involve academic economists in their program design and evaluation activities in many ways, from informal email or phone conversations (asking for references, contacts, opinions) to formal involvement in specific assessment activities. In some cases we can devote significant time to field research ourselves. In other cases, we might need to work through the bright and enterprising students we know (whether undergrads, or M.A., or Ph.D students), who are often eager to undertake internships through which they participate in programs and research in the field. Students can gain valuable field experience and necessary thesis topics, while contributing great creativity, and serving as our eyes, ears, and representatives in the field.[13] Academics' skills and interests may be tapped at low cost. Many academics are expected to engage in research as well as teaching as part of their scholarly activity, and thus have opportunity for involvement. And our motivation for involvement is strong, because we know it would enrich our research and teaching, while also allowing us opportunity to be of more direct service to the poor than is the case in much of our work.

Academics at times may even be able to help pull in additional impact assessment funding. Academic-NGO teams may, for example, be able to obtain funding from the World Bank research committee, or other funders of social science and policy research. A strong case can be made that impact assessments (as long as the results are well-disseminated) provide widespread benefits, and thus are worthy of financial support by the world's large development actors. Perhaps academic economists could be enlisted by a coalition of NGOs to prepare a proposal to the World Bank and several large bilateral development organizations for the creation of an NGO impact assessment facility, which would help finance NGO impact assessments. The same facility could also serve as the repository of impact assessment results.[14]

The Association of Christian Economists (ACE) Development Connections Web Site

In the interest of facilitating and promoting collaboration between academics and practitioners in the area of poverty reduction and economic development, especially in the areas of program design and evaluation, the Association of Christian Economists (ACE) has created the "ACE Development Connections" web

site at http://www.gordon.edu/ace/devconnect/. The site provides
a variety of useful links and resources, as well as contact information for organizations and individuals with a variety of skills
and interests related to the work and evaluation of Christian NGO
development activities. ACE looks forward to growing collaboration with practitioners and to the improved impact in Christian
poverty reduction efforts that will result—by God's grace.

References

Baker, Judy L. 2000. *Evaluating the Impact of Development Projects
on Poverty: A Handbook for Practitioners*. Washington, D.C.: The
World Bank.

Chung, Kimberly. 2000. "Qualitative Data Collection Techniques,"
in *Designing Household Survey Questionnaires for Developing
Countries: Lessons from 15 Years of the Living Standards
Measurement Study, Volume 2*. Margaret Grosh and Paul Glewwe,
eds. Washington, D.C.: The World Bank, pp. 337–364.

Feinstein, Osvaldo N. and Robert Picciotto. 2001. *Evaluation and
Poverty Reduction*. Washington, D.C.: The World Bank.

Grosh, Margaret and Paul Glewwe, eds. 2000. *Designing Household
Survey Questionnaires for Developing Countries: Lessons from 15
Years of the Living Standards Measurement Study*. Washington,
D.C.: The World Bank.

Magnani, Robert. 1997. *Sampling Guide*. Food and Nutrition Technical
Assistance Project. Washington, D.C.: Academy for Educational
Development, http://www.fantaproject.org/downloads/pdfs/
sampling.pdf.

Rossi, Peter H.; Howard E. Freeman and Mark W. Lipsey. 1999.
Evaluation: A Systematic Approach, Sixth Edition. Thousand
Oaks, CA: Sage Publications.

Schaffner, Julie. 2003. "Questions to Guide the Design of Impact
Studies," paper prepared for the conference "Economists,
Practitioners and the Attack on Poverty: Toward Christian
Collaboration," http://www.gordon.edu/ace/devconnect/
conference/schaffner.pdf.

Valadez, Joseph and Michael Bamberger. 1994. *Monitoring and
Evaluating Social Programs in Developing Countries: A*

Handbook for Policymakers, Managers and Researchers.
Washington, D.C.: The World Bank.

Wooldridge, Jeffrey M. 2002. *Introductory Econometrics: A Modern
Approach*, Second Edition. Mason, OH: Thomson South-Western.

Notes

[1] The author gratefully acknowledges valuable feedback on previous drafts
from Cara Carter, Paul Glewwe, John de Haan, Stephen Schaffner, and Stephen
Smith.

[2] An informal survey conducted by Judith Dean and myself in 2001 uncovered
significant interest among Christian development practitioners in learning
more about impact assessment methods. But in personal communication, John
de Haan, the Executive Director of the Association of Evangelical Relief and
Development Organizations (AERDO) indicates regret over his inability to
generate more enthusiasm for impact assessment in the organizations with
which he works.

[3] For a more thorough discussion of impact assessment design for Christian
development organizations, see Schaffner (2003). Good general references on
impact assessment in the context of poverty reduction in developing countries
include Baker (2000), Feinstein and Piciotto (2001), and Valadez and Bamberger
(1994). Email discussion groups on related issues include the UK-based
REMAPP (http://www.mande.co.uk/docs/remapp.htm) and the U.S.-based
IAEVAL (http://groups.yahoo.com/group/IAEVAL/).

[4] Chapter 15 of this book describes the example of World Vision in defining its
objectives and developing good ways of measuring outcomes.

[5] Readers familiar with evaluation discussions, such as that in the text by Rossi,
et al. (1999), will see that I am suggesting evaluations that stretch beyond the
more limited scope of "impact assessment" *per se* to include some "program
theory assessment" and "program process assessment."

[6] For a detailed discussion of questionnaire design, and for model questionnaire
modules, see Grosh and Glewwe (2000).

[7] On qualitative data collection methods, see Chung (2000).

[8] Basic statistical principles suggest that the level and distribution of incomes
in a (sufficiently large) random sample of GLI borrowers should bear close
resemblance to the level and distribution of incomes in the full population of
GLI borrowers; and confidence interval calculations allow assessment of how
accurate sample mean income is likely to be as an estimate of population mean
income.

[9] For a discussion of the sampling methods that must underlie quantitative
research, see Magnani (1997).

[10] For more on these approaches, see Baker (2000), Feinstein and Picciotto
(2001), and Rossi, et al. (1999).

[11] For example, if GLI chose to set up microlending programs in communities

that had been hit particularly hard by structural adjustment (with much of the impact of these shocks hitting after the date at which the baseline data were collected), then macrocircumstances may have been declining more rapidly in the intervention villages than in the comparison villages. Simple before-after comparisons for GLI villages might show outcomes declining, even though the program improved incomes, because macroconditions were deteriorating. Recognizing that role of macroconditions by comparing the before-after change in intervention villages to the before-after change in comparison villages will render a somewhat more positive view of the program, but will still understate program impact, because conditions would have deteriorated even more in GLI villages in the absence of the program than they did in the comparison villages.

[12] A good introductory textbook on regression methods for social science research and additional econometric methods is Wooldridge (2003). Econometrics is not an easy subject to teach oneself, however. Anyone interested in learning these techniques is strongly urged to take an application-oriented course in the subject.

[13] Whether the student needs to be a Christian is an issue to be contemplated. Many of the students I could send to such internships would not be Christians, but would be sympathetic to the purposes of Christian organization and would work with good will.

[14] I gratefully acknowledge email conversations about sources of funding for academic-NGO research with Paul Glewwe, Martin Ravallion, and Vijayendra Rao.

15

Shaping Assessments
to the Organization's Values and Needs

Jaisankar Sarma and Bernard Vicary (World Vision)

For non-profit organizations like World Vision it is important that their mission and values are consistently reflected in their approaches for program planning, management, and impact assessment. Over the past few years, World Vision has developed a set of indicators and assessment methodology that is being implemented in all its development programs around the world. The organization has tried to ensure that the indicators and the assessment methodology give expression to its understanding of development in concrete ways. World Vision developed methods that are relevant at the local level and are cost effective. This chapter draws on our experience with macrolevel, organization-wide impact assessment at World Vision to emphasize three points. First, before engaging in impact assessment, an organization must define clearly what its development objectives and values are. Only then can it identify the impacts it might like to measure. Second, stakeholder participation in designing and implementing the assessment is useful for improving its quality and usefulness. Finally, it is valuable to integrate both qualitative and quantitative methods for gathering information.

In this chapter, we focus on indicators and methods that World Vision has developed to track changes over time in program communities. While these are not impact assessments *per se*, as they do not attempt to infer how much of the change was caused specifically by World Vision programs, they involve many of the same issues that must be grappled with in larger impact assessment exercises. It is also helpful to bear in mind that World Vision defines the term impact as "significant or lasting changes in peoples' lives

Table 1. World Vision's
Transformational Development Framework.

"As followers of our Lord Jesus Christ, we celebrate God's vision for all people from all cultures and we believe that the preferred future for all boys and girls, families and their communities is:
wholeness of life with dignity, justice, peace and hope."

Domains of Change	Scope of Change
1. Well-Being of Boys, Girls and Their Families in the Community	Capacities of families and communities to: • Ensure the survival of girls and boys • Enhance access to health and basic education • Provide opportunities for spiritual and emotional nurture • Develop a sustainable household livelihood with just distribution of resources and enhance the capacity of children to earn a future livelihood • Protect girls and boys from abuse and exploitation • Reduce risks and prevent, cope with, mitigate and respond to disasters, conflicts and pandemics such as HIV/AIDS
2. All Girls and Boys Empowered as Agents of Transformation	• Girls and boys participate in the development process in an age-appropriate manner, becoming agents of transformation in their families and communities, both now and in the future.
3. Transformed Relationships	• Restored with God through faith in Jesus Christ • Equitable, just, peaceful, productive and inclusive relationships within households and communities that impact on economic, social, political, spiritual, environmental and ecclesiastical aspects of life • Responsible relationship with the environment • Includes all who participate in the process of transformational development (donors/sponsors, churches, organizations, staff and their families, boards, the poor, the non-poor) changing their worldview and lifestyles to be more consistent with Christ's concern for the poor

4. Interdependent and Empowered Communities	• Presence of a culture of participation, with families and whole communities empowered to influence and shape their situation through coalitions and networks at local, national, regional and global levels, based on mutual respect, transparency and ethical/moral responsibility
5. Transformed Systems and Structures	• Includes all elements that contribute to transformational development, such as access to social services, citizen participation, means of production, just distribution of resources in the state, civil society and private sectors, structural, systemic and policy issues • Impacts on social, religious, economic and political domains at local, national, regional and global levels

World Vision's role:
Work alongside the poor and oppressed as they pursue their transformational development, in partnership with sponsors/donors, governments, churches and other NGOs.

or a situation whether planned or unplanned, positive or negative, directly or indirectly, that a program or project helps to bring about" (World Vision DME Steering Committee, 2005).

Identifying Program Objectives and Aligning Impact Assessment Indicators and Methods with Them

Impact assessment should seek to identify not just program reach and immediate results, but the lasting effects on lives, communities, and relationships. The scope and objectives of impact assessment should be aligned with an organization's notions of what constitutes development or success. This section describes how World Vision approached this problem. World Vision's understanding and practice of development has evolved over the years, from a welfare approach to community development to broader transformational development. In 1998, World Vision initiated a study of its development models and those of other organizations. Data was collected through focus group discussions involving development practitioners and other stakeholders on their own mental models of development. The study resulted in World Vision articulating its own development framework called the "Transformational Development" frame. World Vision's framework now defines transformational development as "*a process through which children, families, and communities move towards wholeness of life with dignity, justice, peace and hope.*" World Vision has articulated five "domains of change" that are essential for transformational development, and are described in Table 1 (World Vision Transformational Development Network, 2002).

It is often said "you become what you measure." Therefore, we strive to "measure what matters." World Vision has often been strong in measuring financial performance and other aspects typical of "upwards accountability," but has sometimes been less rigorous in holding itself accountable to the people and processes that matter most. As World Vision has defined its understanding of transformational development, it has also been developing a set of indicators to reflect this—to help see how reality matches up to our rhetoric! Over the last five years World Vision has developed a set of *transformational development indicators* (TDI) for measurement in all development programs of World Vision. A systematic process consisting of literature review, stakeholder consultations, development of indicators and assessment methods, field-tests for validation, and revision of indicators and methods was followed in order to finalize the indicators and the methods. TDIs are now being phased in across World Vision's development programs worldwide, more than 1,500 in total.

The twelve current transformational development indicators are described in Table 2. Their purpose is to show the status of quality of life of communities, families, and children where World Vision facilitates community-based, sustainable, transformational development. World Vision believes that the TDIs, as core indicators of the TD Frame, demonstrate the basic quality of life in all contexts of its development work. The process and results of measuring these indicators are designed to be valuable to communities, development programs, World Vision national offices, the wider World Vision partnership, and key external stakehold-ers. Results from using the TDIs will provide evidence about the integrity of World Vision's development work in relation to the organization's common understanding of transformational devel-opment. The picture provided by development programs across the entire World Vision partnership will enable World Vision to reflect on mission effectiveness, leading to adjustments in partner-ship policy and practice. TDI results will also give the partnership a foundation for action research on various issues relating to pro-gram quality and management (Sarma and Vicary, 2002).

The following sections discuss key lessons learned during the development of these indicators and approaches to measurement.

Involving Stakeholders

Many stakeholders view the evaluator who leads an assess-ment process as an expert who can judge the merit or worth of the program that is being evaluated. They expect an evaluator of com-munity development programs to tell them in what ways the pro-gram has or has not achieved the program's goals and objectives, or empowered people to manage holistic sustainable development in their community. In contrast, it is important to view the develop-ment program evaluator more as a facilitator than as an expert in development work. To be sure, an effective development program evaluator must have an understanding of sound principles of devel-opment work. However, evaluation is more likely to have a positive influence on the program and development overall, if the evaluator facilitates judgments by internal stakeholders (e.g., project staff) and external stakeholders (e.g., community members), rather than pronouncing his or her own judgments. Why is that true? Evalua-tion of my situation by someone else is threatening. If I am told that my situation is not up to standard, my natural response is to defend myself. My natural response is to resist changing my attitudes or behavior, even though an expert says that such change is necessary. But if I reach my own conclusions about the quality of my situation, and that quality matters to me, I am more apt to make adjustments to improve the situation (Cookingham, 2002).

Table 2. Transformational Development Indicators.

Title	Indicator	Definition	Data Source	Measurement Process
Water	Percent of households who have year round *access to an improved* water source.	*Access to an improved* water source means 15 or more litres of water per person per day, from a potable source within 30 minutes of the household. Potable source means a tap, protected well, or other protected water source.	Primary data from household survey.	Primary data: 30 cluster random household survey, verified by principal caregiver report.
Nutrition	Percent of boys and percent of girls, aged 6—59 months, *stunted.*	*Stunted* means the child has a Z–score below minus 2 standard deviations (SD) from the median height-for-age of the NCHS/ WHO standard. This indicates moderate and/or severe malnutrition.	Primary data from household survey.	Primary data: 30 cluster random household survey, verified by age, height and weight measurements.
Primary Education	Percent of boys and percent of girls who are *enrolled* in or have *completed* the first six years of formal education.	*Enrolled* means currently enrolled in the appropriate year of formal education for the child's age. *Completed* means successfully passed the sixth year of formal education while of the recommended age for that level. Appropriate level and age are determined by the country's Ministry or Department of Education. These first years of formal school are often identified as primary or elementary school.	Primary data from household survey.	Primary data: 30 cluster random household survey, verified by principal caregiver report.

Diarrhoea Management	Percent of children 0—59 months with *diarrhoea* in the past two weeks, whose disease was *acceptably managed*.	*Diarrhoea* means more than 3 loose stools passed in a 24 hour period. *Acceptably managed* means the child received increased fluids (preferably ORT or recommended home fluid) during the disease and while recovering.	Primary data from household survey.	Primary data: 30 cluster random household survey, verified by principal caregiver report.
Immunization	Percent of children aged 12—23 months *fully immunized*.	*Fully immunized* means the child has received all National Ministry of Health (MOH) recommended vaccines before 12 months. Must include immunization against diphtheria, pertussis, tetanus, measles, poliomyelitis and tuberculosis.	Primary data from household survey.	Primary data: 30 cluster random household survey, immunization status verified by MOH individual vaccination cards.
Household Resilience	Percent of households adopting *coping strategies* within the past year.	*Coping strategies* means an adaptive coping strategy, sale of a liquid or productive asset, so as to mitigate the impact of external shocks and /or environmental stress factors in order to provide the household's basic necessities.	Primary data from focus group discussions and household survey.	Primary data: Focus group discussions to identify local coping strategies, specific to the communities, to be used in a survey. 30 cluster random household survey, verified by principal caregiver report.
Poorest Households	Percent of *poorest households*.	*Poorest households* means those households identified to be the most socially and/or economically disadvantaged within a community.	Primary data from wealth-ranking exercises.	Primary data: Series of wealth-ranking exercises involving community leaders and community members from sample communities.

Title	Indicators	Definition	Data Source	Measurement Process
Caring for Others	Community members care for each other.	*Care for each other* means that men, women, boys and girls perceive that they care for others and others care for them in their community. *Care for each other* is defined around dimensions regarding use of community resources, gender relations, valuing and protection of children, well-being of vulnerable persons and conflict prevention/resolution.	Primary data from focus group discussions.	Primary data: Guided focus group discussions with men, women, boys and girls. Information analyzed and indexed by a rating committee using specific rating guidelines.
Emergence of Hope	Communities' emergence of hope in their future.	*Emergence of hope* means that men, women, boys and girls perceive and demonstrate hope in their future. Dimensions of this *emergence of hope* include peoples' perceptions of the past and the present, attitude towards the future, self-esteem and spirituality.	Primary data from focus group discussions.	Primary data: Guided focus group discussions with men, women, boys and girls. Information analysed and indexed by a rating committee using specific rating guidelines.
Christian Impact	*Christian capacity & intentionality* of program teams.	*Christian capacity and intentionality* means active staff spiritual nurture, strong church relations, and appropriate witness to Christ.	Secondary data from document review.

Primary data from focus group discussions. | Secondary data: Review of program documents.

Primary data: Guided focus group discussion with Christian program staff. Information analyzed and indexed by two consultants using specific rating guidelines. |

Community Participation	*Community participation* in development.	*Community participation* means that men, women, boys and girls perceive they actively participate in all aspects of their development, with particular focus on program planning, implementation, monitoring, and evaluation.	Primary data from focus group discussions.	Primary data: Guided focus group discussions with men, women, boys and girls. Information analyzed and indexed by a rating committee using specific rating guidelines.
Social Sustainability	*Social sustainability* of community development.	*Social sustainability* is defined as the capacity within local community organizations to sustain the long-term viability and impact of development processes. This capacity is focused on how conditions for social sustainability are created through the character, functioning, resource mobilization and networking skills of community organisations.	Secondary data from document review. Primary data from focus group discussions.	Secondary data: Review of documents from development programs and community organizations. Primary data: Guided focus group discussions with office bearers and members of community organizations. Information analyzed and indexed by a consultant using specific rating guidelines.

Involving stakeholders means more than simply allowing them to have their say. It is viewing both internal and external stakeholders as partners. First and foremost, World Vision's understanding of transformational development demands an assessment methodology that is inclusive of all relevant stakeholders as partners. Transformational development does not belong to World Vision, or any other external agency. Our place is that of walking and working alongside communities together with other partners in the journey, such as churches, governments, other NGOs, and donors. Such involvement is important because it communicates to all the stakeholders that we are all partners together in the development process, it increases the range of information available to evaluation, it enhances ownership for the assessment findings, it increases the likelihood of acting on the recommendations arising out of the assessment, and it promotes communication and capacity building.

Practical steps that can be taken to involve stakeholders in the assessment process include (a) identifying stakeholders and their role in the program, (b) consulting stakeholders to assess their information needs from the assessment process; (c) defining stakeholder roles and planning for stakeholder participation in the process of assessment, and (d) having findings and draft reports validated by the stakeholders.

TDI as global indicators for World Vision were developed with the full participation of internal stakeholders of World Vision. A formal advisory network was set up with specific terms of reference to guide the process of development of TDI. The advisory network consisted of representatives of important stakeholder groups such as program staff, technical experts, senior management, and funding office representatives. TDI went through 3 rounds of testing and learning in more than 60 programs in over 30 countries to ensure the usefulness of the specific indicators to the field practitioners, determine the validity of the assessment methods and understand organizational implications of implementing the system, viz., capacity building needs, resources required, management and systems support. Consultations were

held with the program staff who tested the indicators to gather
their input. Numerous changes were made to the indicators based
on what was learned. Without this elaborate process of stakeholder
involvement and input, TDI implementation process would have
been much less effective within the World Vision partnership.

Combining and Developing Methods of Information Gathering

Most of the projects funded by bilateral and multilateral donors tend to predominantly use quantitative methods for assessment. Participatory methods such as Participation Learning and
Action (PLA) are used only as diagnostic tools for program design
purposes, not for impact assessment. Kassam (1998) discusses
the reasons for a bias towards quantitative methods of impact
assessment. The institutional demands to justify the significant
investment of large sums of money and to lubricate the chain of
accountability make it imperative to obtain the so-called hard data
on project performance. Participatory evaluation is not fully understood in terms of its value and methodological validity. Those
working in funding agencies do not have the resources to plough
through large amounts of detailed texts generated by participatory
evaluation methods. Finally, in many quarters, development work
is still perceived predominantly as a technical exercise rather than
as a complex and dynamic process of transformation.

Quantitative assessment methods such as cluster surveys—
which limit participation by beneficiaries—and qualitative methods that are participatory in nature, should not be exclusive and
are often best used together. For example, qualitative methods
should be used to develop questionnaires to be used in survey
work. Qualitative methods can also be used to further explore and
research the results of a survey. There are several benefits of using
integrated approaches in assessment: (a) consistency checks can
be built in through the use of triangulation procedures that permit
two or more independent estimates to be made for key variables,
(b) different perspectives can be obtained, (c) analysis can be conducted on different levels, and (d) opportunities can be provided

for feedback to help interpret findings (Baker, 2000). Survey methods can provide good estimates of individual, household and community wellbeing, but they are less effective for analyzing social processes or for institutional analysis.

Some TDI measure tangible aspects of well-being of children and families through household surveys. These indicators are similar to some used in the millennium development goals, and they use well-established quantitative methods of data collection and analysis. Some TDI focus on relationships and empowerment in communities, and for these we have developed innovative methods of qualitative data collection and analysis, using focus groups, document reviews and wealth-ranking used in Participation Learning and Action methodology (PLA). One example is worth mentioning here. One TDI that was initially field-tested was the "household's ability to meet basic needs without incurring debt." The indicator was quantitative and the method was household survey. It considered issues related to income and consumption as key indicators for household welfare. Feedback that we received from the field tests brought to light several problems with the indicator and the method used. People considered some of the questions on income, expenditure and indebtedness to be too private to share or in some cases, questions of such nature raised peoples' expectations of the program to unrealistic levels. Another major problem was that while we considered income level and consumption to be indicators for household welfare, the communities felt that vulnerability during times of crisis as the main indicator of household welfare. World Vision developed a new indicator to address the issue. The TDI on household resilience studies changes in household coping behavior due to some shock or emergency. The indicator method uses a combination of qualitative and quantitative methods. Data for this indicator is primary data collected through a two-part process of focus group discussions and household survey. The first part is a focus group of key informants who discuss the local context of coping strategies, select 10 out of 20 questions given in the standard questionnaire and make the questions specific to their context. For example, the following questions need to be made specific to the local context.

- In the past year, did your family eat wild food more frequently than usual to have enough food to eat? (*name the wild food*)

- In the past year, did your family sell (or consume) more of your small livestock than usual in order to have enough food to eat? (*name the common livestock in the community*)

The output of this discussion is a contextualized questionnaire that is specific for a given program. This new indicator and the method seem to have found better acceptance among our field practitioners and communities that we work with.

References

Baker, Judy L. 2000. *Evaluating the Impact of Development Projects on Poverty: A Handbook for Practitioners.* Washington, D.C.: World Bank.

Cookingham, Frank G. 2002. *Monitoring and Evaluation Manual.* Monrovia, CA: World Vision.

Sarma, Jaisankar and Bernard Vicary. 2002, *Transformational Development Indicators Field Guide: Volume 1, Getting Started.* Monrovia, CA: World Vision.

Kassam, Yusuf. 1998. "The Combined Use of the Participatory Dialogue Method and Survey Methodology to Evaluate Development Projects: A Case Study of a Rural Development Project in Bangladesh." *Knowledge and Policy.* 10(1/2):43-.

World Vision DME Steering Committee. 2005. "Learning through Evaluation with Accountability and Planning." Monrovia, CA: World Vision.

World Vision Transformational Development Network. 2002. *Transformational Development—Core Documents.* Monrovia, CA: World Vision.

Section IV

Christian Engagement in Poverty Reduction Policy-Making

16

Development Challenges
for the New Millennium:

Dialogue and Partnership Issues for Faith
and Development Institutions

Katherine Marshall (World Bank)

This chapter describes the origin of recent engagement between the faiths and faith-based development organizations, on the one hand, and the large secular development institutions, on the other. It describes the development over the past six years of new forms of dialogue among these groups about the challenges of global poverty. It sets out the challenge to Christian and other faith organizations posed by the Millennium Development Goals, describes the genesis of the World Faiths Development Dialogue, and explores some practical ways for faith-based organizations to become involved in the formulation of policy toward poverty alleviation, notably through the Poverty Reduction Strategy Paper (PRSP) process.

Millennium Development Challenges and Goals

In looking to the vital challenges and issues for our times—war and peace, social justice, the scourge of HIV/AIDS, child welfare, and environmental protection—the links between the agendas, concerns and core purpose of those who work on international development and those whose central focus is faith and religion are striking and legion. Perhaps no common challenges are as clear as the imperative and urgent need to address the HIV/AIDS pandemic and the crisis to global governance and support for international development assistance posed by corrupt practices. However, with notable exceptions, dialogue between these two worlds has historically been weak and fragmented, characterized by considerable tension and missed opportunities for positive action. Reflection and action to strengthen the links, and to address some real concerns that have impeded joint action, is critically needed.

The 2000 U.N. Millennium Summit,[1] which was preceded by an extraordinary meeting at the United Nations of leaders of the world's faiths, spurred both new thinking and new engagement among development and faith leaders at the global level about the roles of religion and interfaith dialogue in meeting the core challenges facing humanity, defined particularly in terms of the fight against global poverty. The September 2000 Millennium Declaration by world leaders proclaimed: "We will spare no effort to free our fellow men, women, and children from the abject and dehumanizing conditions of extreme poverty, to which more than a billion of them are currently subjected." The Summit put a spotlight on the roles of faith leaders as agents of change, and the lessons to be learned by and from different partners in addressing society's challenges. These challenges were amplified following the events of September 11, 2001 and their aftermath.

The Millennium Development Goals (MDGs) emerged from this engagement of world leaders in 2000.[2] They reflect an effort to frame and encapsulate many global agreements reached in recent decades, and a new determination to mobilize energy, resources and passion behind tangible and quantified imperatives. They are presented in the form of a "covenant" through which progress can be judged. 2015—not far before us all—is a date when we (as a global community) are committed to take stock of how well we have done to defeat the ancient scourges of want, ignorance, hunger and strife. The goals are straightforward—halve poverty, halt the spread of communicable diseases, ensure that all children go to school and at least finish primary school, work to protect and improve the environment, etc. But they present still a formidable challenge and the current prognosis is that in many areas the MDGs will not be achieved.

The MDGs reflect "ancient wine" in new bottles and labels.

They are simple and incontestable goals. They are, however, an essential backdrop to current thinking about the role of the faiths in world development, because they symbolize a new awareness of the need to galvanize stronger global partnerships and an urgent global commitment to making better progress towards social justice. An essential part of this effort must be to appreciate better the complex and varied roles that faith institutions play in the development arena, from contribution to broad ethical and policy debates from global to personal levels (for example in making the human imperative of fighting poverty an obligation of each of us), to on-going derivation of practical insights about interventions at the community and family level. Without faith institutions engaged, the fight to achieve education goals, to address gender inequities, and to combat the scourge of HIV/AIDS, among many others, cannot be won. Therefore, never has the need for thoughtful dialogue been greater.[3]

World Bank Dialogue with Faith Groups

The World Bank (one of the leading protagonists in the development "world") has historically engaged directly with faith institutions in only limited ways. In the course of its efforts to engage more with "civil society," however, the Bank has begun working with many faith-based nongovernmental organizations on a wide range of development projects.

What has led the World Bank to engage more directly with faith institutions? A first motivation has been new recognition of the important role that faith institutions have played in education, health, and the promotion of development more globally, as witnessed in the development of the MDGs. The World Bank and other secular development actors have also recognized the skill and energy that faith institutions bring to poor communities, working to empower poor people and to advance community development agendas. This often wins remarkably high levels of trust. These facts are highlighted powerfully in the *Voices of the Poor* surveys conducted by the World Bank (Narayan and Petesch, 2002). In additional to skills and energy, faith institutions also contribute substantial financial resources to development efforts. These flows are notoriously poorly documented, but we know, for example, that over half of the resources within the U.S. philanthropic world flow through faith-based institutions. Finally, the world's faiths have from time immemorial grappled with the fundamental ethical issues that underlie the development challenge and worked towards greater social justice. Never have such prophetic voices been needed more in the face of the complex challenges that confront us today.

Reflections on the role of faith institutions have also been spurred by the sometimes highly visible and often contentious questioning of World Bank policies and programs towards debt, structural adjustment and cost recovery from faith institutions. Voices from pulpits, temples, and Friday prayers ricochet in both developing and developed countries. Globally, faith groups influence global public policy in many ways, including the orchestration of major global summits and the building of consensus for development aid (witness their impact through the Jubilee 2000 campaign on poor country debt and at global meetings on HIV/AIDS).

The World Bank today is keenly aware that faith institutions are important players on development issues, with whom better dialogue is needed. These institutions have much to offer development practitioners in responding to the challenges of poverty and social justice.

The World Faiths Development Dialogue

An effort to further dialogue began in February 1998 in Lambeth—the lovely old Palace on the Thames River, where an ancient gnarled fig tree reminds visitors of the times when King Henry VIII provoked radical changes in England's relations between church and state. Jim Wolfensohn, then President of the World Bank, and George Carey, then Archbishop of Canterbury, invited leaders from the world's major religions to discuss how they viewed the global challenge of poverty. The first meeting of the group, at Lambeth, was rather tentative and strained.

Many faith leaders were critical of the World Bank, especially its promotion of what was termed "structural adjustment," and concern about the growing weight of debt on poor countries was widespread. World Bank officials were frankly baffled and frustrated by the much of the criticism since they saw themselves in the vanguard of the fight against global poverty. All participants were forced to recognize how far apart the worlds of faith and of development had grown. More than fifty years of development history had brought very little organized cooperation between them, leaving them with vocabularies that seemed to come from different planets. But the meeting brought into the light a deep sense that these worlds were joined in a common purpose in the fight against poverty.

The sequel to this meeting was a continuing and focused process of dialogue, looking both to define broad objectives and ethical imperatives and to derive lessons from practical, on the ground experience of working in poor communities. Three areas illustrate these initial efforts and their promise. Working through the World Faiths Development Dialogue (WFDD), a consultation process provided ideas and concrete suggestions to two major policy exercises led by the World Bank: the World Development Reports on Poverty in 2000 and Services to the Poor in 2003. The role that faith communities have played in the emerging process of country poverty strategies has been brought into the light. Finally, exploratory interfaith groups in Guatemala, Ethiopia and Tanzania have showed that concrete challenges such as national health policy, approaches to food security, and articulation of common ethical principles for the education system can unite groups long divided by history and conflict. The WFDD remains a small organization, based in the UK, with a permanent staff of only four people, but its network spans the globe and it offers great promise as a bridge among different actors committed to global social change.[4]

The effort to engage in robust dialogue, leading to action, has been driven by the strong personal commitment of the two leaders concerned (Jim Wolfensohn and George Carey). The dialogue is grounded in the deeply felt common purpose that was the central outcome of the 1998 Lambeth meeting. The World Bank articulates its mission in two phrases: "our dream is a world free of poverty" and "to fight poverty with passion and professionalism." Every major world religion has as a central anchor in compassion for those who suffer, a deep obligation of the fortunate to help those in need and a fire for social justice. Beyond the common starting point lie worlds of complications—in how the World Bank and other institutions view and fight poverty, and in how religions explain it and exhort us to respond. But the core is there; this is a central problem for us all. The dialogue builds on three other strong areas of common concern: the deep engagement of faith institutions in social services, a recognition that faith institutions have a special "ear" for voices of the poor because they are so present in poor communities and are trusted by poor people, and the strong common concern for building peace—both preventing conflict and rebuilding when it comes to an end.

After the Lambeth meeting, the path proved more complex than expected. The idea of dialogue, seemingly straightforward and sensible, drew sharp criticism, mainly from the secular development actors. Why was this so? Most important was fear that the engagement with religious organizations might exacerbate interreligious tensions that were fueling conflict and even affecting the rise of fundamentalist movements, associated in the developing world with terror and in the developed world with controversial stances on such issues as women's reproductive health rights. The complex lines between "church and state" were an immediate concern for some and they were concerned that an explicit development community and World Bank focus on religion might muddy the waters of respective roles of church and state. It took some years of exploration to understand the concerns, to move to address the real challenges of respecting the hard-won separation of church and state, and to define better what dialogue meant—not debate, not explanation, not just words, but a real effort to understand and find better ways to work in partnership. Perhaps the most significant challenge and avenue that has emerged is continuous and explicit efforts to link the broad global dialogue on issues such as approaches to health or HIV/AIDS to specific and current experience at the community level. The World Faiths Development Dialogue in the form of a very modest but important institution is now well launched and the process of dialogue and learning is advancing across a wide range of institutions and initiatives.

A second important marker along the path was September 11, 2001. This brought the links between religion and development into much sharper and much more complicated relief. No one could plausibly argue thereafter that a better understanding of religions was not vital. At the same time, the difficulties of dialogue appeared even greater still than before, and the list of questions much longer: Was religion changing? In what direction? Was it conducive to peace and stability or against it? Did religion favor a dialogue or a clash of civilizations? The World Faiths Development Dialogue continues to be confronted directly and immediately with these questions.

A major recent milestone was a meeting in Canterbury, England on October 6–8, 2002, again co-chaired by Jim Wolfensohn and the Archbishop of Canterbury (Marshall and Marsh, 2003). A group of leaders from the world's major religions, major development institutions, foundations and the private sector gathered to consider how their various partnerships could be strengthened to combat poverty and to work together toward the realization of the Millennium Development Goals. Their exchange was pitched squarely at moving beyond talk and dialogue to more effective action. The meeting was marked by a common commitment to make a difference in the world, even as important differences were aired in a candid, forthright and constructive manner. Participants agreed totally about the need to translate promises into reality through consistency, drive, and humility. The meeting agenda, focused on the core of the global development agenda and the MDGs, with special focus on poverty, education, HIV/AIDS, community empowerment and development, and issues around conflict and development in countries under stress, afforded a solid basis for practical agreements on follow up in key areas, notably education, HIV/AIDS and gender. The admonition of Lord Carey, that "paths are made by walking" has been followed since with a focus on bringing faith and development actors closer together in all the critical areas involved, but especially on the implementation of community-based programs combating HIV/AIDS in many African countries.

The dialogue thus engaged underscores that great potential synergy can come from partnership and dialogue among development and faith organizations. There are many avenues for such joint work, including (taking the case of the World Bank) more focused engagement through the Poverty Reduction Strategy Papers and Country Assistance Strategy (CAS) consultations, World Development Report consultations, education (in the context of the Education for All initiative), and HIV/AIDS strategies and programs at country levels. There are still, though, many missing links. Development practitioners and the World Bank specifically will need to work to be more aware of the vital institutions, experience, insights, and ideas of faith institutions, while faith institutions would benefit from more efforts to delve more deeply into the history, underlying principles for action, and operating modalities of the development institutions.

Poverty Reduction Strategy Papers

One mechanism through which faith-based organizations, and people driven by faith concerns, can participate in design and application of poverty-eradication policy is through engagement in the development of Poverty Reduction Strategy Papers (PRSPs).[5] The international community agreed (in mid-1999) to develop and rely on this mechanism to help ensure that nationally-owned participatory poverty reduction strategies would provide a basic anchor for strategic work and all programs, from debt reduction to community development programs, particularly in heavily indebted poor countries. This approach builds on the Comprehensive Development Framework,[6] which reflects a vision of country-driven, results-oriented, and comprehensive programs for development, in which a beacon is always focused on fighting poverty.

Dialogue and action to enhance links with faith institutions in PRSP development is a good illustration of the practical application of the emerging dialogue among world faiths and development institutions. It creates great potential for productive involvement of faith organizations in development efforts. To date the experience has been mixed, with wide variation across countries and regions in the extent to which this potential has been realized.

Recognizing the untapped potential of the PRSP process, the WFDD hosted a consultation on the PRSP experience in Canterbury, UK, including participants from fifteen countries, in July, 2002. In each country represented, PRSPs had been elaborated, all involving specific and quite elaborate processes of consultation with civil society groups, broadly defined, and there was consensus that each process had brought benefits both of stronger strategic focus on strategy and broader public understanding of the issues involved. However, the stories also detailed missed opportunities and frustrated understanding of what engagement in national processes involved and how to use the instrument more effectively. There was a shared sense in the group that even the act of participating in the national process was positive, in that it highlighted the importance of common engagement, allowing deep reflection about values, beliefs, and advocacy for poor communities. Prophetic reflections identified the desire to tap into deeper sources of motivation, and to promote genuinely sustainable life styles. Practical discussions focused particularly on the complex linkages among service delivery mechanisms of public and private institutions, including faith institutions, which often were less engaged than others in dialogue on critical short and long term policy issues. It was striking how widely actual experience varied, not only country-by-country, but among faith communities. The central and enduring conclusion is that the PRSPs and similar instruments offer a fruitful avenue for continued action and exploration, but that much more effort and focus is needed if they are to fulfill their potential. Faith groups may have an important role to play in monitoring and implementing the PRSPs, and it is crucial that they have the capacity to participate in these processes. A common refrain was the need for training to offer "economic literacy" and in this manner help voices to be heard. WFDD is currently engaged in running a series of workshops to deepen the understanding of issues and share experience.

Conclusion

There is much scope for strengthening partnerships between faith and development organizations. The traditional divides between the worlds reflect well known skepticism on both sides about working together—stemming from different values, different norms, different languages, and different approaches. More important, though, many basic issues that are central to the world of development—poverty alleviation, dynamic approaches to ensuring access to high quality education, social justice, and social safety nets—are core issues in all of the major religious traditions, with intellectual and moral roots that can be traced back thousands of years. Theologians from every religion have grappled with the whys and hows of poverty and misery. Faith institutions have long played a pivotal role in providing services to the poor, and in working to overcome the underlying roots of poverty. It is therefore heartening to see growing appreciation that the role of faith-based groups is vital for success and sustainability in the global fight against poverty. The door is open, the path ahead is clearly marked.

For further information and additional publications, contact the Development Dialogue on Values and Ethics Unit at the World Bank (www.worldbank.org) and the World Faiths Development Dialogue (www.wfdd.org.uk).

References

Marshall, Katherine and Richard Marsh. 2003. *Millennium Development Challenges for Development and Faith Institutions.* Washington, D. C.: World Bank.

Narayan, Deepa and Patti Petesch. 2002. *From Many Lands: Voices of the Poor.* Washington D.C.: World Bank and New York: Oxford University Press.

Notes

[1] UN Millennium Summit website: http://www.un.org/millennium/summit.htm

[2] Among other good sources about the MDGs are http://www.worldbank.org/poverty/mission/up4.htm

[3] Marshall and Marsh (2003) focuses on the MDGs and the faith development agendas.

[4] See website for more information: www.wfdd.org.uk

[5] For more information see http://www.worldbank.org/poverty/strategies/index.htm

[6] For background see http://web.worldbank.org/WBSITE/EXTERNAL/PROJECTS/STRATEGIES/CDF/0,,pagePK:60447~theSitePK:140576,00.html

17

Why Trade Matters for the Poor

Judith M. Dean[1] (U. S. International Trade Commission)

International trade can play a major role in the promotion of economic development and the alleviation of poverty...We recognize the particular vulnerability of the least-developed countries and the special structural difficulties they face in the global economy. We are committed to addressing the marginalization of least-developed countries in international trade and to improving their effective participation in the multilateral trading system. *The Doha WTO Ministerial Declaration* (2001)

World trade has the potential to act as a powerful motor for the reduction of poverty . . . but that potential is being lost. The problem is not that international trade is inherently opposed to the needs and interests of the poor, but that the rules that govern it are rigged in favour of the rich . . . [W]here good policies enable poor countries . . . to participate in markets on equitable terms, trade can act as a force for poverty reduction. *Oxfam, Rigged Rules and Double Standards* (2002)

In the years leading up to the new millennium, many poor countries made dramatic reductions in trade barriers. Reform was significant in scope and magnitude, even in countries that had long maintained high levels of protection and extensive restrictions on foreign exchange. Perhaps the most remarkable changes occurred in Latin America, where trade restrictions fell, in many countries, nearly to the levels of the East Asian "tigers." However, liberalization also began to accelerate in South Asia—especially in India and Bangladesh in the early 1990s. Within East Asia, significant reform occurred in some ASEAN members during the 1980s, and began in China and Viet Nam in the 1990s. Only in Africa was there little progress towards a liberalized trade regime (Dean, et al., 1994).

Surprisingly, Oxfam and the WTO are singing a similar song regarding freer trade. Granted a few of Oxfam's verses are not found in the WTO's songbook, and vice versa. But the main theme is the same. Trade is seen as a powerful force for growth and poverty reduction, and developing countries need to be able to effectively participate in it. But developing countries have been impeded from fully taking advantage of the benefits of trade, and this needs to change. To achieve this, trade policy in both poor and rich countries must be reformed, as well as procedures in the WTO.

How is it that both Oxfam and the WTO come to the conclusion that freer trade will, in general, help reduce poverty? Economists know that trade liberalization generates both winners and losers, but at the national level the gains from freer trade should outweigh the losses. In theory, the winners could compensate the losers such that everyone is better off. But couldn't the poor be among the "losers" from freer trade? If so, how could we be sure that adequate compensation took place? Both the WTO and Oxfam actually expect that most of the poor will be among the "gainers" from freer trade. In the sections below, this paper explores some of the reasons why.

Since understanding who the poor are is critical to understanding the potential role of trade in improving their well-being, the first section discusses some of the common characteristics of poor populations across countries. The next section highlights the importance of increased income for poverty alleviation, and briefly explores why freer trade tends to raise income, and may generate faster growth. The central part of the WTO/Oxfam argument—the detrimental role of trade barriers imposed by both developing and industrial countries—is explored in the subsequent sections. Finally, the limitations of trade reform in alleviating poverty, and the necessity of reforming other domestic policies is considered. Freer trade does have the potential to be a powerful force to reduce poverty. Academics and practitioners concerned about poverty should support reform of both industrial and developing country trade policies. However, they should also be aware that freer trade alone will not eradicate poverty.

Common Characteristics Across Poor Populations

The links between trade and poverty are complex and can be ambiguous (Winters, 2000).[2] Trade reform affects the poor in terms of their ability to earn income, and their ability to buy goods with that income. Thus, the net impact on poor people depends critically upon where they work, what skills they have, and what they consume. To understand how poor households might be impacted by freer trade, we must probe more into who the poor are and why they are poor. If trade reform is expected to raise the earning power of poor households, or to reduce their cost of living, then we would expect it to be beneficial for poor households. Better yet, if trade reform were to actually address some of the fundamental causes of poverty, it could be expected to have long-lasting beneficial effects.

Despite the many differences between poor households in different countries in the developing world, there are certain common characteristics which help us understand how different policies may affect their well-being. The majority of the poor still live in rural areas, and, most often earn incomes in the agricultural sector. In Burkina Faso, Ghana, Mauritania, Nigeria, Uganda, Zambia, and Zimbabwe in the late 1990s, for example, more than half the rural populations fell below national poverty lines, while (with the exception of Nigeria and Zambia) less than 20 percent of urban populations fell below these lines (World Bank, 2000). Poor individuals also tend to have relatively little education. A recent demographic survey found 12 countries where more than half the 15 to 19 year olds in the poorest 40 percent of households had no formal education at all (World Bank, 2000). Outside of agriculture, poor workers tend to be employed in small scale, lower-skilled, labor-intensive industries such as apparel. A very large proportion of poor households' incomes is spent on basic necessities like food and housing.

The causes of poverty are multiple and far too complex to cover in-depth here. However, a few factors appear to be fundamental to both understanding the origins of poverty and finding effective solutions: lack of income and assets, voicelessness, and vulnerability to shocks (World Bank, 2000). Most of the world's poor own few physical or human assets (land, skills, education, good health), and the return to these assets is often low and volatile. Access to financial assets, such as savings and credit, are often nonexistent. Where there is absence of rule of law, or corruption in law enforcement, the poor often suffer disproportionately (usury, bribery, and indentured servitude). In the face of adverse shocks, families with few assets also have little to sustain them. Floods, crop failures, high inflation, government collapse, job loss, and sickness, can easily push these families into dire poverty. To the extent that more open trade addresses these fundamental factors, it can help reduce poverty.

Trade, Growth, and Poverty

Since the majority of the world's poor still live in the lowest income developing countries, expanding national income is critical to reducing poverty. One of the most widely agreed upon conclusions in economics is that international trade raises the overall income of a country.[3] There are two fundamental reasons for this welfare improvement. First, countries have access to many goods at relatively cheaper prices than in their domestic market; they also find more profitable markets in which to sell many other goods. Second, production of goods in which the country has a comparative advantage expands, while those sectors displaying comparative disadvantage shrink. Since this is a reallocation of productive factors from less efficient sectors to more efficient sectors, overall real GNP rises.

In addition to this one-time increase in the level of national income, more open trade may have a more enduring impact on the growth rate of national income. Many empirical studies have posited that freer trade increases a country's growth rate by raising the productivity of a country's labor and capital. The channels through which this can occur include exposure to increased competition in the global market; access to new technology via trade in information or imitation of new products; increased foreign direct investment which may bring new technology; economies of scale in production, as firms now sell in a global market; and access to cheaper imported inputs. Since growth is of critical importance in reducing poverty (Dollar and Kraay, 2002; Ravallion, 2001; Berg and Krueger, 2003), trade liberalization may help reduce poverty through its contributions to overall growth.

Using country-level data, researchers have found a large amount of evidence that more open economies do appear to grow faster. Recent work shows that the positive effects of trade openness on growth are evident for different time periods, many different measures of trade openness, and for both industrial and developing countries (e.g., Harrison, 1996; Edwards, 1998; Greenaway, 1998, 2002). New evidence also suggests that the links between trade openness and growth may be indirect–trade liberalization inducing more investment, and thereby more growth (Baldwin and Seghezza, 1996; Wacziarg, 2001). This work is not without its limitations (Rodriguez and Rodrik, 2001). Trade liberalization is very difficult to quantify, and other factors interrelated with trade policy often impact growth simultaneously, making it hard to discern the effects attributable to trade alone. As Berg and Krueger (2003) note: "Clearly opening to trade does not guarantee faster growth. But one striking conclusion from the last twenty years of evidence is that there are no examples of recent take-off countries that have not opened to an important extent as part of the reform process."

Trade Liberalization by Developing Countries: Benefits to the Poor

One of the most common features of trade restrictions across the developing world, has been their *bias against agriculture*. Import-substitution development programs entailed high trade barriers to promote the growth of capital-intensive, import-competing manufacturing industries. These barriers inevitably depressed the relative price of agricultural products, reducing returns to farmers. This was compounded by overvalued exchange rates, which kept imported inputs into manufacturing cheap, but made agricultural exports expensive in the eyes of foreign buyers. Some countries (particularly in Africa) required farmers to sell their crop through state-owned marketing boards. These monopsonies usually taxed the crop heavily, implying that farmers ultimately received a very small fraction of the world price for their crop. These practices were so common that researchers sometimes use an aggregate measure of bias against agriculture as a proxy for the trade restrictiveness of a country (Harrison, 1996). The dismantling of these trade restrictions, and foreign exchange distortions, has meant a rise in the return to agricultural production. Since agriculture remains a principle means of income of many of the poor, this move toward more open trade directly addresses one of the fundamental causes of poverty.

Oxfam (2001) discusses several examples of the benefits to smallholder agriculture after reforms. After significant reductions in agricultural taxes, and rights to sell in export markets, Viet Nam shifted from a small net importer of rice to a major exporter. The widespread growth in rice production also stimulated demand for rural labor. Oxfam cites a dramatic drop in the proportion of Vietnamese below the national poverty line during this time. In Uganda, taxes on coffee exports and overvalued exchange rates had pushed many small farmers into subsistence. When Uganda removed the export taxes, moved toward a market-oriented exchange rate, and removed trade barriers on agricultural inputs toward the end of the 1980s, coffee production rose. Oxfam notes a dramatic drop in the percentage of Ugandans below the national poverty line as a result. They also note that higher farm income promoted diversification in production, and improved nutrition. Crop diversification helps reduce the effects of adverse shocks faced by poor families, and better nutrition helps build up human assets. These again are fundamental factors that directly help reduce poverty.

The type of restrictive trade regime described above also embodied a *bias against low-skilled, labor-intensive manufacturing*–the type of manufacturing in which many developing countries have a comparative advantage, and many poor workers are employed. Reductions in manufacturing trade barriers have raised the relative profitability of sectors such as textiles, clothing, electronics, and shoes. Since these industries employ relatively low-skilled workers, are small scale, and require little infrastructure, expanded output and employment in these sectors have meant higher incomes for many of the most vulnerable urban workers. Oxfam cites studies of Mauritius and Bangladesh, where expansion of textiles and apparel industries have significantly increased employment of low-skilled workers, many of whom are women.

In addition to the fundamental gains from trade discussed above, more open markets give a country access to a wider variety of goods. Quite often trade restraints exist against basic consumer goods such as clothing or household products, creating a *bias against low-income consumers.* Until the mid-1990s, India effectively banned the import of all consumer goods, leading to relatively high prices and low quality for these basic items. Oxfam notes that the Vietnamese government retains very high tariffs on bicycles, raising the cost so high that millions of poor families can't afford them. Since such items make up a disproportionately large share of the expenditure of poor households, the cost of such trade barriers falls more heavily on the poor. Removal of this bias is an additional source of gain for the poorer groups in developing countries. By making better quality consumer goods available at lower prices, freer trade can help raise the purchasing power of poor households.

Trade Liberalization by Industrial Countries: Benefits to the Poor

It is important to note that the largest share of benefits from trade liberalization generally accrue to the liberalizing countries themselves. Thus, developing country welfare will likely be more impacted by removal of their own distortive policies, than by removal of industrial country trade barriers. However, Oxfam (2001) argues, correctly, that industrial country trade policies work against the ability of developing countries to benefit from trade. First, these trade policies *damage developing country agricultural exports.* A well-known example of this is the EU, whose trade barriers, internal price supports, and export subsidies have generated excess production of many goods which are major exports of many poor countries. This excess output has been dumped on global markets, significantly reducing the prices poor exporters receive for these products. U.S. internal price supports for dairy and other farm products also contribute to this problem. A recent IMF study reported findings from the OECD that "total transfers from [industrial country] consumers and taxpayers to farmers averaged about 30 percent of gross farm income in 2001, cost over $300 billion (1.3 percent of GDP), and amounted to six times overseas development aid" (IMF, 2002). The largest share of this farm "support" is through trade barriers.

Liberalization of industrial country agricultural markets should generally result in higher prices for agricultural products in global markets, raising incomes for many developing countries that are net exporters of agricultural products, and for the poor within those countries, since many are net suppliers of agricultural products. But the overall effect on poverty in poor countries is clouded by additional complexities. Results from an IMF simulation (2002) suggest that removal of industrial country agricultural "support" would lead to gains for Sub-Saharan Africa, Latin America, and South Asia (with Sub-Saharan Africa gaining the most), and losses for North Africa and the Middle East. In contrast, Panagariya (2002) argues that regional analysis masks differences across countries, and that in fact a very large number of low-income countries are actually net food importers. If Panagariya is right, this should increase the likelihood that many poor people will lose from this liberalization.[4] However, others argue that it is the urban consumers in these countries who would lose from higher food prices, not the poorest who tend to be rural farmers.

Most studies agree that the impact of industrial country agricultural trade liberalization on poor countries will depend upon the specific agricultural products that they export (import). In addition, related domestic policies (such as developing country export taxes, marketing boards, fertilizer subsidies, etc.) can often play a critical role in determining the welfare effects of industrial country liberalization (Anderson, et al., 1998). For example, an increase in the world price of cocoa might not lead to a higher price paid to developing country cocoa farmers, if they must sell to a state marketing board which taxes away most of their earnings on the crop.

The Doha Declaration states that the WTO members "[commit themselves] to comprehensive negotiations aimed at: substantial improvements in market access; reductions of, with a view to phasing out, all forms of export subsidies; and substantial reductions in trade-distorting domestic support" (WTO, 2001, par. 13). Since many poor households are likely to benefit from agricultural trade liberalization in the industrial countries, it would be especially useful to identify the poor households who are net buyers of the agricultural products whose prices will rise and find ways to reduce their vulnerability. It may be that with better infrastructure and new technologies they can meet more of their food needs through their own production. For some it may be necessary to provide alternative ways to increase incomes faster than their cost of living. NGOs working close to these groups can play an especially valuable role in this undertaking.

Second, *the most restrictive industrial country trade barriers are imposed on developing country products.*[5] Oxfam notes that the manufactured goods that face the highest (peak) tariffs in industrial countries are exactly those goods in which developing countries have a comparative advantage. This tends to inhibit growth in these developing country industries, and works against the benefits described above. Apparel is a particularly critical example. This system of trade barriers began in 1974, and by 2000 restrained imports of more than 106 apparel products from more than 40 developing countries. The combination of non-tariff and tariff barriers tended to raise the average U.S. price of a garment by about 34 percent in 1999 (USITC, 2001).[6]

While the non-tariff barriers on industrial country apparel imports are supposed to be removed by 2005, there is grave concern that industrial countries may back away from this commitment, leaving market access extremely limited and distorted (Dean, 2002; Spinanger, 1997; Krishna and Tan, 1998).[7] The WTO Declaration commits "to negotiations which shall aim . . . to reduce or as appropriate eliminate tariffs, including the reduction or elimination of tariff peaks, high tariffs, and tariff escalation, as well as non-tariff barriers, in particular on products of export interest to developing countries." (WTO, 2001, par. 16). One estimate (cited in Oxfam, 2001) suggests developing country exports could expand by 11 percent, simply by removing the trade barriers on goods facing peak tariffs. This would clearly translate into significant expansion in employment and output in these industries in poor countries.

Third, developing countries are increasingly the targets of anti-dumping charges. U.S. industries are allowed to file complaints that exporters are "dumping"—selling their products in the U.S. market at "less than fair value." The Department of Commerce then determines the "dumping margin"—the gap between the actual price and the "fair price"—and the USITC determines if this dumping has caused significant injury to the U.S. industry. Many studies have found the U.S. system predisposed to finding dumping. If injury is found, the U.S. imposes an "anti-dumping duty" (a kind of discriminatory tariff) on the imports in question. As of November 2002, the U.S. had anti-dumping duties against many developing country products. Noteworthy are those on 47 Chinese products and anti-dumping or countervailing[8] duties against 14 Indian products, some of which have been in place since the 1980s (www.usitc.gov).

Under the present system, exporters from developing countries often do not have the skilled personnel necessary to file the required evidence nor to defend themselves against these charges. The penalties can be extremely high. Oxfam cites the example of EU anti-dumping duties of 25 percent against bed linens from India, from 1997–2000. Even though the EU ultimately voted that these duties were unjustified, and suspended them, the damage to the Indian industry (reductions in output and employment) during these three years was significant. Without reform, this system of anti-dumping will continue to impede developing countries' ability to benefit from participation in global trade.

Trade Liberalization: Necessary but not Sufficient

The extent and type of trade restrictions maintained by both developing countries themselves, and by industrial countries, have increased the marginalization of poor countries from the world trading system. These trade barriers have tended to depress incomes in industries where the poor work, increased the risk which poor households face, and raised the cost of products that are a large part of poor households' consumption. Thus, there is good reason to believe that a large proportion of poor households would directly benefit—be the "gainers"—from globally freer trade. However, at least two caveats should be recognized. First, trade reform takes place in the context of other policies. Thus, its effects can be magnified or impeded by these other policy choices. Second, trade policy cannot, by itself, solve the poverty problem.

Trade Reform Does Not Occur in a Vacuum. Potential benefits of trade may not accrue to the poor because of other policy choices made by governments.[9] As Oxfam notes, these policy choices are not inherently linked to trade policy, and hence are avoidable. Winters (2000) cites an example used in an earlier Oxfam study which illustrates the point. In the 1990s, Zambia abolished the official purchasing monopsony for maize. However, the activity was taken over by two firms that kept purchase prices low, and did not serve remote areas. Here, lack of competition and lack of access to a market prevented benefits of maize trade from reaching farmers. In contrast, abolition of the official purchasing monopsony for cotton in Zimbabwe led to three buyers emerging, including one owned by farmers. Here, the increased competition led to higher prices for farmers. The distinction in these two cases, rested not on trade liberalization at all, but on the promotion of competition among private buyers, and access to those buyers.

Trade Reform Alone Is Not Enough. The evidence presented in the *World Development Report 2000* shows quite clearly that freer trade alone cannot solve the poverty problem. While acknowledging the many difficulties in measuring poverty with any accuracy, the World Bank presents estimates using an international poverty line (the share of the population living on less than $1 per day) and an alternative relative poverty line (the share of population living on less than one-third of the average national consumption). Using the international poverty line, it appears that poverty in the developing world is shifting towards South Asia and Sub-Saharan Africa. Between 1987 and 1998, the share of population living on less than $1 per day fell dramatically in East Asia and the Pacific (excluding China) from 23.9 percent to 11.3 percent, and remained low in Latin America (about 15 percent). However, the share of the population living on less than $1 a day in South Asia and Sub-Saharan Africa remained roughly the same (40 percent and 46 percent, respectively). Even with the alternate relative poverty measure these same trends appear.[10]

Given the dramatic trade liberalizations in some of the East Asian and Latin American countries during this time period, in contrast to little or no liberalization in South Asia and Sub-Saharan Africa (respectively), it is likely that freer trade played a role in reducing or maintaining poverty levels in East Asia and in Latin America. However, other factors, such as wars and AIDS in Sub-Saharan Africa, financial crises in East Asia, and natural disasters in South Asia, Sub-Saharan Africa, and Latin America, have had a tremendous impact on poverty in these regions. War and the lack of rule of law may be critical in explaining the very sharp increase in poverty in Eastern Europe and Central Asia during this time period. Clearly trade policy alone cannot counteract the impact of these shocks on poor households. In addition, though the majority of poor households may benefit from freer trade, there will always be some who lose in the short run, and will need direct help to offset these costs during the transition.

To echo both the Doha Ministerial Declaration and the Oxfam study, increased isolation from global markets would deprive the poor of the tremendous opportunities offered by international trade. Trade can be a powerful force to counteract poverty, but the present restrictions on that trade deprive poor countries and poor households of its benefits. Changes in the trade policies of both industrial and developing countries should improve the real purchasing power of poor households, thereby helping to build up physical and human assets and to reduce vulnerability to shocks. However, freer trade must be accompanied by complementary domestic policy reforms. Without these, the benefits of trade may be greatly reduced.

References

Baldwin, Robert and Elena Seghezza. 1996. "Testing for Trade-Induced Investment-Led Growth," National Bureau of Economic Research Working Paper 5416.

Berg, Alan and Anne O. Krueger. 2003. "Trade, Growth, and Poverty: A Selective Survey," IMF Working Papers WP/03/30.

Dean, Judith. 2002. "Removing Textile and Apparel Trade Barriers: The Impact on Developing Country Exporters," manuscript prepared for the Office of the U.S. Trade Representative.

Dean, Judith; Seema Desai, and James Riedel. 1994. *Trade Policy Reform in Developing Countries Since 1985: A Review of the Evidence,* World Bank Discussion Paper No. 267 (November).

Dollar, David, and Aart Kraay. 2002. "Growth is Good for the Poor," *Journal of Economic Growth.* 7:3, pp. 195–225.

Edwards, Sebastian. 1998. "Openness, Productivity, and Growth: What Do We Really Know?" *Economic Journal.* 108:447, pp. 383–398.

Greenaway, David; Wyn Morgan, and Peter Wright. 1998. "Trade Reform, Adjustment and Growth: What Does the Evidence Tell Us?" *Economic Journal.* 108:450, pp. 1547–1561.

Harrison, Ann. 1996. "Openness and Growth: A Time-Series, Cross-Country Analysis for Developing Countries," *Journal of Development Economics.* 48:2, pp. 419–447.

IMF. 2002. "How Do Industrial Country Agricultural Policies Affect

Developing Countries?" *World Economic Outlook* (September), pp. 81–91.

Krishna, Kala and Ling-Hui Tan. 1998. *Rags and Riches.* Ann Arbor: University of Michigan Press.

Martin, Will and L. Alan Winters. 1995. *The Uruguay Round and the Developing Economies*, World Bank Discussion Paper 307.

Oxfam. 2002. *Rigged Rules and Double Standards.* Oxford: Oxfam.

Panagariya, Arvin. 2002. "Trade and Food Security: Conceptualizing the Linkages," manuscript available at http://www.columbia.edu/~ap2231/policy.html.

Ravallion, Martin. 2001. "Growth, Inequality, and Poverty: Looking Beyond the Averages," *World Development.* 29, pp. 1803–15.

Ray, Edward and Howard Marvel. 1984. "The Pattern of Protection in the Industrialized World," *Review of Economics and Statistics.* 66: 3, pp. 452–58.

Rodriguez, F. and Dani Rodrik. 2001. "Trade Policy and Economic Growth: A Skeptic's Guide to the Cross-National Evidence," in *NBER Macroeconomics Annual 2000.* Ben S. Bernanke and Kenneth Rogoff, eds. Cambridge, MA and London: MIT Press, pp. 261–325.

Spinanger, Dean. 1999. "Textiles Beyond the MFA Phase-Out," *World Economy.* 22:4, pp. 455–76.

Tokarick, Steven. 2003. "Measuring the Impact of Distortions in Agricultural Trade," IMF Working Paper WP/03/110.

Wacziarg, Romain. 2001. "Measuring the Dynamic Gains from Trade," *World Bank Economic Review.* 15:3, pp. 393–429.

Winters, L. Alan. 2000. "Trade and Poverty: Is There a Connection?" in *Trade, Income Disparity and Poverty.* D. Ben-David, H. Nordstrom and L. Alan Winters, eds. WTO Special Study 5. Geneva: WTO.

Winters, L. Alan; Neil McCulloch, and Andrew KcKay. 2004. "Trade Liberalization and Poverty: The Evidence Thus Far," *Journal of Economic Literature.* 42:1, pp. 72–115.

World Bank. 2000. *World Development Report 2000/2001.* Washington, DC: Oxford University Press.

WTO. 2001. *Ministerial Declaration.* WTO Document WT/MIN(01)/DEC/1.

USITC. 1997. *The Dynamic Effects of Trade Liberalization: an Empirical Analysis.* Publication 3069.

USITC. 2002. *The Economic Effects of Significant U.S. Import Restraints,* Third Update.

Notes

[1] The views expressed here are solely those of the author. They do not represent in any way the views of the U.S. International Trade Commission, or any of its individual Commissioners.

[2] A detailed, in-depth survey of trade liberalization and poverty was published by L. Alan Winters (2004) after this conference. This survey is highly recommended for those readers who want a thorough explanation of the numerous intricate issues involving the impact of trade liberalization on poverty, as well as a thorough examination of the empirical evidence to date.

[3] Panagariya also argues, for example, that though the EU market is highly distorted, the "Everything But Arms" preferential agreement actually gives lowest income countries preferential access to the EU market where they already receive higher prices for their products. EU liberalization would eliminate this preference, and, *cet. par.*, reduce these countries' welfare. For more detailed arguments see Panagariya (2002) and Tokarick (2003).

[4] Early evidence of this can be found in Ray and Marvel (1984). USITC (2002) documents, in addition to apparel and some agricultural products, peak tariffs on products such as frozen fruits, fruit juices and vegetables, and footwear.

[5] This is a lower bound estimate.

[6] There are serious problems with Oxfam's analysis of this issue.

[7] Levied against countries which have "unfair subsidies" on their export goods.

[8] The absence of infrastructure may also reduce a country's ability to reap the benefits of freer trade. Here we confine the discussion to distortive domestic policy choices that can explicitly reduce or reverse otherwise beneficial effects of freer trade.

[9] Latin America shows a much higher percentage of the population in poverty by this measure.

18

Macroeconomic Stability and Poverty Reduction

Andrew Levin (Federal Reserve Board)[1]
Stephen L. S. Smith (Gordon College)

Macroeconomic instability can have severe consequences for the poor, both directly and by drawing policymakers' attention away from longer-term poverty reduction. It can also wreak havoc on even the best efforts of non-profit development organizations. At the same time, the policies implemented to end the instability (such as cuts in government spending, and currency devaluation) can themselves raise poverty, at least temporarily.

For all these reasons individuals and organizations involved in poverty reduction may naturally be drawn into considering stabilization issues, and even towards direct engagement in macroeconomic policy debates. NGOs' grassroots connections to the households directly affected by stabilization policies render some of the costs of instability and of stabilization policies painfully clear. But debates about stabilization can seem arcane and technical. And detailed analysis of stabilization policies is not something many NGOs feel equipped to do.

This chapter aims to assist the conversation about macroeconomic stability by offering a summary of economic thinking on the topic, with particular emphasis on its relation to poverty. This is not a survey of the vast economics literature that exists on stabilization. Instead, we hope to provide a straightforward and intelligible guide to some of the issues posed by macroeconomic instability and stabilization policies.

We begin by describing three common scenarios in which macroeconomic instability arises in developing countries. Though particular institutional details vary from country to country and from case to case, there are large common elements. Macroeconomic instability in and of itself hurts low-income households. Instability almost always requires some kind of macroeconomic adjustment; "stabilization policies" are essentially inevitable. Furthermore, the sooner these policies are adopted the better in order to avoid even more substantial problems for the economy in general and the poor in particular.

We then outline policy measures that can help promote greater macroeconomic stability, and consider some of the merits and shortcomings of standard stabilization policies with respect to their consequences for the poor. Much of the controversy regarding stabilization focuses on the potential for stabilization policies to harm the poor.

We argue that, from an ethical point of view which emphasizes care for the poor, macroeconomic stability is itself a worthy aim of economic policy. But actually achieving macroeconomic stability is difficult. Short-run stabilization policies have real costs, even when they are essential for long-term improvements in an economy and for the poor. Thus a crucial challenge for governments facing macroeconomic instability—and for the economists, NGOs and practitioners who advise them—is to craft carefully targeted social service programs that assist the poor and shield them from the harmful short-term effects of stabilization policy while allowing the genuine benefits of stabilization and growth to be attained. This is no easy task. But it is a task to which NGOs bring real strengths and where practitioner-economist collaboration could be particularly fruitful.

Common Scenarios of Macroeconomic Instability

It can be hard for Western observers to appreciate the full significance of macroeconomic instability because Western economies have been more or less stable for the past quarter century or more. These economies have experienced relatively steady economic growth, relatively low inflation and unemployment, and very few economic crises that have threatened to stop a nation's economic life in its tracks. By contrast, many developing countries have experienced considerable macroeconomic instability, manifested in high inflation rates (sometimes well over 100 percent per year), and episodes of sharp decreases in income and employment. When the unemployment rate doubles in the space of a few months, say from 10 percent to 20 percent, it represents a gut-wrenching crisis that leaves few households untouched. Macroeconomic instability is also often accompanied by the breakdown of key economic institutions, such as when a nation's entire banking system is closed down or when certain goods are simply unavailable at any price because some foreign exchange transactions are banned. Macroeconomic instability, in short, can lead to grave national crises which impose huge costs and disrupt lives.

We sketch below three types of macroeconomic instability that emerge in developing countries.[2] These scenarios exhibit several common elements which have large implications for poverty reduction.

Scenario #1: A Debt Crisis. In developing economies governments face many demands for spending. Education, health care, and sanitation spending is urgently needed. Longer-term development requires spending on improved public infrastructure such as electricity, communication, and transportation. The government may also face pressures to subsidize the cost of various goods and services (for middle and upper classes, not just for the poor). Finally, military expenditures may be substantial, reflecting the influence of the armed services and internal or external national security threats.

Developing economy governments also face obstacles to collecting taxes. Historically, import duties and export taxes were substantial, but many countries have chosen to reduce these taxes in order to stimulate international trade and foreign investment (as discussed in Chapter 17 of this volume). In rich countries government revenue is mainly obtained via sales and income taxes, but these are much more difficult to collect when, as is true in poor countries, a large fraction of economic activity is "informal" with no written records. As a result, developing country governments often rely on a patchwork of revenue sources (such as taxes on banking and real estate transactions), many of which are susceptible to corruption, evasion, and ongoing pressure to establish special exemptions for specific individuals and companies.

Given these obstacles to raising public revenue, the government may seek to borrow funds to pay for expenditures. Such an approach may be sensible if the deficit is assuredly short-lived (e.g., in the aftermath of a natural disaster) and the outstanding level of government debt is relatively low. In contrast, large and persistent government deficits can generate a substantial risk of macroeconomic instability.

The evolution of a public debt crisis is comparable in many respects to what can happen with an individual or family. A prudent household has a sustainable level of longer-term debt (such as student loans or a home mortgage), and maintains minimal balances on its credit cards except perhaps in a medical emergency or other unusual event. In contrast, a household that uses credit to finance ordinary expenditures will face a growing level of debt. As time passes, the household will find itself borrowing even more to cover the additional interest charges, and its debt will accumulate at an accelerating pace. And growing dependence on various credit cards and consumer finance loans will typically lead to higher interest rates that exacerbate the financial difficulties. Finally, when no further credit can be obtained, the household will be forced to make even more drastic spending adjustments than would have been required if the debt spiral had been halted at an earlier stage.

Persistent government deficits can trigger a similar sequence of events, except that the adverse consequences affect an entire country, and especially its poorest citizens. If the public debt is still manageable, the government might avoid further borrowing by raising taxes and cutting spending enough to offset its existing interest obligations. Unfortunately, the first government programs to be cut are typically those oriented towards the segment of the population with the least political clout, namely, the poor. Nevertheless, the budget usually cannot be balanced without cutting back on some popular programs that benefit the upper and middle classes. And as the government debt continues to accumulate, increasingly sharp adjustments are required to move towards a balanced budget, and the political consensus required for fiscal stability becomes even more difficult to achieve.

With a mounting public debt, individuals and private institutions (such as banks) holding government-issued securities become more concerned about the possibility of default, and start moving their assets towards alternative investments. To engage in continued borrowing, the government must pay higher interest rates to compensate investors for greater perceived risk. Public officials may seek to alleviate the interest burden by shifting the government's debt towards bonds and foreign currency loans that have relatively short maturity (e.g., three months or less); however, these changes have the unfortunate side-effect of making the government's interest obligations more susceptible to foreign exchange rate movements and other short-term fluctuations.

Thus, the later stages of a debt crisis involve an element of self-fulfilling prophecy: as investors become increasingly anxious about the possibility of government default, the government must pay higher interest rates that exacerbate its financial problems and thereby make the default more likely. Such concerns about macroeconomic stability also make it more difficult for households and companies to borrow at reasonable interest rates, thereby contributing to a drop in private spending and higher unemployment. The economic slowdown causes a decline in tax revenue, putting further pressure on the deficit and raising perceptions that the government's budget outlook is not sustainable.

At the culmination of the crisis, the government suspends its debt payments and formally defaults. Unlike an individual household, the government then faces a complex and protracted process of negotiating new terms with all of its creditors. Until these negotiations are completed, the supply of credit may dry up not only for the government but for domestic households and companies, including many small firms that rely on short-term trade credit for normal operations.

Thus, a debt crisis typically leads to a very sharp contraction in economic activity, with rising unemployment and falling wages. This has particularly severe consequences for low-income households, which will be pushed towards or into poverty. In fact, developing country poverty rates are strongly tied to overall national income growth, so slowdowns or contractions tend to raise poverty directly.[3] And as the government is finally forced to balance its budget, the brunt of the adjustment may occur through drastic cuts in programs that benefit the poor. Even after the government succeeds in renegotiating its debt and restoring a degree of stability to financial markets, the adverse consequences of the crisis may continue to be felt for many years in the form of higher interest obligations and lower spending on programs oriented towards poverty reduction and longer-term growth.

Scenario #2: High Inflation. In addition to providing various services such as education, the government is responsible for maintaining a stable value of the currency. Low and stable inflation is not only important for economic development, but is also crucial for poverty reduction: low-income households conduct most or all of their transactions in cash, and have limited ability to protect themselves against high inflation.

When public spending exceeds tax revenue, the government may be tempted to print money to cover the deficit. From a short-term perspective, issuing additional currency may seem relatively painless compared with the prospect of spending cuts, tax hikes, or further borrowing (especially if the government would have to pay high interest rates on any new debt). Nevertheless, "resorting to the printing press" has detrimental consequences for the economy, especially for its poorest members.

Suppose the local currency is the peso. If the government expands the total amount of pesos in circulation while the real quantity of goods and services in the economy is essentially unchanged, then each peso will have less purchasing power. More specifically, the prices of goods and services will tend to rise at roughly the same rate as the supply of money. For example, if the government expands the money supply by ten percent during the month of January, then households might find that a liter of milk which cost 20 pesos at the beginning of the month rises in price to about 22 pesos by the end of the month.

As money-financed deficits push up the inflation rate, low-income households will tend to experience a direct fall in their standard of living, even if their nominal incomes are being adjusted upward at fairly frequent intervals as a result of cost of living increases. Their reliance on cash means that they lose purchasing power with every price increase that takes place between wage rate adjustments. If a worker keeps the income received on pay day in the form of cash and spends it gradually over the course of the month, a high rate of inflation will mean reduced purchasing power later in the pay period. Lower spending may be needed early in the pay period to ensure that enough cash remains to pay higher prices later in the month. In contrast, a wealthy household could deposit the pension payment into a bank account for which the interest rate is automatically adjusted in parallel with inflation, leaving its standard of living unaffected. Inflation's impact on living standards is even greater for the poor who are recipients of pensions or other incomes whose values are fixed in nominal terms and do not tend to be adjusted for rising prices. For them, the erosion of living standards induced by inflation continues not just between pay periods but across pay periods, sometimes leading once-meaningful sources of income to become trivial in real terms.

Inflation also tends to erode the savings of low-income households, who have few alternatives to keeping their savings in cash. Over the past couple of decades, a number of developing countries have experienced very high and persistent inflation, with monthly rates of 20 to 30 percent that correspond to an annual rate above 500 percent. With such high inflation rates, any cash savings will be virtually wiped out over the course of a year or two. In contrast, households with access to bank accounts and other interest-bearing assets can largely shield their wealth from the "inflation tax."

Furthermore, in an economy with ongoing high inflation, the government often faces increasingly severe difficulties in collecting tax revenue, while the wages of public employees and the costs of other government services may rise roughly in line with the inflation rate. Thus, the government may be forced to rely even more heavily on printing money to finance the widening public deficit, pushing the inflation rate up even further.[4]

Whenever inflation rises due to printing money, the private sector has an increasingly strong incentive to reduce the need to hold currency. For example, firms may start sending their extra cash to the bank multiple times per day instead of waiting until just before closing time. With declining demand for currency, the government must print money at an even faster rate in order to finance the public deficit. The situation is roughly similar to that of a municipality with a shrinking tax base; in such a situation, raising the tax rate will generate a temporary rise in revenue but will subsequently cause even further shrinkage of the tax base.

Given these factors, an economy with ongoing high inflation faces substantial risk of sliding into an inflationary spiral referred to as "hyperinflation," with even more severe consequences for the poor. At the worst point of such a crisis, inflation can peak at over 100 percent per month, with annual inflation exceeding 1000 percent. As inflation reaches these levels, prices may be adjusted on an hourly basis, so that working families have trouble maintaining their standard of living even if wages are paid out once a day, while those on fixed incomes face a seemingly hopeless situation. Such an episode occurred in Argentina in 1989: as consumer inflation rose to more than 3000 percent, the fraction of the population living below the official poverty line reached an all-time high.

Unfortunately, the only known cure for hyperinflation is to balance the government's budget deficit in conjunction with stabilizing the supply of money. With a depressed level of tax revenue, this prescription may require the government to make drastic cuts in public spending, at least temporarily, with correspondingly adverse effects on low-income households. Having eliminated the budget deficit, the government can then bring the printing press to a virtual halt. As the supply of currency begins to grow at a much lower rate, inflation typically falls very sharply. Nevertheless, ongoing fiscal prudence is required to ensure that inflation remains at a fairly low and stable level.[5]

Scenario #3: Financial Crisis. The Asian financial crisis of 1997-98 demonstrates that sound fiscal and monetary policies are not sufficient to ensure macroeconomic stability: over the previous few years, nearly all the countries in this region maintained balanced budgets or even surpluses, while inflation remained low and stable. Thus, we now consider the extent to which the banking system can become the Achilles heel of the economy.

In almost all countries the banking system operates on a fractional-reserve basis. Each bank only keeps a small fraction of its deposits on reserve (either in the vault or at the central bank), and uses the rest of the money to finance business investment, property mortgages, and other types of bank loans. In normal circumstances, a moderate quantity of funds will be withdrawn from the bank on any given date, and this amount will be largely offset by new deposits of other customers and by repayment of existing loans. If any residual shortfall needs to be covered, the bank simply borrows on a short-term basis from some other bank that has excess reserves. In most countries, the government also provides some degree of explicit or implicit deposit guarantees; that is, if a given bank becomes insolvent, the government will pay off the depositors using funds generated by deposit insurance fees from other banks.

In a fractional-reserve banking system with a deposit insurance mechanism, each individual bank has an inherent incentive to shift its lending towards relatively high-risk projects for which the borrower is willing to pay a relatively high interest rate. If most of the projects in the bank's portfolio turn out to be successful, then the owners of the bank receive a relatively high rate of return. And if too many borrowers default on their loans, then the owners of the bank simply walk away, the bank is closed down, and the government pays off the depositors. Given these incentive problems, government supervision and regulation is essential to ensure that the banking system maintains sound lending practices.

Unfortunately, oversight of the banking system has been insufficient in many cases, not only in developing countries but in some industrial economies (as shown by the U.S. savings and loan crisis of the 1980s and the protracted Japanese banking problems of the following decade). In such circumstances, financial institutions engage in an excessive amount of high-risk lending. As long as the economy continues to boom, these banks earn high rates of profit. But when the economy begins to slow, a greater fraction of high-risk projects tend to fail; if these borrowers cannot make the required interest payments, their loans are reclassified as "nonperforming" or written off entirely.

Such imprudent lending problems can threaten the entire banking system, including banks with sound loan portfolios. At an early stage, a few specific banks may go out of business, and the deposits from those institutions are simply shifted to other banks. However, as the public becomes increasingly aware of the ongoing deterioration of banks' balance sheets, many depositors may decide to completely withdraw their money from the banking system, perhaps even moving the money out of the country altogether.[6] As a result, even more banks become unable to meet the demands of their depositors and must close their doors. (An excellent illustration of such an episode may be found in the classic movie, "It's a Wonderful Life.")

As the financial crisis evolves, the government is faced with taking over an increasing number of failing banks. If the banking system has been subject to inadequate regulation, then the value of loans of failed institutions may fall far short of the value of deposits. Thus, a banking crisis may cause the government to incur very large obligations quite rapidly, and it must come up with funds either by issuing new debt or by printing currency. In favorable circumstances, the government might obtain funds by issuing new debt at moderate interest rates (as in the resolution of the U.S. savings and loan crisis). But in other settings, as in the Asian crisis of 1997-98, the cost of rescuing the banking system may be so large as to push the government into a debt crisis (Scenario #1) or skyrocketing inflation (Scenario #2).

In either case, the financial crisis will tend to have serious consequences for poverty reduction and economic development. There will inevitably have been some disruption in bank lending, with firms running short of working capital and, along with households, losing access—at least temporarily—to their bank accounts. So it is hard to navigate a financial crisis without a fall in incomes and a rise in unemployment, which hurt the poor directly.

Macroecomic Stability and the Poor

Several common threads are apparent across these scenarios that are relevant for thinking about poverty reduction. First, macroeconomic instability, by its very nature, hurts the poor. The high inflation and economic disruptions (such as slow or negative income growth, job loss, and breakdowns in the banking system) that occur with instability all harm the poor. This implies that macroeconomic stability—steady growth, low inflation, and no crises in the financial system—benefits the poor and is a worthy aim for economic policy makers even if looked at in terms of nothing but its effect on the poor.[7]

Second, once instability emerges some kind of stabilization policies are inevitable. The damage caused by crises is so large that governments must act. In each of the scenarios above, acting sooner is preferable to acting later in that the disruptions caused by instability are less pronounced and smaller adjustments are necessary to achieve stabilization.

Finally, the kinds of stabilization policies appropriate to the various scenarios are similar. Moving a country out of macroeconomic crisis almost always will require some mix of the following "stabilization" policies: adjustments in monetary policy that stabilize the inflation rate; measures to balance the government budget (including tax increases, spending cuts, and privatization of state-owned firms); and policies that stimulate exports and generate foreign exchange to make payments to creditors (including exchange rate adjustment and trade liberalization).

However, stabilization policies may themselves harm the poor. Is this avoidable, even if stabilization itself is unavoidable?

What can be said about the best stabilization policy choices to achieve macroeconomic stability that minimize the harm suffered by the poor? We consider these important questions below.

Attaining Macroeconomic Stability—Long Run Issues

Although there is no simple recipe for ensuring macroeconomic stability, certain essential elements can be identified. It is helpful to distinguish between long-term and short-term factors, and we begin with the long-term.

First, the existing evidence supports the notion that a stable democratic political system is conducive to macroeconomic stability and long-term growth. While an authoritarian state may appear to be stable over some length of time, longer-term political stability requires the establishment of a representative democracy with guaranteed rights for minority groups. And an independent judicial system is needed to ensure that the political system remains representative and that minority rights are protected.[8]

Second, certain principles of sound fiscal policy are conducive to minimizing the risk of excessive budget deficits that might lead to a debt crisis (*Scenario #1*). Pressures for excessive military spending may be reduced by ensuring that the armed forces operate under the ultimate supervision of civilian authorities. Privatization of state-owned enterprises may be expected to alleviate pressures for excessive government payrolls as well as tendencies to provide subsidized goods and services to middle-class and high-income households. The tax system should be relatively simple and readily enforceable, with very few exemptions for specific companies or individuals. For example, a value-added tax is largely self-enforcing. Since each firm pays tax on its revenue less its costs of materials, the firm has a strong incentive to provide accurate information about its payments for raw materials and other inputs, which in turn enables the tax agency to determine the revenue of the firm which supplied those materials.

Third, certain principles of sound monetary policy help avoid high inflation and minimize the risk of hyperinflation (*Scenario #2*). In particular, the central bank should operate as an independent government agency, insulated from short-term political pressures. Monetary policy should be oriented towards a clear objective of low and stable inflation, so that the printing press is not used to finance ongoing budget deficits.

Finally, government oversight of the banking system is essential to avoiding a financial crisis (*Scenario #3*). Thus, sufficient resources need to be devoted to enable the banking supervisory agency to perform its functions effectively. More broadly, the government must ensure that the entire private sector is subject to transparent accounting standards, which in turn serve to facilitate the proper functioning of the banking system as well as other financial markets.

These policy prerequisites for long-term macrostability are not generally controversial, though implementing them can be difficult. Key elements on this list (such as central bank independence, and the ability to regulate financial markets) reflect institutional capabilities and reforms that may take years to accomplish.

Attaining Macroeconomic Stability—Short Run Issues

What are controversial are the particular policies countries use to achieve stabilization when they are in crisis, under pressure from international lenders, and anxious to stabilize quickly. As noted above, budget cuts, tax increases, privatization, currency devaluation and trade liberalization are the policies on the menu for rapid implementation when countries need immediate fixes. They are not unrelated to the long-run policies discussed above. For instance, privatization of a money-losing national airline is probably in line with long-term healthy fiscal practice. Balancing the budget, even on an emergency basis, opens a window for sound monetary policy management over the long-run. Currency devaluation may be essential for rebuilding foreign exchange reserves and attracting capital inflows. Trade liberalization can stimulate long-term growth and job creation among low-skilled workers.

But all of these policies may hurt the poor, at least in the short run, and often do. Tax increases may fall disproportionately on the poor. Government spending cuts may slash programs that especially helped the poor and women and children. Privatization may result in higher unemployment. Currency devaluation, which makes all imports more expensive, drives up the cost of staple items such as cooking fuel oil on which the poor depend. Trade liberalization takes time to deliver extra jobs in exporting sectors of the economy, while causing immediate suffering in industries that lose trade protection. NGOs and other observers have offered these points, among others, in criticism of stabilization policies.

There is some ambiguity about exactly how much harm occurs. Many studies show that the poor are worse off after the imposition of stabilization policies than before. Unfortunately, it is often difficult to ascertain whether these adverse effects should be attributed to the stabilization policies or to the preceding instability.[9] Some studies that attempt to separate out the effects of the instability and the subsequent policy find that the poor may not be as harmed in the short term as commonly supposed. For instance, Sahn et al.'s (1997) analysis of stabilization in ten countries in sub-Saharan Africa in the 1980s and early 1990s found that education spending was so highly tilted towards the middle and upper classes that when governments cut education spending in fiscal retrenchments the effect on the poor was negligible. They also found that devaluations improved the poor's access to foreign exchange. On paper, devaluations implied higher prices for imported items, but prior to devaluation the shortage of foreign currency kept certain goods from the poor entirely.[10] But these findings do not generalize to all stabilization cases. A definitive universal answer to the question *does stabilization hurt the poor?* will probably remain elusive because it hinges on exact details of implementation and institutions that vary from case to case.

And, fortunately, fruitful collaboration between economists and practitioners need not await a definitive answer to that question. Given that stabilization policies of some kind are inevitable once macroeconomic instability emerges, and given that stabilization hurts at least some of the poor in the short and medium terms, practitioners and economists alike should give serious consideration to finding ways to prevent the costs of adjustment from falling heavily on the poor. Surely there are potentially fruitful grounds for collaboration and study in this area of designing suitably targeted social safety programs. What might be involved?

First, it is helpful to recognize that the effects of stabilization on the poor are not uniform. While the economic policy changes inherent in stabilization often create a distinct group of "losers," other groups of poor households may gain. This means that the effort to create compensatory policies should be directed towards those groups among the poor who most need the help without compromising the gains made elsewhere.

A vivid example of this is seen in the case of Filipino vegetable growers in the temperate mountains of northern Luzon. They have suffered from dramatically lower prices for the vegetables, such as carrots, that they supply to urban dwellers now that the Philippines has liberalized its agricultural trade and Chinese carrots flood the market.[11] Yet, because the Philippines is a net importer of these vegetables, the real income gains to the urban poor of cheaper vegetables almost certainly exceed poor farmers' losses. The appropriate policy response should be a targeted one that focuses on these small vegetable farmers rather than, say, a national-level response in trade policy that helps farmers by undoing a real gain for the urban poor. Careful analysis of who among the poor most needs help, and who does not, is essential for constructing the best social safety net policies.

Second, creating properly-targeted social safety nets is an enormous challenge. It is not at all clear what works best. Means tested programs (common in the west) are of limited use in developing countries because of their complex bureaucratic requirements. Current thinking focuses on labor intensive employment programs, which can be located precisely where need is great, and which attract precisely those most in need of help (namely, those for whom low-paying but guaranteed work is superior to other options). Sometimes cash transfer programs are used in which participants are chosen in some way other than means testing. But in each of these types of programs the overall outcome can hinge on details of program design.[12]

All these considerations mean that NGOs and practitioners, with their well-developed grassroots capabilities and their international connections, could play a vital role in program study, design, and diffusion of knowledge about successful strategies. Best practice social safety net programs will not emerge without a large investment in study and design. The depth of this challenge suggests that there is much room for vigorous NGO action.

Conclusion

What lessons do we draw from this overview? Macroeconomic instability can have severe consequences for the poor, a key fact that should condition economist, NGO, and practitioner response to stabilization policies. In an environment of democratic governance, long-term stability can be achieved by an appropriate mix of institutions and policies, including an independent central bank, a broad and equitable tax system, and effective supervision and regulation of the financial system.

Once macroeconomic crises emerge, stabilization policies are inevitable. Even though well-designed stabilization policies should bring substantial long-term benefits to the poor, they may harm the poor in the short-run. Evaluating stabilization policies' effects on the poor requires distinguishing between particular groups among the poor, who may fare quite differently.

Macroeconomic stabilization by its very nature requires national-level policies that have different effects on different groups. National governments face difficult but unavoidable decisions about tradeoffs between present costs and future benefits, and about which sectors and groups in the economy will gain and lose in the short run. Targeted social programs are essential for helping the poor during stabilization while simultaneously allowing a government to pursue stabilization's long term benefits for everyone. But creating safety nets is inherently difficult. NGOs can be instrumental in helping to design the best such programs, as their knowledge and grassroots level experience offer essential insights.

References

Barro, Robert J. 1991. "Economic Growth in a Cross-Section of Countries," *Quarterly Journal of Economics*. 106:2, pp.407-444.

Deininger, Klaus and Lynn Squire. 1996. "A New Data Set Measuring Income Inequality," *World Bank Economic Review*. 10:3, pp. 565-91.

Fischer, Stanley. 2004. *IMF Essays From a Time of Crisis*. Cambridge, MA: MIT Press.

Fischer, Stanley, Ratna Sahay and Carlos A. Végh. 2002. "Modern Hyper- and High-Inflations," *Journal of Economic Literature*. 40: 3, pp. 793-836.

Linder-Hess, Maria. 2003. "Economic Globalization: What Price Will Small Farmers Pay?" *A Common Place*. November.

Sahn, David E.; Paul A. Dorosh and Stephen D. Younger. 1997. *Structural Adjustment Reconsidered. Economic Policy and Poverty in Africa*. Cambridge, UK: Cambridge University Press.

Schaffner, Julie. 2005. *Economic Development in the Modern World: Practical Analysis of Poverty Reduction Strategies,* manuscript.

Notes

[1] The views expressed here are solely the responsibility of the authors, and should not be interpreted as reflecting the views of the Board of Governors of the Federal Reserve System or of any other person associated with the Federal Reserve System.

[2] Macroinstability can arise for reasons other than the ones discussed here. For instance, we do not consider the consequences of economic shocks generated outside the economy, such as sudden changes in the price of an important traded commodity or an economic downturn in a trading partner that lowers the economy's exports. The scenarios we outline here are the classic problems that arise when developing countries' own monetary and fiscal policy choices, combined at times with bad luck, generate real difficulties.

[3] See, out of a large literature on this subject, Deininger and Squire (1996).

[4] Another problem with inflation can emerge when a government fixes the value of a country's exchange rate in terms of a foreign currency. Such a fix offers the benefit of stable prices for imported goods, but relies on the government having sufficient foreign currency reserves to maintain it. With high or even moderate inflation, foreign buyers of the country's goods will find that those goods—at the fixed exchange rate—are more expensive than goods from other countries. The consequent decline in exports is often associated with reduced employment and lower household income, and may cause the central bank to

lose substantial foreign currency reserves. In some instances, specific exchange rate arrangements (such as a currency board) may help avoid or alleviate these problems, but are only likely to be successful if other conditions for overall macroeconomic stability are also in place.

[5] Fischer (2004) surveys the economics research showing the high cost of inflation on the poor.

[6] In many countries, the government maintains a system of deposit insurance oriented towards maintaining public confidence in the banking system; such arrangements have been reasonably successful in many industrial economies but less so in the developing countries.

[7] There are other important arguments in favor of stabilization, not the least of which is that it is almost always a precondition for economic growth and long-term improvements in the material wellbeing of the poor (see Fischer, Sahay, and Végh, 2002). But the point we stress here, that economic instability in and of itself hurts the poor, can be lost in hectic public discourse during economic crises.

[8] See, for instance, Barro (1991).

[9] See Sahn et al. (1997:10-11) on this point, and for an excellent survey of the methodological issues involved in evaluating the effects of stabilization policies.

[10] The "cross-cutting" nature of stabilization policies' impacts on poor households also makes it hard to assess their overall effect on wellbeing. For instance, a household may lose access to a particular government health program when benefits are cut. But if inflation stops and the household's adults have steadier jobs due to the resumption of growth, they may not be worse off overall.

[11] See Linder-Hess (2003) for a sympathetic account of the plight of the farmers near Baguio City.

[12] Schaffner (2005) discusses theoretical and practical issues in safety net program design.